DON'T TRUMP ON US:

MAKING OUR UNIONS GREAT AGAIN

BY

BILL BARRY

For Joan, Willie and Alex

© by Bill Barry   2018

Other books by this author are
Closing Up the Open Shop: A Guide to Internal Organizing
I Just Got Elected, Now What: The New Union Officers' Handbook (3nd edition)
Union Strategies for Hard Times (2nd edition)
From First Contact to First Contract: A Union Organizer's Handbook
The 1877 Railroad Strike in Baltimore

Send all comments and correspondence to:
    4204 Elsrode Avenue
    Baltimore, MD 21214-3107
    Billbarry21214@gmail.com

TABLE OF CONTENTS

CHAPTER 1—INTRODUCTION — P. 1
CHAPTER 2—INDIVIDUAL CHANGES — P. 28
CHAPTER 3—CHANGING THE UNION STRUCTURE — P. 36
CHAPTER 4—NEGOTIATIONS — P. 65
CHAPTER 5—GRIEVANCES — P. 92
CHAPTER 6—ORGANIZING — P. 99
CHAPTER 7—POLITICAL ACTION — P. 119
CHAPTER 8—DISPLACED MEMBERS — P. 149
CHAPTER 9—UNION EDUCATION — P. 157
CHAPTER 10-UNION FINANCES — P. 165

APPENDIX 1—THE ORGANIZING MODEL OF UNIONISM — P. 174
APPENDIX 2-UNION LEADERSHIP — P. 175
APPENDIX 3—POLITICAL ACTION — P. 176
APPENDIX 4-ANALYSIS SHEET — P. 177
APPENDIX 5--"NO JOBS" OP-ED — P. 178
APPENDIX 6—PLACES TO LEARN ABOUT UNIONISM — P. 180
APPENDIX 7—THE RECOGNITION AGREEMENT — P. 181
APPENDIX 8—CASH VALUE OF A UNION CONTRACT — P. 184

CHAPTER 1—INTRODUCTION

"It was the best of times, it was the worst of times, it was the age of wisdom, it was the age of foolishness, it was the epoch of belief, it was the epoch of incredulity, it was the season of Light, it was the season of Darkness, it was the spring of hope, it was the winter of despair, we had everything before us, we had nothing before us, we were all going direct to Heaven, we were all going direct the other way . . ."
Charles Dickens. *A Tale of Two Cities* (1859)

Donald Trump might be the worst thing that ever happened to unionism in the United States.

Or the best.

Or both.

Or neither.

The times are so crazy that one reporter claimed about Trump's election that "Outside of the Civil War, World War II and including 9/11, this might be the most cataclysmic event the country's ever seen." The tumult grew exponentially in the following year, with the rise of the alt-right, the Nazi demonstrations, the Charlottesville murder, and the counter-demonstrations—the Women's March, the Poor Peoples March, the #MeToo movement, the DACA demonstrations and constant controversy on social media. The conflicts became even more outlandish, childish, global—and dangerous, as the war cries against countries like Iran, North Korea and Venezuela grew louder.

While the turmoil in the "shithole" Trump administration is getting everyone's attention, the danger is that every discussion is about Trump, partly because he is (unfortunately) such a compelling figure who has figured out how to make himself the center of political and social opinion. More importantly, blaming everything, or anything, only on him, however, skips much deeper problems for unions with much more complex solutions.

Watching "the crisis president," can be distracting but we need to start organizing for ourselves so that unionism can capture this enormous energy to change our workplaces and our society. Considering the beating that unions have been taking, it is a great chance for us to reconstruct our movement. People are moving, our members are moving (in many directions at the same time) but can we grab the moment?

The 2016 elections at every level demonstrated many deep divisions within the ruling class and its major political parties and within the union movement. It's like everything is in motion and up for grabs so life in the time of the Trump cannot be a spectator sport. Millions of workers who have, in effect, coasted because they assumed that their unions or the government could protect their lives, must become more militant.

In the first year of the new administration, there was much discussion and, most importantly, much activity from workers who never before saw a need to express their opinions--

at work, at their union meetings, on social media and in the streets. Sometimes their actions are negative, like voting in enormous numbers for Trump in 2016 and waving Nazi flags, and sometimes they are positive, like participating in demonstrations or proposing new union movements and political campaigns. Today clearly could be the revolutionary time that Dickens described.

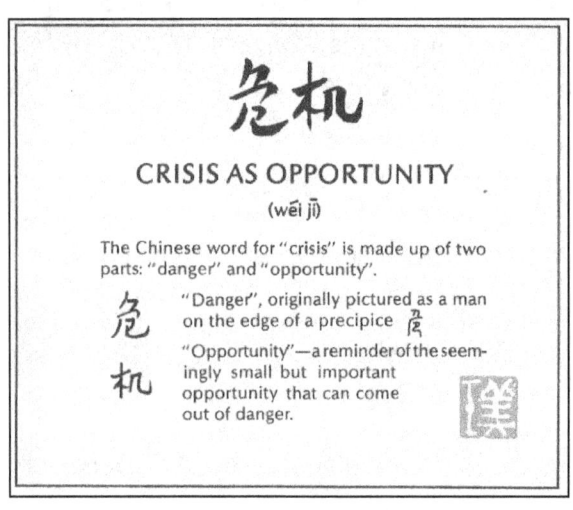

The situation perfectly illustrates the Chinese character for "crisis." Comprised of two parts— "danger" and "opportunity"—the character represents the challenges that we face, both the small percentage of unionized workers and the huge majority of angry, frustrated non-union workers. While they are demonstrating for, or against, "social" issues, like respect for women, protection for immigrants, higher minimum wage, jobs—and isn't the demand for jobs a "social" issue?--all of these issues can be, and should be, union issues.

Political scientists from the Universities of Connecticut and Denver, claimed that the Women's March in January, 2017, was "the largest day of protests in US history"-- somewhere between 3.3 million and 4.6 million marchers--and that "1 out of every 100 Americans marched to protest the new president's regime." As we stress the importance of global unionism to meet the new global economy, it was encouraging to see that sister protests across the globe attracted nearly 300,000 more attendees, 100,000 of them in London, with marches in solidarity from Iraq to Antarctica.[1] Some of the controversies got so hot that people complained of "resistance fatigue." We must use this excitement to rebuild our union movement? The #MeToo movement, for example, is a discussion about power in the workplace. Millions of people discussed and defended workers—both men and women--who have been abused by their bosses. If ever there was a potential union issue, this is it because a union gives workers power in our workplaces, so we don't have to put up with any kind of shit.

As an organizer in North Carolina, Juan Miranda stated:

> "The conditions that allowed for Trump to appeal to working-class people through an openly racist platform are the same conditions that are ripe for the rapid growth of solidarity, class consciousness, and mass action. As horrific as it was, Trump was able to inspire and mobilize many distraught and struggling people because he was able to deliver a simple message that spoke to what people wanted and gave them someone to blame. This is exactly what we should be doing, except we know who the real enemies are. We are already seeing opportunities as many who hoped for Trump to bring desired changes are now learning that he was never really a friend to working people. With the potential for more war, fewer good jobs, and the gutting of the public

---

[1] Matt Broomfield. *The Independent*. January 23, 2017.

school and healthcare systems, poor and working people are yet again being pinned down. These attacks present an opportunity to reach people who we have previously ignored."[2]

We should even create the new logo—MOUGA—Making Our Unions Great Again!

* * * * * * * * * * * * * * * * * * *

Once upon a time, most American workers knew the rules of life's game. We could get steady jobs—in coal mines, in steel and auto plants, in offices and schools and hospitals—and with hard work and union protections, we would live well. We knew what our futures would be like and what the future for our children would be like. As will be discussed more in Chapter 4, we are confronting a global economy that is tremendously different and rapidly evolving. With enormous changes in technology and in corporate structure, there is no more "normal."

All the institutions that so many people have taken for granted— economic cycles of recession and revival, the nature and attitudes of our employers, government at every level, the two main political parties, culture and participation and, most importantly, our unions--are now dramatically changing, whether we like it or not.

And it's not just Donald Trump.

In the period after the Civil War, the US economy went through tumultuous changes. As mass production expanded, the effects on people, both those in the United States and those immigrating to the US, were extraordinary: businesses were consolidated into corporations, the robber barons gained political power, and work processes were deskilled. The workshop economy and the artisan working class were destroyed and everything these skilled workers knew as "normal" was disrupted by the new economic structure. Millions of migrants were set in motion: internal migrants inside the US, pushed off farms and out of workshops, moved into the cities and took factory jobs while more millions of immigrants came to the US, looking for better lives. The lives of generations of workers were forever changed. The Civil War and the freeing of 4 million slaves were not solely responsible for these dramatic changes but they were a significant factor,[3] in the creation of a world that, for workers, seemed new and threatening.

As the US economy began to dominate the world, management demanded total control over the working class. Great social divisions—exactly like today—split workers along different lines, providing an opportunity for new movements and new ideas to rebuild our unions, confronted by an intensified anti-union movement. Small local unions with volunteer officers grew into national unions with fulltime paid staff and large treasuries. Unions saw the value of solidarity and created the Knights of Labor, the American Federation of Labor (AFL) and the Industrial Workers of the World (IWW).

We were confronting a similar transformation, even before Trump's election. The loss of employment and the dramatic decline of our standard of living was already the major challenge for unions because the old "normal" of recessions and economic revival is gone. Trump so

---

[2] Sarah Jaffee. "The Next Operation Dixie." *Dissent*. Summer, 2017.
[3] Mark Lause. *Free Labor: The Civil War and the Making of An American Working Class.*

expertly grabbed this "jobs" issue during his campaign, and even pivoted the "social" issue into an economic one and got a lot of votes from our members.

The most important word for workers is "jobs," but the simple loss of jobs, as industries shut down to move to non-union areas, or out of the country over the past 50 years, is simply no longer the only change. As described in Appendix 5, we are in a new economic world where technology and new business structures are eliminating jobs by the millions—jobs that will never come back, no matter how loudly Trump honks. Whole groups of workers can be affected by cultural changes, like coal miners, or by new technology, like landline telephone company workers or postal workers, who may go the way of the workers who manufactured the Smith-Corona typewriters.

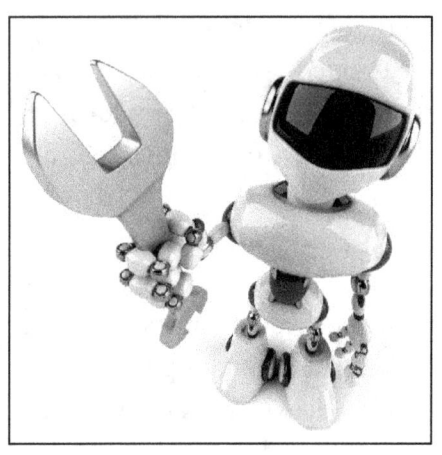

One consulting firm estimates that by 2030, as many as one-third of American jobs may disappear because of automation. Another estimated that by 2030, somewhere between 16-54 million jobs will be displaced by Artificial Intelligence (AI), or "robotics" as we know it.

These seismic changes are an enormous challenge for unions. accustomed to negotiating with one employer over basic issues like wages and benefits. As the whole world is being transformed, we have to plan ahead, not just for next week's grievance or next year's contract but to recreate our unions to deal with a radical new world—or else.

Airbnb is now the biggest hotel company in the world, although they don't own any properties. Uber is just a software tool, they don't own any cars, and are now the biggest taxi company in the world. There is even a $100 agricultural robot in the future so farmers in third world countries can then become managers of their field instead of working all day on their fields.

The problems of this world for us are enormous and you need to go no further than one day's Business section of the *New York Times* to see the challenges. At Ford Motor's "state-of-the art factory" in Hangzhou, China, "at least 650 robots, resembling huge, white-necked vultures, bob and weave to assemble the steel structures of utility vehicles and midsize sedans. Workers in blue uniforms still do some of the welding but much of the process has been automated." Ford was driven to this intense automation because "Blue-collar wages are now $4 to $5 an hour in large prosperous cities. . . Automation is a competitive necessity." The article describes the total automation of the welding and painting processes and while the director of China manufacturing for General Motors, proclaims that "Robots aren't the threat," clearly the drudgery of the assembly line work—with union pay and benefits--for which so many are nostalgic, is gone forever.[4]

---

[4] Keith Bradsher. "A Robot Revolution in China as Car Manufacturers Look to Cut Costs." *New York Times*. May 13, 2017.

In the same section, there was a discussion of the proposals by the Trump administration to change tax policies as "a range of economists, both conservative and liberal" claim "the government's focus. . . should be on raising the economy's speed limit, for example, by encouraging investments that increase productivity."[5]

In other words, more robots.

Donald Trump's promised these displaced workers to turn back the clock, to bring back "normal." Whether it was workers at the Carrier plant in Wisconsin, coal miners in West Virginia or steelworkers in Pennsylvania and Ohio, he proclaimed his power to reverse the changes. His first tweet as president-elect—echoing Franklin D. Roosevelt in 1932--promised that "the forgotten man and woman will never be forgotten again."

Over the past several years, a whole culture that I call "post-industrial pornography," has emerged to tell the sad tales of workers—mostly white industrial unionized workers—who lived, as if by entitlement, the American Dream, only to have it yanked away when their factories closed. This group, the deplorables, have been ignored for many years by the Democrats but became the centerpiece of the Trump's 2016 campaign. In his last campaign stop on November 8, 2016, in Grand Rapids, MI, Trump proclaimed: "The corrupt politicians and their special interests have ruled over this country for a very long time. Today is our Independence Day. Today the American working class is going to strike back, finally."

Look at Trump's inaugural speech:

"For too long, a small group in our nation's Capital has reaped the rewards of government while the people have borne the cost. Washington flourished – but the people did not share in its wealth. Politicians prospered – but the jobs left, and the factories closed. The establishment protected itself, but not the citizens of our country. Their victories have not been your victories; their triumphs have not been your triumphs; and while they celebrated in our nation's Capital, there was little to celebrate for struggling families all across our land. . . . The forgotten men and women of our country will be forgotten no longer. Everyone is listening to you now. . . . what people want is great schools for their children, safe neighborhoods for their families and good jobs for themselves. . . these are and reasonable demands of a righteous people and a righteous public."

If you just saw this statement printed, you would think an international union president had taken a forceful approach and was trying to rouse the members to fight the bosses. It is a sign of Trump's instinctive political sense that he captured, and then perverted, the anger of millions of workers. It also shows the vacuum within our unions that allows a guy like Trump—"my button is bigger than your button"—to appear as a champion of workers.

Trump was careful during the 2016 campaign never to demonize labor unions. "I have great relationships with unions," he told *Newsweek*'s Matthew Cooper in July 2015. "The union

---

[5] Binyamin Appelbaum. "Economists Skeptical of Trump Tax Plan." New York Times. May 13, 2017.

people, the people in unions, they seem to really want to vote for me," he told the South Carolina Radio Network in Feb. 2016. "I can live with unions in certain locations." [6]

"To a considerable extent, Trump preempted labor's political agenda. He peeled off rank-and-file support and backing among the broader working class by speaking plain language on such issues as trade, jobs, law enforcement, regulation and immigration. Trump promised fundamental change, pledging to 'drain the swamp.' In his campaign, Trump also exposed weaknesses in labor's political armor that raise serious questions about its future influence; a shrinking labor movement, particularly one with significant political cleavages, simply has less potential to deliver the vote."[7]

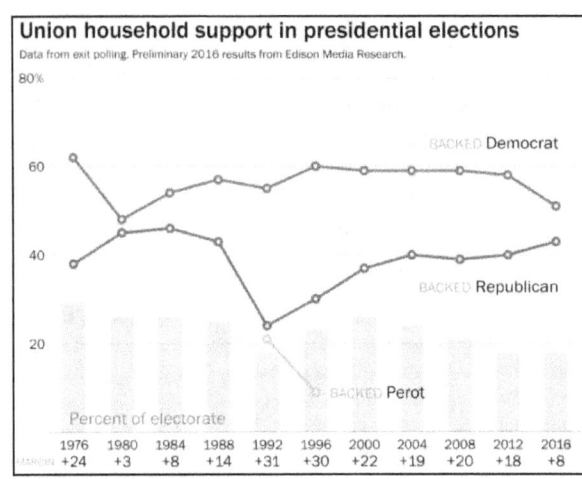

Is it a surprise that voters in union households still turned out for Democrats — but Clinton won union households by only 8 percent, according to exit polling, the smallest margin since Ronald Reagan's re-election in 1984. The 2016 exit polls show that 43 percent of voters in union households voted for Trump. In Ohio, he won the union vote by 9 percentage points after Obama carried the state's union households by 23 percent in 2012.

One statistic that is especially important for the 2016 election is while "by 2015, the number of union members had fallen to 14.8 million, and the number of white men in unions to 6.2 million. That's a drop in density from 48.4 percent to 41.9 percent -- just over the last 16 years. That means that Trump did as well as Reagan in 1984 *despite* more of those union members being nonwhite. One reason why may be women who are members of unions. In 2012, Mitt Romney beat President Obama by 20 points among white women without college degrees. Trump beat Clinton with that group by 28 points."[8] By one estimate, "About one-third of the [United Auto Workers] members cast a vote for Mr. Trump and another 8 percent either didn't vote for president or went with a third-party candidate, breaking from historical trends."[9]

Trump followed up his campaign by meeting with officers of the Carrier Corporation to demand that they block the transfers of 1,000 jobs to Mexico, and got the state of Indiana to provide a $ 7 million incentive to keep the jobs, praising Carrier for investing another $16 million in their factory in Indianapolis. As one worker responded, "'I'm ready for him to come,' said Robin Maynard, a 24-year veteran of Carrier who builds high-efficiency furnaces and earns

---

[6] Timothy Noah. "Does Labor Have A Death Wish?" Politico. November 7, 2017.
[7] Marick F. Masters, Raymond F. Gibney and Robert R. Albright. "Labor Blues: President Trump." *Labor Studies Journal*. September, 2017.
[8] Phillip Bump. "Donald Trump got Reagan-like support from union households." *The Washington Post*. November 10, 2016.
[9] Cristina Rogers. "UAW Working to Organize Employees at Mississippi Nissan Plant." *Detroit Free Press*. July 18, 2017.

almost $24 an hour. "Now I can put my daughter through college without having to look for another job."[10]

We all know by now, of course, that Carrier soon announced that 600 jobs were being moved to Mexico and that a lot of their investment would be to automate sections of the factory, likely resulting in a further reduction in the number of workers needed to run the plant.

"We're the ones that made the $9.7 billion that they collected. We can understand companies having to go overseas if they're losing money. We get it. But Carrier is the top A.C.- and furnace-making company in the nation, getting money hand over fist. Just don't bullshit us."[11]

* * * * * * * * * * * * * * * * * *

Enough about Trump. What about us?

You can't find a solution if you don't know what the problem is, and many union members look at Donald Trump as if he were our only problem. While "one longtime union staff member told me that Trump's victory was 'an extinction-level event for American labor,'"[12] the problem of anti-unionism is much deeper and has been going for more than a century, even if the controversy over such large numbers of union members voting for an anti-union candidate is still a hot topic.

Our situation is illustrated by the story of the boiling frog. The organizing director for the old Amalgamated Clothing & Textile Workers was Jim Walraven and he often told this story from his childhood in Sweet Valley, GA. If you have a pot of water on a stove, and you place a frog in it and slowly turn up the heat, the frog will stay in the pot until it dies. On the other hand, if you get the water boiling and toss in the frog, it will jump right back out.

We are the boiling frog. While many union officers have reacted with expressions of concern over the election of Donald Trump, their reaction to this latest of attacks has not been to look at our movement to see what needs to be done but to make excuses and to basically sit tight and hope for the best. They ignore that all our "strategies" for the past 70 years have failed.

WHY DOES AMERICA NEED UNIONS?

Since 1978, the percentage of American workers in labor unions has been cut in half.

Also since 1978, average pay has increased 997% for CEOs and 10.9% for workers. Coincidence?

OCCUPY DEMOCRATS

Numbers demonstrate that the decline in unionism since the end of world War II. According to the Department of Labor figures for 2017, unions have dropped from 37 percent of the workforce in the late 1950's, down to 20.1 percent in 1983 when the Department of Labor started keeping count, down to 10.7 percent in 2017, the lowest rate in more than 75 years, even with a slight gain of 262,000 members in 2017.

---

[10] Nelson D. Schwartz. "Trump to Announce that Carrier Plant Will Keep jobs in U.S." *New York Times.* November 29, 2016

[11] Natasha Bach. "Carrier Factory 'Saved' by Donald Trump to Lay off 200 more workers." Fortune. January 11, 2018.

[12] Harold Myerson. "Donald Trump Can Kill the American Unions." *The Washington Post.* November 23, 2016

In the private sector, union members were 24.2 percent of the workforce in 1973 but today only 6.5 percent of the work force, a figure comparable to 1900. In 2017, 7.2 million employees in the public sector belonged to a union, compared with 7.6 million workers in the private sector. Although the union membership rate for private-sector workers edged up by 0.1 percentage point in 2017, their unionization rate continued to be substantially lower than that for public-sector workers (6.5 percent versus 34.4 percent). We represented the same 14 million that were members at the end of World War II. As one commentator stated several years ago: "A generation ago, labor unions were often a familiar feature of the American workplace, but in private businesses across the country, unions have been shrinking. Today fewer than one in 15 private sector workers belong to a union, compared with almost one in four in 1973."[13]

So we have been pushed back almost 120 years in percentage of workers represented, and pushed back more than 70 years in sheer numbers. Another ominous statistic is that union membership rates continued to be highest among workers ages 45 to 64. In 2016, 13.3 percent of workers ages 45 to 54 and ages 55 to 64 were union members. More importantly, the number of workers age 16-24 who are members of a union is only 4.4% and the number of workers 25-34 is only 9.2 percent so a whole generation of young workers has no union experience. The one glimmer of hope in the 2017 BLS report is that of the 858,000 net new jobs for workers under age 35, almost one in four (23 percent) was a union job.

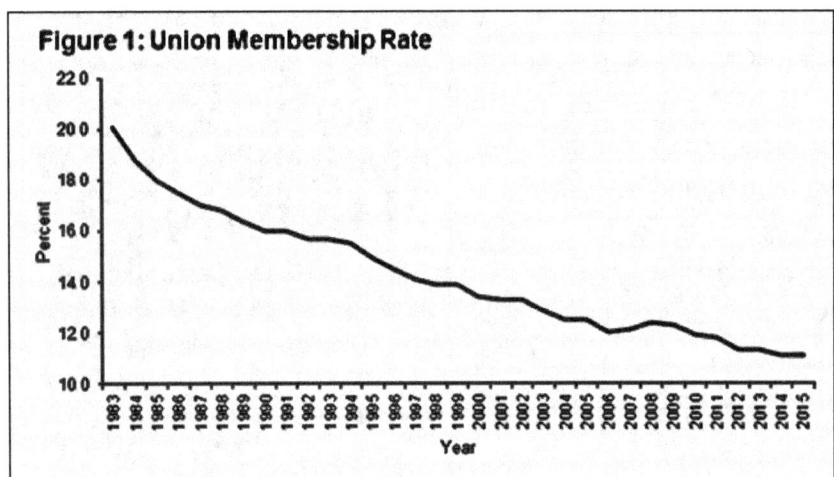

Figure 1: Union Membership Rate

Union membership in 2017 in the public sector was 34.4 percent, more than five times higher than that of private-sector workers, a figure that has basically held steady since 1980. Within the public sector, the union membership rate was highest for local government (40.3 percent), which includes employees in heavily unionized occupations, such as teachers, police officers, and firefighters, making public employee unions the juiciest of targets for the anti-union movement.

Most importantly, an indication of "the southernization of the United States," membership was dramatically compressed into a few states: "Over half of the 14.8 million union members in the U.S. lived in just seven states (California, 2.5 million; New York, 2.0 million; Illinois, 0.8 million; Michigan and Pennsylvania, 0.7 million each; and New Jersey and Ohio, 0.6 million each), though these states accounted for only about one-third of wage and salary

---

[13] Anna Bernasek. "The Shrinking American Labor Union." *New York Times*. February 7, 2015.

employment nationally[14] Need you be reminded that Ohio, Michigan, Pennsylvania went for Trump in 2016 and that Chris Christie was a two-term governor in New Jersey?

If you want a fabulous interactive map that show the decline of union membership 1964-2014 in each state, check out
https://www.npr.org/sections/money/2015/02/23/385843576/50-years-of-shrinking-union-membership-in-one-map

A surprising statistic is that "About two-thirds (65.4 percent) of workers age 18 to 64 and covered by a union contract are women and/or people of color.
- Almost half (46.3 percent) are women.
- More than a third (35.8 percent) are black, Hispanic, Asian, or other nonwhite workers.
- Black workers are the most likely to be represented by unions: 14.5 percent of black workers age 18 to 64 are covered by a collective bargaining agreement, compared with 12.5 percent of white workers and 10.1 percent of Hispanic workers.[15]

Another urgent statistic is that there are 1.6 million "free riders"—workers covered by a union contract who are not members. This group, almost 12 percent of union members, not only deprives our unions of resources but is the basis for decertification campaigns and should be targeted by internal organizing campaigns.

Clearly, there is a movement is to eliminate unionism completely in the United States. Labor historians often focus on a succession of historical moments, like the Trump election, which are described as climactic or "turning points." Joseph McCartin called the PATCO strike "the strike that changed America," and many union members mark the strike as "the beginning of the decline," while Tom Juravich and Kate Bronfenbrenner called the 1990 Ravenswood strike "the Revival of American Labor." The point is that the decline of our movement has been steady for the past 70 years—yes, there have been some dramatic attacks like the PATCO strike, and occasional resistance, like the Ravenswood strike, but missing the structural decline distorts any discussion about solutions.

One crisis that became an opportunity for our bosses was the recession of 2007-2009. The U.S. Department of Labor reported in November, 2008, that employers slashed 533,000 jobs—the most in 34 years—as the Great Recession surged. The unemployment rolls had risen for seven months before that and continued to soar for another 10 months before topping 10 percent and beginning to level off late in 2009. These hard times provided what Naomi Klein calls "the shock doctrine"—a situation when the big capitalists take advantage of a social crisis to push through policies while "citizens are too emotionally and physically distracted by disasters or upheavals to mount an effective resistance."

Using the Great Recession as an excuse, companies and public agencies in negotiations came after long-standing union contracts, demanding two-tier (or three-tier or more) wage structures, extorting health insurance co-pays and cancelling pensions. Unions have not

---

[14] Bureau of Labor Statistics. January 19, 2018. https://www.bls.gov/news.release/pdf/union2.pdf
[15] "How Today's Unions Help Working People." Economic Policy Institute. January 25, 2018.

recovered any of the previous benefits, even though the stock market hit a new high in January, 2018.

One historian sees unionism in apocalyptic terms, comparing us to the last living people in the movie *On The Beach,* where a group of survivors from an atomic bomb are waiting for the end of the world.

"Formed in 1955 with a merger meant to end two decades of bitter infighting, the AFL-CIO's primary purpose was to consolidate and administer the post-war collective bargaining regime. There was a reason why its new headquarters building overlooked the White House. The premise of that regime was that labor was a limited partner with capital in a relationship mediated by the federal government. This arrangement made workers and their unions particularly vulnerable to the rise of neoliberal globalization. Moreover, a labor movement whose mission focused on collective bargaining with individual employers, and with many of the fundamental functions of working- class solidarity outlawed or constrained, left little scope for a national labor organization to mobilize and lead an organized working class in campaigns against capital. . . . Today, labor's influence has been reduced to a few diminishing private-sector outposts. Capital has long moved on, embracing a neoliberal world order with no place for unions or any restraints on its mobility or autonomy. [16]

* * * * * * * * * * * * * * * * * * *

The speech that Donald Trump gave in Warsaw, Poland, on July 6, 2017, could apply to unionism as well: "We have to say there are dire threats to our security and to our way of life. You see what's happening out there. They are threats. We will confront them. We will win. But they are threats."

There are more than 15 million union members, plus another million or so union retirees, plus our families and neighbors. We are not small and helpless—especially if we start building global unions--but we need to learn how to stand up and roar to take advantage of the social turmoil all around us. Yes, there is danger but there is also huge opportunity and many unions have significant financial resources to support campaigns. This book will talk about the desperate need for union members to adjust our attitudes and change our strategies to rebuild our unions—to "confront the dire threats to our way of life."

For several generations, workers accepted The Servicing Model of Unionism [Appendix 1], so their union is a service they buy with their dues dollars, like cable TV, and they sat back and

---

[16] Mark Dudzic. "The AFL-CIO "On The Beach." *New Labor Forum.* June 1, 2017.

expected "The Union" to take care of all their problems. They were hired into a workplace where a union already existed, with a strong contract and effective enforcement, and knew nothing about the struggles that it took to make all of this happen.

Over these decades, like the years after the Civil War, the bosses demanded total control of the workplace and, more importantly, total control over the direction of the company. We conceded it to them so the challenge by the unions over management decisions—"Management Rights"--has been narrowed. As a result, companies can close, move, merge, replace us with robots or declare bankruptcy and we have no power to contest the decision. In town after town, when companies, close, union members blame The Union—or politicians—for not doing anything to challenge the decision.

Unions have been reactive, only responding to management. We must change this attitude as well as our strategies for dealing with this new world. As a first attitude adjustment, we have to tattoo the word "proactive" on our foreheads. Being proactive means making things happen, planning and aggressively organizing, not waiting until things happen to us and then trying to make the best out a bad situation.

We also need to appreciate that our anti-union opponents have something that we lack: a strategic plan, like the one outlined by Lewis Powell in his famous directive to the Chamber of Commerce in 1971. The Powell Memo is thorough and comprehensive, and encouraged an expansion of activities through the Chamber of Commerce (the equivalent to our AFL-CIO). Powell advocated expanding business control at every level, and especially in schools, the courts, political action, "books, paperbacks, pamphlets" (so pre-social media!), paid advertisements and control of the media.

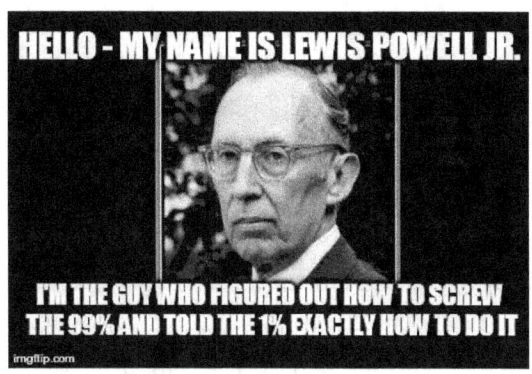

While Powell looks at the power of the conflict as a debate, and criticizes businessmen who "have shown little stomach for hard-nose contest with their critics, and little skill in effective intellectual and philosophical debate," he is talking about building a movement at a time of crisis: "The overriding first need is for businessmen to recognize that the ultimate issue may be survival — survival of what we call the free enterprise system, and all that this means for the strength and prosperity of America and the freedom of our people." With the change of a few words, this challenge could apply to unionism today, which is indeed facing a crisis of survival.

Powell's evaluation of corporate officers at the time can also apply to union officers today: "The painfully sad truth is that business, including the boards of directors and the top executives of corporations great and small and business organizations at all levels, often have responded — if at all — by appeasement, ineptitude and ignoring the problem."

We certainly should adapt Powell's "solution" as our own: "Strength lies in organization, in careful long-range planning and implementation, in consistency of action over an indefinite period of years, in the scale of financing available only through joint effort, and in the political power available only through united action and national organizations."[17]

The success of the Powell Memo is illustrated by the abysmal numbers for union membership today. For Powell, defending "free enterprise" meant expanding corporate power and his memo is just one articulation of a strategy that has been followed in the intervening years by groups like ALEC (American Legislative Exchange Council) or the Koch Brothers' People for the American Way, as well as by The Chamber of Commerce.

If this discussion of corporate strategies seems a little lengthy, it is directed at union members, and non-union workers, who think that the attacks by their boss are isolated and limited only to their workplaces. Their responses, then, are also limited to individual workplaces and not to a comprehensive strategy involving all workers—not just in the US, but in the world. Powell was talking about building a movement and we need to do the same thing.

Let's focus on some specific long term attacks on unionism that show Trump is a symptom, not the illness. The passage in 1947 of the Taft-Hartley Act, which allowed states to pass open shop legislation—cleverly misnamed "Right to Work"-- was a major attack on private sector unions and one important factor in the low percentage of union membership today. In many of these 27 open shop states (plus Guam), there are locals with barely 50% membership, cutting off bargaining power and leaving the unions ripe for decertification campaigns.

With membership in private sector unions down to below 7 percent, the next front is to attack public sector unions where membership is still almost 40 percent of all public workers. Public sector unions in many states have negotiated "agency fee" contract clauses so non-members must properly pay a "fair share" fee for union representation, even if they do not become members. It is these clauses that are being attacked, using the courts, as Lewis Powell urged, with bogus Constitutional law challenges.

One challenge for public sector workers came at the end of 2015, when the case *Friedrichs v California Teachers Association*, that could have outlawed the collection of agency fees from public employees, was moving to a decision by the Supreme Court. There was a flurry of activity from union presidents to try to start internal organizing programs and to sign up the non-members but the sudden death of Supreme Court Justice Antonin Scalia, and the blocking of the decision, allowed them to go back to business-as-usual.

The anti-union movement is relentless, however, and now there is a new case, *Janus v AFSCME*, ready to be heard in the spring, 2018, before a Supreme Court which appears set to endorse it. The results of the attacks on public sector workers on a limited basis are catastrophic.

The example of Wisconsin is a powerful example of their destructive success. Governor Scott Walker supported the passage in 2011 of the Wisconsin Act 10, proclaimed "The Wisconsin Budget Repair Bill," eliminating agency fee requirements, as well as limiting union rights in negotiations and requiring annual recertifications. Union membership in Wisconsin dropped from 354,882 members in 2010 to 218,233 in 2016, a decline of 38.5 percent. Membership in The Wisconsin State Employees, AFSCME Council 24, fell 60 percent and its

---

[17] Lewis Powell. Memo to the Chamber of Commerce. August 23, 1971

annual budget plunged from $6 million to $2 million. Hard up for cash, the union considered selling its building, which was underused anyway as staff reductions left many offices empty. In Oshkosh, among the city's 560 city workers, union membership fell to 225, or 47%, down from 450, or 87%. Since Act 10 was enacted, membership in Local 1 [in Madison] has plummeted to 122 from 1,000.[18] "Records filed with the Internal Revenue Service show the three AFSCME councils operating in Wisconsin — umbrella groups for union locals — saw their combined revenues drop from $13.8 million the year Walker was first elected to $6.2 million by 2013. The downsizing prompted those three councils recently to merge into one." With the loss of income, unions lose bargaining power and the services diminish. Members who believe in The Servicing Model of Unionism simply quit the union, creating a deadly downward spiral.

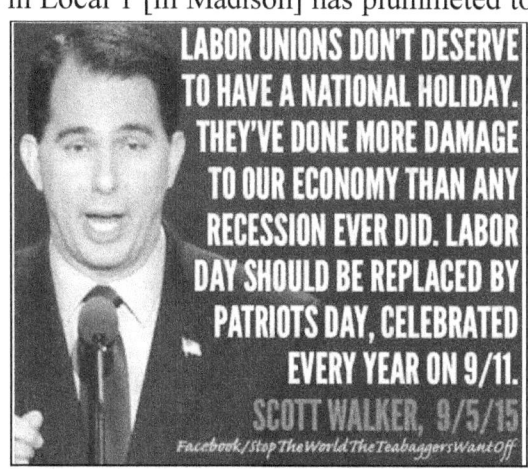

Building on his "success" attacking the public-sector unions, Walker then attacked private sector unions.

> "Walker took the fight to public worker unions in his first term, but in his second — as he readied his presidential run — he has broadened the battle to include private-sector unions, something he previously indicated he would not do. As turmoil erupted in 2011 over his initial anti-union moves, Walker gave a statewide 'fireside chat' on public television in Wisconsin in which he hailed private-sector unions as 'our partners in economic development.' Unlike most in organized labor, Terry McGowan, the business manager of a construction workers union headquartered in Pewaukee, a Milwaukee suburb, endorsed Walker's re-election last year. McGowan said he did so after receiving personal assurances from Walker that he would not go after unions in the private sector. But in his new term, Walker has signed anti-union 'right-to-work' legislation, scaled back pay protections for many building projects and trimmed state-funded roadwork that provides jobs for McGowan's members. McGowan now says Walker double-crossed him. 'To me he lied,' said McGowan, who heads the 9,100-member Operating Engineers Local 139. 'He looked me in the eyes and told me that it was all safe.'"[19]

The failure of unionism, as a movement, was that Scott Walker was elected in 2010 in a "union" state that Obama won in 2008 by 14 percentage points. Walker survived a recall vote in 2012 and then was re-elected in 2014. After the recall vote in 2012, "Wisconsin Gov. Scott Walker says 'there's no doubt' that union members were among those who voted to keep him in office in Tuesday's recall election. The network exit poll for the special election showed that

---

[18] Steven Greenhouse. "Wisconsin's Legacy For Unions." *New York Times*. February 24, 2014.
[19] Bob Secter. "Walker's anti-union crusade pivotal to White House run, damaging to labor." *Chicago Tribune*. July 28, 2015.
[20] Susan Jones." 38% of Voters from Union Households Voted for Walker." CNS News.Com June 6, 2012.

Walker won the votes of 38 percent of voters who said they were a union member or lived in a household with a union member."[20]

Another challenge for unionism is equally strong: where industries located in the US, often unionized, once dominated the world, now these facilities are spread across the globe to places many of us cannot find without a map. Unions that claimed to be "international" unions because they had locals in the US and Canada, and maintained bargaining power with national contracts, now find themselves overwhelmed. The loss of this power is the result of many factors: in many industries, work has moved, just as it has for the past 100 years only now the work is being moved out of the US and into foreign countries, destroying unions in the process. The "electronic economy" allows work—like call centers—to be done anywhere in the world.

Our unions are then failing as their industries in the United States fail and also in terms of "market share," the percentage of workers in an industry that are represented by a union. As US Steel announced the layoff of 25% of its salaried workers in April, 2016, the numbers were grim: once the largest steel producer in the world, the company employed more than 300,000 workers in the years after World War II. With the layoffs announced Wednesday, the company will employ about 20,000 workers in North America. It was ranked last year as the 15th-largest steel producer in the world."[21] Republic Steel is now owned by Grupo Simec, based in Guadalajara, Mexico and still maintains plants in the US but with a work force of only 2,000 workers. China is now the top steel producer in the world, followed by Japan and India.

And all of this before Donald Trump.

In a cruel and destructive irony, Trump's boasts will devastate the US steel industry. "Foreign steel makers have rushed to get their product into the United States before tariffs start. According to the American Iron and Steel Institute, which tracks shipments, steel imports were 19.4 percent higher in the first 10 months of 2017 than in the same period last year. That surge of imports has hurt American steel makers, which were already struggling against a glut of cheap Chinese steel. When ArcelorMittal announced the layoffs in Conshohocken [of 150 of its 207 workers], it blamed those imports, as well as low demand for steel for bridges and military equipment.[22]

In a speech in June in Cincinnati, Trump proclaimed: "Wait till you see what I'm going to do for steel and your steel companies."

I guess we have seen.

Once upon a happy time, unions like the United Auto Workers (UAW) and the United Steelworkers of America (USWA) represented all of the workers in their industries under national contracts. In 2013, "UAW members produced only 54 percent of the cars and trucks made in the United States last year. That compares with 85 percent of cars and trucks built in the U.S. in 1999. One reason is the growing number of non-union plants built by foreign auto

---

[21] Alex Nixon. "U.S. Steel will lay off 25 percent of its salaried workers." *Chicago Tribune*. April 6, 2017.
[22] Ana Swanson. "Trump Promised to Protect Steel. Layoffs are Coming Instead." *New York Times*. December 22, 2017
[23] Micheline Maynard. "The UAW Is Losing Its Grip On Auto Industry Labor." *Forbes*. February 20, 2014.

companies, mainly across the south. Another reason is the sales growth by those companies, ranging from Honda and Toyota of Japan to BMW and Mercedes-Benz of Germany, to Korea's Hyundai and Kia."[23] UAW campaigns to organize workers at the "run-backs" factories, those that have relocated into the US, have failed—at Volkswagen in Tennessee in 2014, at Nissan in Mississippi in August, 2017, and at Fuyao Auto Glass Plant outside Dayton, OH in October, 2017.

The UAW which has a "national" contract with General Motors, now finds that GM has facilities in almost 20 different countries, from England to Vietnam, none of which is covered by a UAW contract. The UAW has lost more than 1 million members since 1979 and 10% of its members now are graduate students.

And all of this before Donald Trump.

In the construction industry, where building trades unions have been strong, there is now a clear open shop movement. In a "candid speech" on June 28, 2017, Lou Coletti, president of the New York City Building Trade Employers Association, stated: "We're an organization that's in transition, ninety-five percent of my construction managers are building open shop. There are trades that have made changes, and if they made changes, their prices are at the table and it works and if it doesn't, then we don't get the job. It's that simple. We're a contractor group, not a labor group. We know we've lost a tremendous amount of market share in the residential marketplace as well as the interior marketplace. It's a fact. We're in an open shop environment—that isn't going to change."

The motto of the Building Trades Employers Association, by the way, proclaims that it recognizes "that a vibrant unionized construction industry is essential to the economic future of New York City."[24]

In response, Gary LaBarbera, the president of the Building & Construction Trades Council of Greater New York, could only respond lamely that "Gotham Was, Is and Always Will Be a Union Town. . . We've worked with the city of New York over recent years to create strong Project Labor Agreements (PLA) covering over $8 billion of construction projects and saving the City and taxpayers over $347 million. . . [working] to reduce wages and cut construction costs, but union have also made historic changes to collective bargaining agreements including work rule changes."

LaBarbera attacked the safety records of non-union—or "rat"—contractors, by noting that "more than 30 workers have been killed over the past 30 months, and 90 percent of those fatalities were on nonunion sites,"[25] avoiding a discussion of the value of a union officer boasting about reducing wages for his members.

---

[24] Sally Goldenberg. "As Construction Safety Debate heats Up, Contracting Group Acknowledges Shift away from Unions." *Politico*. July 5, 2017.
[25] Gary LaBarbera. "Gotham Was, Is and Always Will Be, a Union Town." *Commercial Observer*. June 20, 2017.

Companies are dramatically changing their structures, creating non-union divisions in complicated management shuffling that construction unions call "going double-breasted." The Communications Workers of America (CWA) went on strike against Verizon for both of their most recent contracts, in 2011 and 2016. The CWA, along with the IBEW, represented 45,000 Verizon workers in 2011 but only 39,000 workers in 2016, while Verizon Wireless—an example of how technology is changing the workforce—now has more than 100,000 workers, all of whom are non-union except for about 120 wireless retail workers. As an example of the dangers of allowing the non-union division to grow, Verizon in 2012 successfully forced landline workers (and retirees) to start paying health insurance co-pays for the first time, a significant loss for the members and retirees in a company where they had successfully resisted such demands for many years. As will be discussed in Chapter 4, the changing structure of employers—new divisions, new owners, like private hedge funds and vulture capitalists, with bad attitudes toward unions is a major challenge for us that came long before Donald Trump was elected.

* * * * * * * * * * * * * * * * * *

As if we didn't not already have enough problems dealing with our own supervisor in our own town, we are now all workers in a global economy and our unions must adjust. Just as small craft unions evolved to deal with large national corporations after the Civil War, now we have multi-national companies, which really seem to exist only in offshore post office boxes. Their relentless drive for maximum profits is being felt in every town in the United States, and all around the world, as workers face what is called ""precarisation of labor." A "precariat" is defined as "a social class formed by people suffering from precarity, which is a condition of existence without predictability or security."

The precariat is part of the "gig economy," in which "workers" disappear, replaced by contractors, "contingent workers" or temps. "Steven Berkenfeld, an investment banker who has spent his career evaluating corporate strategies, says companies of all shapes and sizes are increasingly thinking like this: 'Can I automate it? If not, can I outsource it? If not, can I give it to an independent contractor or freelancer?' Hiring an employee is a last resort, Mr. Berkenfeld adds, and 'very few jobs make it through that obstacle course.'"

"Bank of New York New York Chairman and CEO Gerald Hassell vowed to 'drive down the labor component of our company' with technology that can perform tasks currently done by people. Other companies view contracting as a stopgap until more jobs are automated, freeing firms to dispense with some workers altogether."

One reader remarked:" As a retired employee who was loyal to his company for 36 years and frankly felt the company was loyal to me, I find this to be a very depressing article. There really is no difference now between on-shore outsourcing and off-shore outsourcing. Employees are no longer contributors to the overall corporation success but small cogs in the machine which can be discarded at will. If anything shows what Trump's challenge to 'Make America Great Again' truly is, this article does it. I am glad I worked those years, got my pension and can look back at some success. What are so many current workers going to look back on?[26]

The most dramatic opposition to the gig economy was the suicide of taxi driver Doug Schifter, who killed himself with a shotgun in front of New York City Hall to protest the expansion of Uber and other competitors. Schifter, a member of the New York Taxi Drivers Alliance, "had driven more than five million miles throughout his tenure, through five hurricanes and 50 snowstorms" but now was working a 100-hour week, where a 40-hour week was "normal" in the past. "He had lost his health insurance and accrued credit card debt and he would no longer work for 'chump change,' preferring, he said, to die in the hope that his sacrifice would draw attention to what drivers, too often unable to feed their families now, were enduring."[27]

In the United States, it is the part-time jobs, the gig economy, the contract work without benefits or legal protections.

"On June 7, US Secretary of Labor Alexander Acosta announced the withdrawal of joint employment independent contractor informal guidance, effectively removing what are called 'administrator interpretations' implemented under the Obama administration designed to create employer liability. The decision will serve to further empower the major corporations while reducing their accountability and restricting the rights of workers. . . . The new legal interpretation was designed to provide some form of basic representation to workers employed by companies that refuse to recognize themselves as employers while still maintaining the level of control over the worker that an employer would have. . . Following the 2007-2008 economic crisis and the subsequent "recovery" under the Obama administration, such forms of employment have been on the rise. Since the recession, small businesses have accounted for 67 percent of net new jobs—most of them low-wage, temp or contract work. From 2012 to 2016, franchises accounted for 10.9 percent of new private sector jobs. Franchises now account directly and indirectly for over 13 million jobs in the United States. . . . Furthermore self-employed individuals are not allowed to organize or be involved in collective bargaining of any sort. In fact, for such employees to work together on pricing and conditions would be considered illegal price fixing."[28]

---

[26] Lauren Weber. "The End of employees." *Wall Street Journal*. February 2, 2017.
[27] Ginia Bellefante. "A Driver's Suicide Reveals the Dark Side of the Gig Economy." *New York Times*. February 6, 2018
[28] E.P. Milligan. "Trump administration rolls back "joint-employer" labor provision in favor of big business." World Socialist Web Site. http://www.wsws.org/en/articles/2017/06/13/labo-j13.html June 13, 2017.

This seismic change in employment relations—destroying all of the social and legal avenues for organizing that are familiar to us—are not limited to the United States. In Europe, we see "Labour contracts without health and social insurance. Involuntary part-time. Fixed-term and agency jobs. Across the continent, millions of Europeans must deal with insecure and low-paid employment, though the economy, overall, is doing better than at any point in the last decade. In the euro zone alone, more than five and a half million people found new jobs since the end of 2012. But four out of five are part-time or fixed-term and largely low-paid, according to Eurostat. . . . Nearly half of employees up to the age of 25 are employed on temporary contracts, in Spain this figure is even more than 70 percent."[29]

"This is the legacy of a painful financial crisis that has left employers wary of hiring permanent workers in a tenuous economy where growth is still weak. Under European labor laws, permanent workers are usually more difficult to lay off and require more costly benefit packages, making temporary contracts appealing for all manner of industries, from low-wage warehouse workers to professional white-collar jobs. For those stuck in this employment netherworld, life is a cycle of constant job searches. Confidence can give way to doubt as career prospects seem to fade. Young people talk of delaying marriage and families indefinitely. And though many were grateful for any workplace experience, they were also cynical about companies that treated them like disposable labor."[30]

So everything revolves around the word "job," at least for workers. Where the jobs are, or will be, and what happened to them is a very complicated situation, far beyond the "normal" union negotiations and political action we have known.

* * * * * * * * * * * * * * * * * *

Enough of the bad news. While the election of Trump obviously represents a danger, it also provides an enormous opportunity to make a break from our recent past. If the change seems abrupt and dangerous, it has provoked some union officers to look at our movement, creating a discussion that is long overdue. There is no longer a simple *status quo*, and everyone who believes that the old days will be brought back are simply whistling past the graveyard. Some of the officers of the Building Trades union officers figured that groveling directly in front of Donald Trump might preserve some of their benefits—pipeline jobs, the Davis-Bacon Act—but clearly every union is under open attack and there will be no survival for any of us if the goal of eliminating unions completely is achieved.

---

[29] Elisa Semantke. "Race to the bottom: Europe's precariat." *Investigate Europe*. November 22, 2017.
[30] Liz Alderman. Feeling 'Pressure All the Time' on Europe's Treadmill of Temporary Work." *New York Times*. February 9, 2017.

As the crisis deepens, it is discouraging to hear a response from top officers who act as if the Titanic were not taking on water. After the release in January, 2017, of the dismal statistics about unions from the BLS, here was the response from the president of the AFL-CIO:

For Immediate Release January 26, 2017   **Contact:** Josh Goldstein 202-XXX-XXXX
Collective Action Is Stronger Than Ever
Statement by AFL-CIO President Richard Trumka on the release of the annual Bureau of Labor Statistics report on union membership:

The sky is falling! The labor movement is dead! These are the canned reactions that of out-of-touch people who want to believe their own story about unions in America will tell themselves when they see today's report. But neither reflects a real understanding about a movement that cannot be defined by government statistics. The truth is, collective action in America is stronger than ever. We've seen the source of our power in defeating the TPP, even when most people told us we couldn't. We've seen it in successfully raising wages at the state and local levels against great political odds. And we'll use it to begin to change the tide for all working people. Because a strong labor movement raises wages for all working families and improves our entire economy. For decades, study after study has proven that all wages in America have a direct tie to union density. And according to today's report, workers in a union made $202 more per week. That's money in people's pocket. That's a government statistic we can get behind.

This response echoes George Meany's famous—or infamous-- statement from 1955: "I used to worry about the size of the membership. I stopped worrying because to me it doesn't make any difference. The organized fellow is the only fellow that counts."

More importantly, as one CWA member told me on January 28, 2017, "It saddens me that Trumka doesn't see a need to be concerned about these numbers. Labor is in big trouble. At the local level we're struggling and fighting to survive every minute of every day. One thing I've learned is if we wait for the leadership to do something, it will never get better. We, the rank and file will continue to fight for workers' rights and work to grow the union."

One characteristic of "great leadership" is claiming credit for something you really didn't accomplish, and Trumka's boast that "we" defeated the TPP" is really inaccurate It is not clear how labor defeated the TPP after enthusiastically supporting a presidential candidate who described the trade deal as one "which will bring together nine APEC economies in a cutting-edge, next generation trade deal, one that aims to eliminate all trade tariffs by 2015 while improving supply change, saving energy, enhancing business practices both through information technology and green technologies" before desperately reversing herself a month before the election.[31]

The elation over the withdrawal in mid-February, 2017, of the proposed Secretary of Labor Andrew Puzder, the president of the conglomerate CKE that owns fast food chains Hardees and Carl's Jr., is another example of taking credit where it is not deserved. Without doubt, Puzder was an abominable choice—fitting in perfectly, of course, with Trump's other

---

[31] Lauren Carroll. "Hillary Clinton flip-flops on Trans-Pacific Partnership." Politifact. October 8th, 2015

selections—as the head of fast food franchises, as an opponent of minimum wage and insulting to every worker. "Attacking a state minimum wage increase, Puzder proclaimed: 'California has gone really from being this golden state, the state of opportunity, to being a kind of nanny state,' he said in 2009. 'You can't be a capitalist in this state.' . . . In the months before California passed a law last year raising the minimum wage to $15 by 2022, many business leaders kept their objections discreet, but Mr. Puzder was blunt: 'How do you pay somebody $15 an hour to scoop ice cream? How good could you be at scooping ice cream?' he asked."[32]

One sign of the political weakness of the union movement was our inability to block Puzder's nomination because of his brutal approach to workers. "He had faced aggressive attacks in recent weeks by Democrats, unions, workers' rights advocates and fast-food employees over labor law violations at his company's restaurants and his opposition to a significant increase in the federal minimum wage. But his decision to pull out was triggered by concerns from a growing number of Senate Republicans about decades-old allegations of spousal abuse and an admission that he had employed a housekeeper who was in the U.S. illegally."[33]

The national AFL, however, was quick to claim credit. In an e-mail blast, we got:

"President Donald Trump's first nominee for labor secretary, Andrew Puzder, is out! This is huge news and wouldn't have been possible without the calls and other actions you took since his nomination was announced. It sends a strong message to Trump that when working people take collective action, we can win. This will not be the last time we'll need to take a stand to stop attacks on our families and communities, but that doesn't mean we can't celebrate our victories. The defeat of Puzder was a big victory and would not have been possible without everything you did to make Puzder toxic on Capitol Hill. It's a reminder of the collective power of working people. Together, we sent a clear message to President Trump that it's time to change course completely, not double down. And he is listening. . . ." [34]

Yeah, right. He's listening. Believe that and I have a resort to sell you . . .

In another on-line posting, "CWA President Chris Shelton said, 'The withdrawal of Andrew Puzder for consideration as Secretary of Labor is a victory for working families and demonstrates the power of grassroots resistance and mobilizing against corporate greed.'"[35]

Facts are stubborn things.

* * * * * * * * * * * * * * * * * * *

The pattern of union standards being spread out to non-union workers has been reversed. When unions were a strong majority of the workforce, our conditions were passed along to the non-union workers; in fact, many anti-union campaigns were founded upon the company's proclamation that they gave their workers "everything the unions get."

---

[32] Jodi Kantor and Jennifer Medina. "Workers Say Andrew Puzder 'Is not the one to Protect them' but he's been Chosen To." *New York Times*. January 17, 2017
[33] Jim Puzzanghera and Lisa Mascaro. "Andy Puzder withdraws as Labor secretary nominee amid Republican opposition." *Los Angeles Times*. February 15, 2017.
[34] "A Huge Win Because of You." Mass e-mail from AFL February 17, 2017.
[35] CWA Newsletter. February 17, 2017.

Now it's gone the other direction so non-union conditions are forced upon us: most unions have health insurance co-pays, many have lost defined benefit pensions and have accepted multi-tier contracts. While unions once had some political power, it has disappeared so that our real issues—higher minimum wage, lower retirement age, better labor laws, support for new organizing—were not even part of the 2016 presidential campaign. The Promised Land has been foreclosed.

While it is important to be critical about solutions, many of the discussions are distorted by a disagreement over the problem. What has caused the collapse of the economy and the enormous shift of wealth and social inequality and what can we do to change it? Immigration (especially of dark-skinned subversives)? Loss of manufacturing jobs? Free trade? The Republican Party?

Many workers—both union and non-union—are bitter over the loss of these conditions but instead of looking for ways to recover, they are searching for targets to blame. As will be described in Chapter 2, the attitude of most workers has been passive: we just assumed that these conditions, created out of centuries of struggle by our union predecessors and handed down to us, would be there forever. We would not have to do anything collectively, would not have to learn any organizing skills and, most importantly, we would not have to take any risks.

The emotions of anger, resentment and fear—of hating a system that is slowly screwing us—has never been more evident but billionaire (or not, depending on his hidden tax returns) Donald Trump was the person who captured our emotions.

In his acceptance speech at the Republican convention, he proclaimed: "I have visited the laid-off factory workers and the communities crushed by our horrible and unfair trade deals. These are the forgotten men and women of our country, and they are forgotten, but they will not be forgotten long. These are people who work hard but no longer have a voice. I am your voice."

" The world is a mess. The world is as angry as it gets," he proclaimed in another speech that could also have been given at an Occupy rally, doubling down on his claim from his inaugural address that "The establishment protected itself, but not the citizens of our country. Their victories have not been your victories; their triumphs have not been your triumphs; and while they celebrated in our nation's capital, there was little to celebrate for struggling families all across our land."

And the conditions are a mess, for sure.

As David Brooks wrote:

> "For every one American man aged 25 to 55 looking for work, there are three who have dropped out of the labor force. If Americans were working at the same rates they were when this century started, over 10 million more people would have jobs. As [economist Nicholas] Eberstadt puts it, 'The plain fact is that 21st-century America has witnessed a dreadful collapse of work.' That means there's an army of Americans semi-attached to their communities, who struggle to contribute, to realize their capacities and find their dignity. According to Bureau of Labor Statistics time-use studies, these labor force dropouts spend on average 2,000 hours a year watching some screen. That's about

the number of hours that usually go to a full-time job. Fifty-seven percent of white males who have dropped out get by on some form of government disability check. About half of the men who have dropped out take pain medication on a daily basis. A survey in Ohio found that over one three-month period, 11 percent of Ohioans were prescribed opiates. One in eight American men now has a felony conviction on his record. This is no way for our fellow citizens to live."[36]

* * * * * * * * * * * * * * * * * *

So now what?

It's all about organizing—that is, moving people in a direction we choose. It is a skill unfortunately lacking in most unions, and union officers, today. As industry developed, there was a conscious plan to remove any intelligence from the worker's day: work was made routine and workers are expected to come to work, follow orders, do what they are told without exercising any judgment, and go home. It became a habit of mind and fit The Servicing Model of Unionism. For union members who wanted to become officers, the organizing skill usually only involved joining an incumbent faction, waiting patiently in line, and then moving up. For decades, they followed the Old Joe or Old Jane pattern in their unions—they were the mythical officers who were successful so we just have to do what they did to also become winners.

As union and community organizer Jonathan Rosenblum wrote:

"Over the last several decades, most leaders failed to lead in a bold, visionary direction to inspire millions to build power through collective organizing and action. Instead they clung to outdated assumptions about labor-management relations and remained stubbornly tethered to a political duopoly that has bestowed on us outsourced and exported jobs, stagnant wages, precarious employment schemes, terminated pension plans, rising health care costs, and an eviscerated social safety net. Most unions focused inward, instead of reaching out. Leaders thought their compromises were protecting good jobs, when in fact they were emboldening hostile corporate adversaries. Today, as union members and leaders, we find ourselves in a dead-end alley, surrounded by thugs brandishing crowbars and long knives. But we didn't just get chased into the corner; too many unions went here willingly. To the extent that we recognize how we got here, we can begin to fight our way out of this corner. But it will be a tough fight. It will require us to reimagine the nature and role of unions, to discard failed strategies and assumptions, and to embrace new, deep labor-community-faith alliances.[37]

One important aspect of organizing is watching how other successful organizers set up their campaigns. As will be repeatedly discussed in this book, it is essential for all of us to deal with the crisis by learning Best Practices, the strategies and successes—and failures and self-examination—that organizations go through. Sometimes we can see Best Practices from other locals in our union, or from other unions in our industry or area. We can also see Best Practices in every other organization that is trying to become stronger in the rapidly changing world.

---

[36] David Brooks. "This century is broken." *The New York Times*. February 21, 2017.
[37] Jonathan Rosenblum. "Unions Facing the Trump Era." *Tikkun*. January 2, 2017.

An important part of rebuilding our unions is admitting there is a problem to be solved and focusing our attention on it, even if we don't know the exact solution. Looking for a Best Practice, listen to Warren Buffet as he discusses the health care crisis: "Our group does not come to this problem with answers. But we also do not accept it as inevitable. Rather, we share the belief that putting our collective resources behind the country's best talent can, in time, check the rise in health costs while concurrently enhancing patient satisfaction and outcomes."[38]

Three points apply to unionism:
- Not having "answers" but not accepting today's weakness as "inevitable"
- Putting collective resources to work to figure out a good strategy
- Including "the country's best talent."

Even if we don't agree with their goals—see Trump, Donald, above—we need to watch them, just as football coaches watch tape of opposing teams to pick up new plays. The new administration has energized everyone—supporters and opponents—and all of them have started "organizing" campaigns. Just check your mail box for the flood of solicitations for Planned Parenthood, Sierra Club ("The Trump Administration has set their sights on unraveling all of the gains made over the past eight years"), ACLU—all of them concluding not just with "Please donate" but with a plea to become a Financial Sustainer—that is, to pay regular dues.

It is also urgent to look at how the anti-union movement expanded to attract our members with social issues like immigration, birth control and abortion, gun ownership or the environment. The right wing includes a section of anti-unionism in every campaign so we—looking at Best Practices—have to do the same in reverse.

To build a union movement, we must connect "social" issues, or other concerns, with our rights to organize. We have to make jobs, income and working conditions "social issues" that can unite the huge majority of our country.

If we talk, for example, about "women's issues," as the Mothers March did, they were the "social" issues that the Democratic Party has sort of endorsed for years. But do not "equal pay for equal work," or "paid sick days" or a "$22 starting wage immediately"—that can only be gained through a union contract-- qualify as "social issues," or "women's issues?" Donald Trump figured it out, trying to shift the debate on woman's issues with his tweet during the January, 2018, Women's March:" Lowest female unemployment in 18 years!"

The most important point about the sexual predators in the #MeToo movement was that women felt powerless and isolated in their workplaces, worried about their jobs if they protested or publicized the sexual harassment. Having a union contract, with a No Discrimination clause,

---

[38] Nick Wingfield and Katie Thomas. "Amazon, Berkshire Hathaway and JP Morgan Team Up to Disrupt Health Care." *New York Times*. January 30, 2018.

and an active steward system to enforce it, with protections for promotion and job security based on seniority and not on sexuality, is so important and can be a terrific organizing issue. And sexual harassment is about power—and who has more power than the boss of a non-union workplace? We need to take these issues and make them union issues, so that workers organizing will prevent more such abusive behavior by people with unlimited power.

> "Most of the sexual harassment allegations to date have been reported by white-collar, professional women, but the problem is thought to be even more widespread among low-wage and immigrant workers. These women often don't speak up because they can't afford to lose their jobs or don't know the procedures for reporting abuse. Undocumented immigrants fear that if they call out their harassers, they could report them to immigration authorities. If they do come forward, lawyers often won't take their cases because the women can't pay upfront, and if damages for lost wages are awarded, they tend to be low, meaning a smaller cut for attorneys' fees. In the restaurant industry, which employs many women, and immigrants, at fairly low wages, the problem is especially pronounced. Two-thirds of female restaurant workers say they have been routinely sexually harassed by managers, according to a 2014 report by the advocacy group Restaurant Opportunity Center United."[39]

To build a union movement, we must connect "social" issues, or other concerns, with our rights to organize. We have to make jobs, income and working conditions "social issues" that can unite the huge majority of our country.

Every campaign we start must have one main goal, however: increasing the number of unionized workers. Everything else would be great but if there are not more of us, none of the other issues will ever become reality.

Part of expanding our membership is exposing the anti-unionism of many of the right-wing "social" campaigns. One good example of connecting these dots—or not—was the campaign against Trump's choice for Secretary of Education. While opposition to Betsy DeVos, especially from teachers' unions, properly raised the issue of her qualifications—never went to public school, never taught in public school, never sent her children to public school—a critical point was missed.

In a detailed study of how the open shop law was passed in Michigan, Michelle Kaminski contrasts the union's cyclical activity with Dick DeVos, an heir to the Amway fortune, who started an anti-union campaign in 2006 by running for governor himself, spending $35 million of his own money. The son of Dick DeVos, Sr., founder of Amway, "Dick sees organized labor as an enemy of freedom and union leaders as violent thugs who have 'an almost pathological obsession with power.' But while DeVos Sr. simply inveighed against unions, Dick took the fight to them directly, orchestrating a major defeat for the unions in the cradle of the modern labor movement."[40] DeVos maintained a long-term vision and when unions proposed a proposed

---

[39] Katie Johnston. "Kitchen workers sue McCormick & Schmick's for sexual harassment." *Boston Globe.* December 12, 2017.
[40] Andy Kroll. "Meet the New Kochs" The Devos Clan's Plan to Defund the Left." Mother Jones. January-February, 2014

amendment to the state constitution to "preserve collective bargaining rights in the constitution, making the state less vulnerable to RTW legislation," DeVos was ready with the campaign that led to the signing of the open shop legislation in December, 2012.

One important point is that DeVos tried one strategy and, when it flopped, he tried a new approach. Looking at the decline of unionism in Michigan, Kaminski states: "The labor movement is caught up in this cycle . . ., generally spending their resources on supporting labor-friendly candidates in the election cycle. This leaves them with fewer resources to develop, communicate and enact a long-term agenda that counters the neoliberal narrative and instead promotes a vision of the future in which working people prosper."[41]

* * * * * * * * * * * * * * * * * * * *

One of the constant themes in the discussion about Trump's election is *nostalgia*—both the pleasant memories of the past and, more importantly, the desperate hope that somehow these good old days can be revived. By promising, for example, to bring back the jobs for coal miners, Trump cleverly played this feeling, offering himself as the Savior for an industrial working class that has been deprived and abandoned by the political parties.

While Trump is right to accuse the political parties of abandoning the working class, it is foolish for workers to hope that somehow the past can become the present. This mindset is one of the major problems for workers in dealing with a rapidly changing world: first, they sit passively, poster children for The Servicing Model of Life, waiting for Someone Else—a savior—to somehow make things rights without any concerted action by the workers themselves. At the same time as Trump was proclaiming his support for unemployed coal miners, England announced its first day since 1882 of not burning coal to generate electricity. It's the end of an era because "Since 2012, two-thirds of Britain's coal-fired power generating capacity has been shuttered." Coal burning power plants are a 'technology' that is simply not coming back and everyone—the miners, their families and, of course, the politicians—better face this reality. "In Switzerland, Belgium and Norway, every day is a coal-free day," Carlos Fernández Alvarez, a coal analyst at the International Energy Agency in Paris, pointed out."[42]

If workers, both union and non-union, want to regain some control over the economy, and over their own lives and futures, it is beyond foolish to simply dream that the past can be brought back by some savior. These economic changes also cannot be solved simply by collective bargaining or a stronger steward system. Union members need to build a movement like they did with the Knights of Labor in the 1880s, or like they did with the extraordinary succession of sit-down strikes in the 1930's, drawing in non-union workers, families and communities, and even some elected officials, in a surge of activity.

---

[41] Michelle Kaminski. "How Michigan Became a Right to Work State: The Role of Money and Politics." *Labor Studies Journal*. December, 2015

[42] Katrin Bennhold. "For First Time Since 1800s, Britain Goes a Day Without Burning Coal for Electricity." New York Times. April 21, 2017.

We have gone through the weepy list of all of our problems, so now let's look for solutions, as workers have done for centuries. Faced with technical and industrial changes, ownership structures and fierce political and social opposition, workers created new organizations and new political movements and we have to do the same. For some union members, it is too easy to blame our officers for doing nothing when they are often overwhelmed by decisions that are complicated beyond their skills. As will be discussed in Chapter 2, a major change is for each of us, dumping the Servicing Model of Unionism and stepping up to make these decisions and to face these very complicated attacks on our lives, our standards of living and on our unions.

One important urge, which will be discussed in more detail in Chapter 7, is for political action, which most workers regard as a spectator sport. When James Comey testified before Congress in June, 2017, it was like the Super Bowl: 20 million people watched, there were groups and parties and discussions for day. While you can argue that it's better to watch a hearing like this than *Too Fast and Furious*, it is still passive and doesn't organize anyone. Most workers think of political action as showing up to vote every couple of years, or maybe donating to a candidate or calling their Congressperson, an attitude reinforced by the Servicing Model of Political Action [Appendix 3].

* * * * * * * * * * * * * * * * * * * *

When you witness the dangerous social movements rampaging around the streets, financed by millionaires and endorsed by the President of the United States, it may seem like a discussion about reorganizing our unions may be too late. We unfortunately know how the Ku Klux Klan rally in Charlottesville, VA, in August 2017, turned out. There had been a rally the month before, to protest the city council's decision this year to remove a statue of Confederate Gen. Robert E. Lee from a public park, once called Lee Park, and now called Emancipation Park. James Moore, a member of the Loyal White Knights of the Ku Klux Klan, said "80 to 100 members and supporters are expected to take part in the protest and that most will have guns with them" since Virginia is an "open-carry" state.[43] When Nazis and violent Klan members mixed with protestors on August 12, the results were fatal for one woman and the social divisions in the country appeared to be huge.

We have met the enemy and it way-y-y-y- more than us.

---

[43] Joe Heim. "KKK marchers say they will be armed Saturday at Charlottesville rally." *Washington Post*. July 7, 2017

NOW GO DO IT

1. How successful has your union been in the last 5 years? Evaluate your contract and the enforcement.
2. If your union has not been successful, why is this so?
3. Talk with 5 of your co-workers during your next lunch break about how to revitalize your union.
4. Does your union fit The Servicing Model or The Organizing Model of Unionism?
5. How much have you participated in union activities in the past year?
6. How many of your co-workers voted for Donald Trump? Why?
7. Have you participated in any demonstrations in the past year?
8. What is the most important union issue among your coworkers? How can you create a campaign around it?

Chapter 2—INDIVIDUAL CHANGES

"Nothing to me is better than the process of feeling uncomfortable as u try and push to improve on your skill/talent. I have no ceiling and I refuse to fall into the trap of complacency!"

LeBron James

It is easy to look at the challenges that unions have as collective organizations and to complain about our officers, but any change starts with each of us, as individual members. While we constantly talk about changing the Servicing Model of Unionism, it is important to understand that it's not enough that to just go to union meetings, or to become a steward and handle grievances the way Old Joe or Old Jane have been doing for 30 years. The world is rapidly changing, and we should quickly change ahead of it, so we control the changes and not get blown away by a guy like Trump.

So how do we change this condition? The reorganization starts at home, so to speak. We have to change ourselves first before taking on the world. The question is whether individual workers are ready to "reorganize" themselves to participate in the process, changing almost everything we do and everything we think.

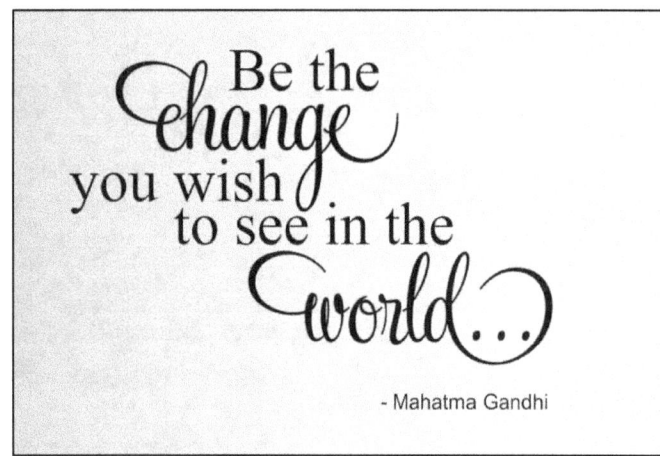

All the union functions have gotten much more complicated, demanding both better skills and a more proactive approach. It is easy to get discouraged, as we are attacked on all sides and as we see some of the distorted national priorities, beyond the Trump election: 4.6 million people watched the heavyweight "money fight" in August, 2017, between Floyd Mayweather and Conor McGregor, generating more than $600 million in revenue.

What if that kind of activity were devoted to building unionism?

The first change is attitude: I have heard so many officers complaining about their employers, about their members—"these millennials just don't understand the union"—about local politicians, about Trump, about Hillary, as if that were enough. They play the Blame Game and think they see the problem without looking for solutions. Our new attitude has to be that we are ready to go to war for our unions, that Pearl Harbor has just been bombed (by the vulture capitalists) and we are the last line of defense for unionism in the US. We better not give it up. Once we have this positive attitude, we need to look at new strategies because the old ones that we have been using since 1945 are no longer effective.

The loss of confidence that many workers have in their own intelligence is the product of many different forces: school, work, and the union structure where a few officers convince the members that they are not clever enough to deal with the boss and his lawyers. The sense of inferiority became a habit that we need to break.

Workers' lives used to run in predictable patterns: we go to work, come home, maybe participate in some family or community activities that we enjoy, rest up and then go back to work. In many unionized industries, these patterns were in place for decades or even for generations, founded on the relative prosperity brought about by both the union contract and a strong national economy. We worked in one place, belonged to one union and were otherwise blissfully isolated from the rest of the union "movement" in the US, and certainly distant from any foreign unions, even as the ownership of our companies went global.

In fact, the success of unionism after World War II may have cut down our militancy. One observer remarked that "in recent decades, American workers have steered clear of such militancy for reasons that range from fear of having their jobs shipped overseas to their self-image as full-fledged members of the middle class, with all its trappings and aspirations."[44]

The percentage of workers who participate in their unions is pathetically low. Informal calculations usually come away with 3-5 percent, documenting a separation of workers from union activities that developed as The Servicing Model became the accepted structure. A few members took all the responsibility and became stewards and officers while the rest paid dues and showed up at contract time. Workers developed excuses for not participating in union activities. Pressures of work, overtime, family responsibilities, commitment to other activities, union meetings on a Sunday afternoon, and reluctance to make decisions—all these are used as excuses to minimize participation.

In many cases, the officers of the union discouraged participation to hold on to their positions; after all, if members started to participate in the union, the next thing they would consider is running for office! Until recently, this structure worked just fine for union members: unionized workers averaged 30 per cent more in wages than non-union workers, with a solid complement of benefits. We had it made. This very prosperity helped isolate unionized workers from the rest of the working class. Problems that other people had, like losing health insurance or houses, were ignored because union members, in general, were not affected.

It is disappointing today how low the definition of "privilege" has become, especially for union members. Political scientists have divided the world into the "haves" and the "have-nots," and provide gruesome statistics that show that the adjusted income for the top 1 percent has risen by 241 percent over the past 40 years while incomes for the rest of us have been flat. The top 20 percent of households control more than 80 percent of the wealth in the country. On a global scale, eight men including Bill Gates, Warren Buffet, Mark Zuckerberg, and Jeff Bezos, have as much wealth as the poorest 50 percent of the population. Scott Stringer, the New York City

---

[44] Stephen Greenhouse. "In America, Labor Has an Unusually Long Fuse." *New York Times*. April 5, 2009.

comptroller, published an annual survey that showed that the 25 best paid hedge fund managers together earned $11 billion in 2016.[45]

"CEOs at the largest U.S. firms now make 271 times more than the average worker, according to calculations by the Economic Policy Institute for 2016 salary numbers. Including stock options, average pay for those at the top of the corporate ladder came to $15.6 million in the group that the EPI examined. While the ratio is still large, it's actually on the downswing — the gap peaked at 376-to-1 in 2000 and was 286-to-1 in 2015. However, it's still 'light years' from the 20-to-1 ratio in 1965 and even the 59-to-1 ratio as recently as 1989, said EPI researchers Lawrence Mishel and Jessica Schieder."[46]

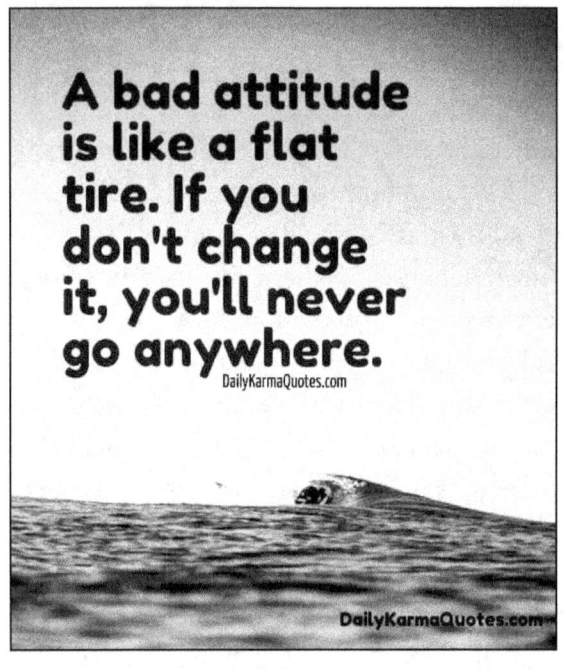

The numbers are so huge and seem so distant that it is hard for an average worker—if such a person exists—to grasp the importance, but each of us sees it in our workplaces: threats to our wages, cuts in our benefits, risky working conditions develop from constant pressure to shift money to this small group.

While this growing social inequality of the "haves" and" have-nots"—stimulated by the crushing of the union movement—is important for organizing purposes to see a third category: the "have-a-littles," a category most union members occupy. If you have a regular place to live (especially if you own it), have regular meals and medical care for your family, a steady, if inadequate income, and possibly some leisure time or retirement, you are ahead of millions of Americans, both in the cities and in rural areas.

I was struck by the gap when I attended several meetings about drastic changes in the Baltimore City bus routes. Opponents got up to testify about the hardships of moving a bus stop, or of skipping stops to create more direct routes. I realized, and so did many of my friends, that it has been years since we rode a bus, in a city where about 1/3 of the population does not have access to a car.

Eighty-four percent of Baltimore students qualified for free and reduced-priced meals this year and one delegate said "If they don't get it at school, they don't get it at all." Not our children, however.

Do you own a house? In Baltimore City, there are about 40,000 abandoned houses—each one of them a working family, pushed out, and each one a potential resource for the homeless but not available. In Los Angeles, in April, 2017, the Housing Authority had a waiting list of 40,000 people for Section 8, with an average delay of 11 years before receiving a voucher. Because of

---

[45] *New York Times.* May 21, 2017.
[46] Jeff Cox. "CEOs make 271 times the pay of most workers." CNBC. July 20, 2017.

the backlog they have stopped accepting new names for the waiting list. In Baltimore City, in one year, there were 151,000 cases in rent court where tenants tried—unsuccessfully in almost every case—to get some fair treatment from their landlords. How many of us have ever had this experience?

Most of us have a regular bank account (and may even have some money in it) and credit cards. As a contrast, payday lenders now make about $46 billion in loans every year, collecting $ 7 million in fees, servicing more than 12 million people who have no other access to credit.[47]

As I think how "privileged" we are, living "normal" lives, I visualize us as all packed together on a raft. Friends are regularly pushed off: they lose their jobs, they get sick or separated, or make "bad decisions" and suddenly, all of the "necessities" that they enjoyed and assumed would be there forever, are gone.

This troubling separation between us, as union members, and the rest of the working-class population affects our commitment to reorganizing our unions. It also blunts any sense of urgency—somehow, we can watch and complain but it won't happen to us, will it? The conversation with angry workers about their conditions, or about political figures like Trump, should always include the question: what are you doing to stop it?

British writer David Goodhart has described the working-class as divided into two groups: the Somewheres and the Anywheres. "Somewheres are rooted in their towns and have 'ascribed' identities—Virginia farmer, West Virginia coal miner, Pennsylvania steelworker. Anywheres are at home in the global economy. They derive their identity from portable traits, like education or job skills, and are more likely to move to areas of opportunity. Somewhere value staying put.; they feel uncomfortable with many aspects of cultural and economic change, like mass immigration. ... [Trump supporters] in Johnstown, PA are classic Somewheres. The steel mills are gone and they are never coming back, but the people remain. The things they value are there, they don't really have the skills to pack up and be an Anywhere and they love Trump because he sticks his finger in the eyes of the anywheres who have made their world worse."[48]

For many workers, even ones in unions, their decline has been dramatic and unpleasant, and seems beyond their control. As the grim scythe of deep changes cuts across all groups, union and non-union, it's time to create a unified movement. Unions still have the greatest resources and we have to understand that our major problems—like the distribution of wealth—can only be solved if everyone's problem is solved.

One serious mistake that many of us make is looking for a miracle cure. I call it the "savior mentality," the belief that someone can wave a wand or give us a magic formula and suddenly all the years of decline will evaporate and we will have a strong local.

One of the great union leaders, Eugene V. Debs summed up this problem in 1905: "Too long have the workers of the world waited for some Moses to lead them out of bondage. I would

---

[47] Stacy Cowley. "Payday Lenders Face Tough New Restrictions by Consumer Agency." *New York Times*. October 6, 2017.
[48] David Brooks. "The Existing Democratic Majority." *The New York Times*. November 11, 2017

not lead you out if I could; for if you could be led out, you could be led back again. I would have you make up your minds there is nothing that you cannot do for yourselves."

An important part of the Trump campaign was his presentation of himself as exactly this kind of savior. "Many have noted that Trump often stirs fear and takes an 'us vs. them' stance in his speeches and other pronouncements. He sets himself up as the hero who can save Americans from a variety of enemies and maladies: illegal immigrants; foreign trade agreements that have sent millions of U.S. manufacturing jobs overseas; Islamic terrorism; and the specter of street violence, though the violent crime rate has trended down."[49]

With his promises and boasting about bringing jobs back, most workers don't care about his tax returns; in fact, the discussion reminds me of a Teamster many years ago who said that he didn't care how much the local officers made, or stole, as long as he got his.

* * * * * * * * * * * * * * * * * * *

Everyone offers wisdom for survival in these tough times, with opinions about what should be done—politicians, of course including Donald Trump, appointed bureaucrats, ministers, radio talk show hosts, the guy sitting next to you at a bar, the woman at church, and the Nazi demonstrators. The media is filled with self-help tips for workers who lose their jobs, as if there were only individual solutions for a massive social problem. Go back to school, exercise regularly, eat right (if cheaper), and watch your money—all these helpful hints assume that a worker and his or her family are on their own and that their lives are simply the reflection of their "choices."

Besides focusing on individual solutions for a broader, social problem, these tips also emphasize one of the biggest problems for workers today: low expectations. Workers are socialized to accept that just getting by may be the best we can hope for, especially in the face of the Next Great Depression. We have been the boiling frog. Workers in the U.S. repeatedly accept with a sense of fatalism the crushing effects of the economy: loss of jobs, loss of health insurance, housing foreclosures, mental and physical stress. Often, as the opioid crisis in white working-class areas, and the "drug culture" in inner cities, shows, people just give up hope.

A candidate who speaks to us about Making America Great Again sounds hopeful, especially when their union officers and politicians of both parties are urging us to lower our expectations and continue with the declining "status quo."

Nowhere does a recommendation come up to encourage greater activity in the union. When the unions collectively are unable, or unwilling, to create a collective response, individual workers are taking stands. We are seeing many instances of resistance, usually on social issues and not connected to our workplaces. Demonstrations about Civil War statues, with people voluntarily turning themselves in to police in solidarity with others who were arrested, demonstrations to protest social policies—but not demonstrations to repeal Taft-Hartley. These terms are not even in the vocabularies of most union members.

---

[49] Thomas Fitzgerald. "How Trump's Speaking Style Drove Home His Message." *Philadelphia Daily News*. February 24, 2017.

One important aspect of this change in attitude is *kaizen,* a term borrowed from sophisticated manufacturing, that literally means "taking something apart and putting it back together better," but can be quickly understood as "continuous improvement." While this proactive attitude gives us intense problems at work, because our bosses are constantly changing conditions, *kaizen* can also help us build stronger unions. In the Servicing Model, union officers react—management does something, we grieve or file a legal response. In the Organizing Model, we are proactive, planning ahead and taking the initiative,

never satisfied. It is an attitude that builds movements, both large and small, and attracts supporters—and even helps sign up non-members in our workplaces. If someone calls you "Mr. Kaizen," take it as a compliment.

Being proactive is essential for each of us as individuals, and for our unions as organizations. As a union steward, for example, we are used to responding—management does something and we react. Often, we have a Reactive *To Do* pad so we don't forget all of our responsibilities—investigate a complaint, file the grievance within the time limit, check for the response. Instead, we need to create a Proactive *To Do* list with goals and timelines for projects to build the union.

Realistically speaking, what can we do? Here are a few practical suggestions:

- Obviously, the first step is to begin to actively participate in our unions. Read your union contract—carefully. Go to meetings and make yourself heard. Volunteer for some of the many activities that the union should be sponsoring and if there are no activities, start some.
- Learn about labor history so you and your co-workers understand where the benefits come from. They were the result of struggle, not gifts from a generous boss or a miraculous gift from Heaven. We made them and we have to struggle again to keep them. One of the biggest mistakes is demanding that manufacturing jobs be expanded, as if they will miraculously pay high wages with great benefits, the way the old steel and auto industries did. These industries paid well because the workers organized and fought to improve their lives. No miracle there. If you can work and listen to music through your ear buds, you could also listen to some union history or labor songs
- Celebrate diversity—go into other departments of your workplace, or to a different geographic area, and learn what they do and what they think and how their union functions. Talk with other members of different sexes, races, religions, seniority or political beliefs.

- Reach out to other workers, both in your own union and in your community. One of the most impressive aspects of the rise of unionism in the 1930's was the commitment to help out *all* workers.
- Show Solidarity—too often individual workers openly protest bad conditions at work or ineffective representation from their union officers. When the backlash hits, they find there are very few legal protections or recourses but a show from co-workers can reverse any attack.
- Be visible in your community. One of the constant complaints about high union officers is that they are virtually invisible. The commercial media basically blacks out any positive achievements of unionism. Stories only appear about strikes—the longer the better—and the corruption of the officers. One of my students directly asked former AFL-CIO President John Sweeny about this issue, and Sweeny replied that he preferred to "stay behind the scenes." If the highest officers hang back, then the members need to step forward. Even writing a Letter to the Editor of your local newspaper is great, like this one:

> **Corporate tax cut makes the case for unions**
> The new tax reduction for large companies is supposed to increase the amount of work and investments that companies will make in America ("Now that the GOP has passed its tax bill, Americans get to find out what's in it (Spoiler alert: It's not good)," Dec. 20). However, most analysts think the money will be used for stock buy-backs. If that is true, the tax reduction does nothing for the American worker. This is where unions have a chance to impact America.
> Watch to see which companies start to buy back stock. If your company is one of them, it is time for unions to use their collective bargaining power to demand that this money be used for increased wages or new product investments. Just a few weeks ago Gary Cohn, the National Economic Council director, was in attendance when the Wall Street Journal asked a group of CEOs whether they were planning to increase their business investment with the new tax cash windfall they would receive — none of them were.
> Unions must help lead the charge and make sure that business leaders use the money in the way President Donald Trump has promised they would. If the people don't take the initiative, the powerful will continue to give the profits to themselves. We need to help the union voices be heard again and support their efforts to increase investment in America.
> Mark Pinsley, Allentown, Pa.
> *Baltimore Sun* December 25, 2017

- If you have been laid off, don't cut yourself off from the union. Go by the hall and suggest some of the activities that were described in previous chapters. If you've been active with your kids' sports leagues, for example, offer to start an informal team for union members (nothing too strenuous, of course) to keep the members together and to try to keep their spirits up. Remember that many of your coworkers are facing economic troubles and need a cheap and friendly social outlet.

- Even if there is no activity planned, use your union hall or a community center as a gathering place. You may hate your boss, and even your job, but the social contacts you make every day at work are a major part of your life. Losing your job can be devastating. Keeping in touch with your friends is essential. The union hall or a community center can be a "third place" for workers in transition, as described by sociologist Ray Oldenburg. Oldenburg identified home (first place) and work (second place) as major centers of people's lives but maintained that a "third place" would "host the regular, voluntary, informal, and happily anticipated gatherings of individuals beyond the realms of home and work." In tough times, workers cannot afford the usual "third places"—restaurants and bars, for example. Unionism was initially based on a sense of community, comprised of workers who lived near, or at, their workplaces and mixed informally with other union members. This sense of community—of solidarity—has been lost. Bring it back.

As we said in Chapter 1, the slogan for this tough period has to be "No More Business As Usual," a motto that most of our employers have taken up. Now it's our turn. It is a huge challenge but the change begins with you and will spread out to your coworkers and community. Get started!

NOW GO DO IT

1. **Get together a group of your co-workers to discuss how to improve the union.**
2. **Find out what each officer of your union does and then figure how you could do it better.**
3. **Create a community discussion on how to build unionism.**
4. **Look at your personal habits—do you think union, shop union, promote unionism.**
5. **Talk with a member from another union to see what strategies they use to deal with their boss.**
6. **Start a Proactive To Do list.**
7. **Develop a list of activities for your union hall to attract families and the community.**

CHAPTER 3—CHANGING THE STRUCTURE OF THE UNION

> "But independent and uncoordinated activity by individual corporations, as important as this is, will not be sufficient. Strength lies in organization, in careful long-range planning and implementation, in consistency of action over an indefinite period of years, in the scale of financing available only through joint effort, and in the political power available only through united action and national organizations."
> Lewis Powell. *Memo to the Chamber of Commerce* (1971)

You learn more from your enemies than from your friends, and the famous Powell Memo is an example of a strategy that every union should follow. His recommendations include proactive planning over a long period, a vision of political power, financing and, most importantly for union officers, working together with people that you often regard as competitors. Powell insists that corporate executives have a responsibility to their class. Union officers have the same responsibility to all workers, even if we have been divided for centuries.

One of the most disturbing reactions by union officers to Trump's election were the cries of catastrophe—as if unionism in the United States was suddenly threatened. The numbers shown Chapter 1 show clearly that unionism has been pushed back dramatically in the US over the past 50 years. Most of the participants—union officers, staff, members and displaced members—have simply hunkered down, hoping that things would somehow miraculously get better if we accommodated. Sad. We have long term structural problems to deal with, not just Donald Trump.

One buzz word is "unitary"—as in referring to a group, like "The United States," or "the labor movement," or "the media," as if everyone in the group thinks the same and has the same goals. Outside media refer to "labor wants. . ." when a high union officer speaks but "the labor movement" is more than 14 million of us, plus the retirees and our families. Each of us has opinions on almost every topic, a division clearly illustrated in the 2016 election.

Unionism in the US has historically been divided, so that our numbers are often in conflict with each other. If you work for 30 minutes in a union shop, you realize how true this is, especially if your union is in contract negotiations. You quickly see that each work force is inevitably divided: by age, by skill, by race and gender, by job classification and seniority, by marital status, by geographic location. Political differences, especially in areas where the workforce is very diverse, simply expand the divisions.

On a national scale, craft unionism has always distrusted industrial unionism. One union claims jurisdiction against another over the assignments of work and co-workers quarrel. Private sector workers think public sector workers are overpaid and pampered, a drag on the treasury funded by taxes on workers. Native-born workers (descendants of immigrants, by the way) rage against immigrants, both legal and "illegal." Employed workers accuse unemployed workers of being "welfare cheats," while unemployed workers lament the low level of public assistance.

The painful example of this division, described in Chapter 1, was the endorsement of Scott Walker for re-election as governor of Wisconsin in 2015 by Terry McGowan, the business manager of an Operating Engineers local, even though Walker announced his intention to destroy the public-sector unions. As soon as the election was over, Walker then proposed an open shop law to undermine private sector unions.

McGowan would have been smarter to proclaim *An Injury to One is an Injury to All*, and he could have then avoided *And Then They Came for Us*.

These divisions are, of course, intensified by sophisticated management consultants, who learned labor relations from Julius Caesar: divide and conquer. (Or as Governor Scott Walker promised a rich donor: "The first step is we're going to deal with collective bargaining for all public employee unions, because you use divide and conquer.... ")

If there was ever an operation that was "insane," by Einstein's definition, it is our union movement. Based on the numbers over the past 70 years, we need to rethink all our practices and strategies. If union officers were managers of a baseball team, and the decline of union membership was the win-loss record, they would all be fired.

Unfortunately, an important measure of an officer's skill is the income of the union, not the participation of the members. This financial standard, which can be measured, is one reason the upcoming *Janus* decision, which could significantly cut union income, provoked flurries of activity.

For union officers, however, change—or even the discussion of it-- can be threatening because they could be held accountable and members might ask questions about the loss of members and bargaining power. Even more threatening, these members might figure they could do a better job and would run for office. "One member said to me about union leadership, 'They're afraid to mobilize their own rank and file. Many are given cushions by their uncle or father. . .. And they think 'If I get someone to do something, I'll build a potential candidate to run against me.'"[50]

The structure of most unions makes it almost impossible for a rank-and-file member to get elected to office: union constitutions restrict elections to three or four-year intervals and often international officers are elected at a convention attended by a miniscule number of members. Some locals have become so large that members cannot possibly reach all of the workplaces.

We have discussed the importance of being proactive as an important part of the Organizing Model. In Chapter 2, we talked about individual's planning activities but every union needs to create a collective Action Plan, with goals, a timeline and funding, and with every

---

[50] Judy Ancel. "310,567 Signatures Block 'Right to Work.'" *Labor Notes*. October, 2017.

member an equal partner. The members and officers should spend time creating goals like maybe cleaning up all old grievances, or getting ready for the next contract negotiations, but how about an internal organizing campaign or a new organizing project? How about looking at health and safety conditions more carefully? Maybe some social activities to get the members families involved? And, of course, political action. Setting up this list involves taking a hard look at the union's condition, even if it puts some of the officers in an unfavorable light.

In any case, set up a project with goals and timelines—what do you want to do in 30 days? 60 days? Six months? A year? Have regular meetings to report back and evaluate your successes and strategies, adjusting where necessary. It is important to delegate responsibility—too often, the same officers take all the responsibility, and this is not good, either in principle or in practice. If you want to get more members involved, here is a chance to offer different activities. Besides, one office trying to carry on all of these different activities simply can't keep up.

You also need to figure out if any of these projects will cost money—for lost time, for travel, if your union is spread out geographically, for refreshments, for outside trainers. In Chapter10, we will look at Union Finances but always figure out what a project might cost. You will also have to look at the bigger structure of your union to see if the District or the International could help with the planning or with some money.

All new strategies must have an organizing component because membership participation is abysmally low in most unions, especially at the local level. Increasing membership participation—and signing up the non-members in open shop situations—will totally change the structure of your union, from the top-down Servicing Model to the bottom-up Organizing Model. Membership participation can be mathematically measured: get a list of everyone covered by your contract and start marking them off when they participate. As part of your Action Plan for the local, keep track of the percentage of members who participate and if the percentage doesn't start to go up, revise your strategies to make participation more attractive.

More importantly, unionism as a movement has also been separated from the rest of the US working class for many decades. The current phrase is "just us or justice?" sums it up. Are union members interested in only bargaining for themselves—"just us"--with little concern for other workers? Do they have a broader sense that unionism represents all workers—"justice"-- so that unions consciously use their strength to organize more workers into the union or to promote "justice" all workers? In the past, unions pushed politically for Social Security, for OSHA and for ERISA at the federal level while lobbying for higher unemployment benefits or better workers compensation laws at a state and local level.

As some unions officers and staff have realized, Solidarity=self-interest. Speaking up for all workers, on issues like public education, public transit or public housing also builds support for the union issues that workers in these industries confront. Rather than bargaining in isolation, unions can build coalitions that both expand a public service and support the improvements for the workers.

Organize, organize, organize!

* * * * * * * * * * * * * * * * * * *

Every union is divided into three distinct groups of members, each of which has selfish and often conflicting interests that challenge the need for solidarity. It is important to appreciate that people at different levels of the union have very different life styles, and as a result have very different attitudes toward changing their unions. As we all do, people make decisions based on economic self-interest: what will help me hang on to a job, even for the short term?

Let's look at the three largest groups, the elected international and district officers, the union staff and the members to see how each could be affected by structural changes in their unions.

Since union officers are elected by members of their own unions, their concerns can be narrow at a time when all of our attitudes and strategies are up for expansion. The elected international and district officers are usually members who have moved up in the union structure, following the pattern of social mobility, to gain access to the considerable resources that many unions have. This group, except for the officers of the United Electrical Workers (UE), is always paid better than the members, usually has special benefits, and is often isolated from the members. The structure of the union and the strategies of the incumbent officers usually are designed to protect themselves, even as our membership numbers decline. Over the past few years, several international unions elected insurgent candidates—those who were not already officers—but in most cases, the officers have joined a political machine which controls the union and establishes a line of succession. These union political machines operate much as the Democratic Party's "super delegates" did in pushing through the nomination of Hillary Clinton—to protect themselves. The similar structures are one reason so many top officers were so loyal to Clinton.

Ambitious members quickly learn that moving up in the union requires participation in the process, a support for a status quo, at a time when such conservativism is dangerous. Officers are not advanced, then, because of successful strategies, new ideas or for serious evaluations on changing unionism's downward trajectory for the past 70 years. Most national union officers place a much higher priority—if their LM-2 reports are an indication—on political action than on organizing to build their unions.

In an evaluation that certainly applies to our unions, W. Edwards Deming noted: ""The only reason an organization has dead wood is that management either hired dead wood or it hired live wood and killed it."

Generally, the international union officers believe that the direction of the union must come from the top-down. A few years ago, a UAW Committeeman remarked to me that he saw the union as an army:" The president says 'March in one direction, we do it.'" Most members do not share this sense of blind obedience but it is often difficult for them to get enough power to force a change, or to even provoke a discussion.

Many of the international unions have offices in Washington, DC, and are as much a victim of the Inside-the-Beltway mentality as members of Congress. As we often say about Congress, "It's not a location, it's a state of mind." The officers run across a very small number of their members at conferences and generally live and socialize separately. With salaries and benefits that are usually substantially higher than their members, their priorities are very different from their members, as was proven by union votes in the 2016 election.

"Like many inside the Washington Beltway, union leaders generally thought things weren't so bad — the unemployment rate has dropped to 4.9 percent, and median household income jumped by a record 5.2 percent last year. But many union officials didn't adequately hear the anger and pain felt by many working-class whites: that they were stuck economically, that Washington wasn't addressing their problems, like disappearing factories and good jobs."[51]

"And American labor leaders, once up-from-the-street rabble-rousers, now often work hand-in-hand with C.E.O.'s to improve corporate competitiveness to protect jobs and pensions, and try to sideline activists who support a hard line. 'You have a general diminution of union leadership that was focused on defending workers by any means necessary,' said Jerry Tucker, a longtime U.A.W. militant. 'The message from the union leadership nowadays often is, 'We don't have any choice, we have to go down this concessionary road to see if we can do damage control,' he said."[52]

The structure of most unions gives these few officers total control over the union's strategies and resources. They can start, stop or avoid, political and organizing campaigns, they can try to block any attempt to expand communication among the members. They can hire, transfer and fire members of the union staff, and often use this authority to intimidate reps that might look at new ideas.

It is important to remember one set of numbers: the political endorsement for the presidency of the US is made by the 58 members of the AFL-CIO Council, so you can calculate what percentage of 14 million members this group represents. The officers of the major unions had become so predictable that the controversy over the presidential endorsement between Bernie Sanders and Hillary Clinton in the summer of 2016 reverberated wonderfully throughout every level of the unions. Many officers were immediately supportive of Hillary Clinton and assumed that the rest of the AFL Executive Council would fall into line.

This predictable endorsement encountered significant opposition at every level of virtually every unions. At the top, six international union presidents, from the ATU, the APWU, the CWA, the National Nurses United (NNU), the UE and the National Union of Healthcare Workers, endorsed Sanders, breaking publicly with the rest of the officers of the AFL.

"As a healthy sign, or dangerous symptom, there was controversy about political strategies within the different unions. After the officers of the AFT endorsed Clinton, 'Almost immediately, there was a backlash among teachers in far-flung locals across the states. The AFT's Facebook page lit up with angry comments from those who favored

---

[51] Steven Greenhouse. "What Unions Got Wrong About Trump." *New York Times*. November 26, 2016.
[52] Stephen Greenhouse. "In America, Labor Has an Unusually Long Fuse." *New York Times*. April 5, 2009.

Vermont Sen. Bernie Sanders instead. Teachers took to Twitter to condemn the endorsement and at least two petitions were circulated online in opposition. Widely read teachers' blogs published screeds against the decision, calling it rigged in favor of Clinton, a longtime friend of AFT president Randi Weingarten. Though a June poll among AFT members showed a majority supporting Clinton over Sanders, the fervor of those unhappy with the endorsement ran high.'"[53]

A significant number of union members first supported Bernie Sanders and then others voted for an openly anti-union candidate. This kind of controversy was especially threatening because the "failure" or "refusal" of "The Union" to listen to different opinions about politics was one basis for the charge by California schoolteacher Rebecca Friedrichs, that her union, the California Teachers Association, had no constitutional right to collect agency fees.

Even after the election, small groups of international union presidents were meeting and discussing new strategies, one of which included encouraging Trumka to "retire" so new energies and ideas could appear at the top of the AFL-CIO. While a challenger to Trumka ultimately did not appear, and the status quo held, the debate is not, or should not be, just about individuals—changing people at the top of a solidified structure.

This was just a short-time failure. The largest calamity—the boiling frog—has been the devastation of the union movement generally, both in numbers and in political strength with almost no response from the top. Maybe the Trump campaign and election will be the stimulus—or maybe the officers of the unions will continue as they are while the membership numbers, and the unions' political power, drop even more. The numbers show that unionism has severe structural challenges that need to be confronted and that change needs to come from the bottom up or extinction looms.

As Sal Rosselli, president of the National Union of Healthcare Workers (NUHW) explained: "Simply stated, it's about concentrating power, resources, and decision-making authority among a few people in Washington, D.C., versus empowering workers and having them in charge of their relationship with their employer. Things like one member, one vote on all decisions that affect them; electing their bargaining committee and being at the bargaining table as opposed to it being someone appointed by the International; voting on their proposals as opposed to it being established by some national committee Stern appointed."[54]

It is discouraging to hear international and district officers discuss unionism as if everything were OK. In early 2016, as the *Friedrichs* case loomed, I attended a central labor council

---

[53] Sam Frizzel. "Hillary Clinton Faces Unrest Among Organized Labor." *Time Magazine*. July 21, 2015.
[54] Mark Brenner. "California SEIU Leader Mounts Battle for Local Control, Union Democracy: An Interview with Sal Rosselli." *Labor Notes*. February 14, 2008.

conference where two high officers in the AFL-CIO were the featured speakers. Instead of grabbing the 300 union members and proclaiming a crisis that needed everyone's intelligence and dedication, they both gave glowing speeches about the value of unionism and the creation of the "middle class"—as if all of us did not already know this--and then thanked us and went back to DC. As you read this, think about your most recent union meeting—did an officer speak with any urgency about the crisis or was it the same complacency?

The death of Scalia, of course, postponed the doomsday scenario but a new case, *Janus v AFSCME*, is working its way up to the Supreme Court and by the spring of 2018, the same threat of a national open shop provision for public sector workers may be realized. It was clear that the loss of dues income provoked some officers—like a frog about to be tossed into boiling water--to support internal organizing campaigns.

The national AFL-CIO convention, held in St. Louis in October 22-25, 2017, passed dozens of resolutions, with enthusiastic speeches in support from the floor, on topics from a right to organize to single-payer healthcare to, in Resolution 19, to "study and incubate best practices for sustaining diverse and inclusive leadership." Will there be a structural change in the movement when the enthusiastic delegates return to their home locals?

At the CWA convention in Pittsburgh, in early August, 2017, President Chris Shelton laid out a different strategy called CWA Strong "and noted that locals already are putting this plan into action. Step 1 for CWA STRONG is increasing membership levels. Step 2 is more mobilization and member engagement. Across this union we must renew our commitment to building our union from the bottom up. At the same time, we must continue to reach out to our community allies who will stand with us against our enemies. A stronger CWA means a stronger foundation for a progressive movement. Locals, large and small, are working hard to sign up agency fee payers and non-members in both the public and private sectors."[55]

While this rhetoric is very positive, once again, only time will tell if he is willing to put the resources and strategic skills into place to support the campaign. It is also troublesome that the loss of members and bargaining power generally did not provoke this campaign, but the possible loss of agency fee rights and income for the union did.

One union president, Fred Simpson, president of The Brotherhood of Maintenance of the Way Division (BMWED), affiliated with the Teamsters, took a more dramatic campaign approach. Stimulated by a survey— "the results were positively scary" said one organizer--that showed that union members, especially the younger ones, felt disconnected from "The Union, Simpson supported a successful campaign to effectively overhaul the union. The union hired a couple of skilled organizers from the outside to develop membership activities and to develop internal organizers but the direction of the campaign was already established, and seems to be one that every union should try to duplicate. This campaign is explained in detail at the end of this chapter.

Another compelling project took place in Canada, where two researchers carried out 53 focus group discussions with more than 430 young members with the goal of "increasing young

---

[55] CWA Newsletter. August 10, 2017.

members' participation in trade union organizations . . .to help young members develop a sense of identity that can lead them to get more involved in union life." These young members "may question the relevance of solidarity" and may have "a political ideology that conveys a rather negative opinion of unions, . . . and general disengagement from any form of political participation, including union action, making the functions and services provided by the unions somewhat irrelevant."

Considerable credit should be given to the union officers who supported this study and committed up to $100,000/year to establish and mobilize youth committees, with "a strong desire to prepare the next generation of union leaders," even if the interviews found that the young members "were not inclined to repeat, or necessarily endorse the union views of the local or national leaders." Reflecting the Servicing Model, "young members appeared to face a significant problem, namely, resistance to change related to practices and traditional repertoires of action at the level of the local executive committees. These obstacles were frustrating for the young members and ultimately discouraged several of them from getting more actively involved in union activities."[56]

It is not just that the mechanics of the campaign are important. It is the attitude of the union officers, who recognized a looming crisis and decided to take decisive action, and to commit the union's financial resources to dramatically change the union structure. It can only be hoped that other union officers will recognize a Best Practice and duplicate it.

Imagine a membership meeting where your local president stands up and announces: "You know, we are in big trouble. What should we do about it? I want to hear from everyone."

Will it happen? "A lot of unions are bureaucratic and clunky," says Richard Freeman, a Harvard labor economist. "Change is hard."[57]

* * * * * * * * * * * * * * * * * *

A second level of the union is the hired staff, the representatives at the international, district or local levels whose responsibility is to carry out the strategies that the officers establish. The staff reps are responsible for the four basic union functions: they handle grievances, lead contract negotiations, carry out political campaigns and are supposed to develop both new and internal organizing campaigns. Not large in numbers, this group is very important because they are the direct contact between the officers and the members and they usually provide years of union experience.

---

[56] Melanie Laroche and Melanie Dufour-Poirier. "Revitalizing Union Representation through Labor Education Initiatives: A Close Examination of Two Trade Unions in Quebec." *Labor Studies Journal*. June, 2017.

[57] Rick Wartzman. "Meet The Millennial Who's Trying To Save The Labor Movement With A Facebook For Unions." *Fast Company*. September 1, 2017.

As unions respond to the Trump victory, this level is most agonized because they see the importance of changing strategies but have very little influence over the officers who set the policies. Often staff reps will hear of good ideas or new strategies but they are either caught in the Servicing Model, where everything is reactive, or they are intimidated by a potentially negative response from an officer.

These union reps who handle grievances and negotiations are in a critical location to change the methods that The Servicing Model has endorsed for decades. Grievances are routinely filed, then processed through to expensive arbitrations. Contract negotiations involve a small committee, often with a blackout on the sessions, and a hasty ratification vote. Basic procedures are not being changed, even as unions are being crushed.

As I do union training, I ask the staff reps:

"How many of you have done anything PROACTIVE for the union is the past two weeks?" and

"How many of you have done anything REACTIVE in the past two weeks."

The answers open up a discussion about how each of us acts, or reacts, as union reps and members. I remind them that change is necessary because the methods for carrying out our union assignments are not working. We can see it by the numbers, and we know it from the challenges we got in our last contract negotiations, and from the pile of unresolved grievances. We may, unfortunately, also be able to measure the decline by the number of members who have taken advantage of an open shop law to drop out.

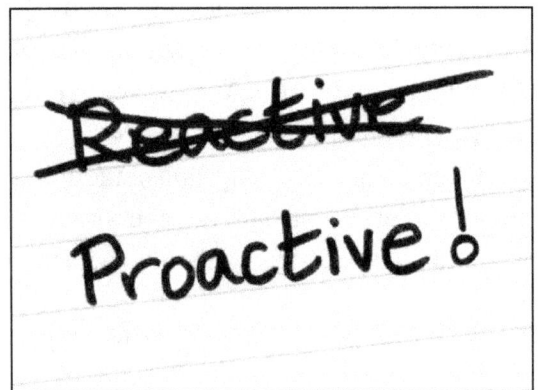

Many union staff members have a severe case of the "grumbles" today—they see that their unions, and unionism generally, are dramatically sliding downhill but they are unable, or unwilling, to try to reverse the movement, even as their jobs are jeopardized. One disturbing aspect, as this book was being prepared, was the reluctance of these reps to speak up in their unions for new strategies: many of them complained about the directions of their locals, or districts or internationals, but when asked, "What have you done to challenge this or to change it," the Excuse-O-Meter was turned on high: "It's not my place," or "They wouldn't listen so why bother" or "I can't get any support." Some of them had suggested major changes for the direction of the union and were ignored or criticized. More importantly, none wanted to be quoted by name or even included in the acknowledgements in this book.

I find a sense of deep cynicism and fatalism setting in among many of the staff I know. As one rep from a public sector union put it after Trump's inauguration: "We have had one 45 minute conference call with [the union] organizing directors since the election. And then a meeting in late February. It's not like there is a bad plan. There is NO PLAN. I'm a colonel holding down a (relatively) important front with 45k members and I'm getting zero direction.

Nothing. I think at some level people know it's over. It's really weird. The aflcio line is 'nothing for the inauguration we will have enough time to fight.' Jesus."

Many of the staff reps come in with radical political beliefs but no union experience—they believe in the cause, but they now also have a job, and eventually families. Since many of the reps do not come out of the units they represent, with recall rights, or have a staff union, they do not have much job security. Getting fired from the staff position seems catastrophic so their issue, as it is for the members, is job security. Advocating new and different policies within the union appears to be like wearing a union T-shirt during an organizing campaign—you leave yourself open to getting fired. As one rep from a state teachers association remarked "I want to retire on my own schedule."

There are job clearinghouses, like www.unionjobs.com, but a new job often means moving and disrupting the family, so they are hesitant to openly challenge the strategies that the officers set, even if a rep knows that disaster will follow. But disaster has preceded them, and once again, they see themselves as sitting on a raft and others sliding off. "'Labor establishments'—trade unions, 'alt-labor' workers centers, and other nonprofits that represent wage-earners' interests—have 14,820 fewer staff positions than during the first year of the Obama administration, about a 9 percent fall from the 164,987 paid employees recorded that year by the U.S. census."[58]

* * * * * * * * * * * * * * * * * *

The third, and certainly most important group, are the members themselves. One significant sign is that they often introduce themselves at training sessions as "just a member," as if they are somehow inferior to staff or officers.

The history of attempts to change the structure of the union from the bottom-up would fill many exciting volumes because there have been campaigns to elect new officers and to set new strategies for as long as The Servicing Model has existed. In fact, some great labor history shows the establishment of The Servicing Model, as radical groups like the CIO were turned into "responsible" unions. A few internal union campaigns have run successfully so several international unions have presidents who came from outside the structure. The Teamsters for Democratic Union (TDU), founded in 1980, became one of the most enduring rank-and-file groups and elected several Vice-Presidents in last year's elections. The TDU maintains constant pressure both on the corruption of union officers as well as strategies for better union activities, like negotiating the new UPS contract next year.

At the opposite end of the rank-and-file movement was the murder-for-hire contract that Tony Boyle, of the UMW, put out on his opponent, Jock Yablonski, in 1969.

One important area for membership pressure is to turn all union activities into a proactive mode—not waiting to react to something the boss does to us, but setting the issues and planning to accomplish them. While this section about changing the members is brief, it is really the most important because any change in your union will have to come from the members, so every chapter is directed at them.

---

[58] Andrew Elrod. "What Happened to Workers Ed?" *Dissent.* Spring, 2017.

* * * * * * * * * * * * * * * * * *

In the history of unionism in the US, structures changed dramatically, usually responding to both economic and social changes as well as to different visions by both workers and prominent officers. For new members in the union movement, this history is important because it helps us to understand how we got to where we are today. At the risk of being repetitious, unionism—just like your individual union contract—did not just miraculously appear but is the product of hundreds of years of struggle, just like the contract is the product of decades of battle with your boss.

After the Civil War, as industrialism grew, unions expanded from small locals into national unions, and eventually created a coalition, the American Federation of Labor (AFL), to advance the movement. As industry grew in the early years of the 20th century, workers created industrial unions and formed a new coalition, The Congress of Industrial Unions (CIO), which was a product of the sit-down strike movement and which split from the AFL in 1937.

Another split came almost immediately when John L. Lewis, the first president of the CIO, pulled the United Mine Workers (UMW) out of the CIO in 1940 in a dispute over the support for Roosevelt in the 1940 election. The UMW reaffiliated with the AFL and remained a member until 1947, when Lewis again pulled the union out in a protest over the refusal of the AFL officers to oppose the Taft-Hartley Act.

Almost prophetically, Lewis proclaimed: "This Act is a trap, a pitfall for organized labor. . .This Act was passed to oppress labor, to make it difficult its current enterprises for collective bargaining, to make more difficult the securing of new members for this labor movement, without which our movement will become so possessed of inertia that there is no action and no growth, and in a labor movement where there is no growth there is no security for its existence because deterioration sets in a unions, like men, retrograde."[59]

One destructive structural change occurred after passage of the Taft-Hartley Act when officers of unions in both federations expelled members, and unions, for membership, or alleged membership, in the Communist Party. Officers like Walter Reuther took control of radical unions like the UAW, created a strong union bureaucracy and The Servicing Model became entrenched.

Some union officers like Ronald Reagan rose to prominence, partly by their roles as spies for the FBI. If there was any doubt about the Trump administration's anti-union attitudes, Secretary of Labor Anthony Acosta announced in August, 2017, that Reagan would be inducted into the Labor Department's Hall of Fame. It is really "fake news" that a man who fired 11,000 air traffic controllers "improved working conditions and quality of life for families," as the induction award claimed. History is written by the winners.

The two federations were separate and competitive for almost 20 years until they finally merged in 1955 to form the AFL-CIO that we know today (and you can easily win a bet by asking your co-workers what "AFL-CIO" stands for on your union membership card or letterhead).

---

[59] John L. Lewis speech. December 12, 1947

Another structural change has been a consistent pattern of union mergers over the past 30 years. Small unions, whose officers were worried about survival, were absorbed into larger unions, often from the same industry but often just to increase membership, as the UAW took in the National Writers Union, the CWA absorbed the Association of Flights Attendants and the USW absorbed the National Pharmacists Association (NPhA).

Over the past 35 years, there have only been a couple of other efforts to bring these structural changes and each came to failure, blocked by the dramatic changes in the economy, by economic recessions and by fierce economic and political opposition from our bosses. The consideration of new strategies was also held back by a union structure that would not change and by individual union officers who valued their positions in the structure more than they respected the movement and who insisted on "business (or unionism) as usual."

Let's look at the recent history of attempts to change the structure at the top.

- In 1979, the AFL-CIO began a large organizing project in the south, the first real effort since 1948 when Operation Dixie promised to shake up the union structure. One campaign was the Houston Organizing Project, a multi-union effort was budgeted at $1 million a year and created to challenge the geographic segregation of unionism. As the recession of 1983 took hold and employers vigorously resisted the AFL-CIO's efforts, however, the Houston Organizing Project collapsed. Today only 4.7 percent of workers in the state of Texas are union members.

- Partly in response to the collapse of this campaign, in 1983 the AFL-CIO executive council began an extensive strategic planning project and a plan was adopted two years later which, among other things, endorsed higher levels of organizing. Between 1985 and 1988, some AFL-CIO officers developed what subsequently became known as "The Organizing Model," which was introduced to member unions in a massive, two-day telephone and video conference call on February 29- March 1, 1988, with skilled organizers from many different unions. The training manual, *Numbers that Count,* was then published and was widely circulated, proclaiming The Organizing Model of Unionism, emphasizing that unions were more effective when they used external, new-member organizing techniques with members who were already organized, and asked especially "Why Do We Act One Way before the Election, and Another the Day After."

In a symbol of our times, this booklet has been out of print for many years.

- In October, 1995, after six months of palace intrigue, John Sweeney became the first insurgent president ever of the AFL-CIO. Sweeney barely defeated incumbent Tom Donohue as part of the New Voice campaign, promising, among other things, to hire and train 1,000 new organizers. The increasingly anti-union actions of the Clinton administration, especially the signing of The North American Free Trade Agreement (NAFTA) in December, 1993, finally stirred this change at the top. It was the first contested election for the position of federation president since 1895, when John McBride of the United Mine Workers challenged Samuel Gompers for the presidency of the AFL. Even though McBride got more votes, Gompers refused to give up the office and was elected, or re-elected in 1896, beginning a pattern of incumbency that ran for 100 years. Many of the changes proposed by the New Voice group—especially the implementing the Organizing Model of Unionism—were met with fierce opposition from state and local union officers and the program withered and died. Sweeney briefly developed a new structure by appointing state AFL-CIO directors, a parallel office to the elected state presidents. The opposition was so heated that the positions were eventually eliminated. The election in 1995 of Richard Trumka as Secretary-Treasurer maintained the tradition of top officers waiting patiently in line, as he was moved up to the president's position when Sweeny retired in September, 2009.

- "The New Unity Partnership (NUP) has stirred up a firestorm of controversy in union circles. Its inception can be traced to the July 4th holiday in 2003 when five national union presidents [SEIU, UNITE, HERE, LIUNA and UBC] gathered for a candid private discussion about the future of the labor movement. The motivation for the summit was concern about the collective inability of unions to reverse their fading fortunes. At this and subsequent meetings the unions considered structural and strategic options to promote union growth, ultimately committing to a form of mutual aid pact to pool resources for coordinated organizing initiatives and to support each other in critical campaigns. The controversy stems not from this tangible outcome, but from the NUP's call to dramatically restructure the entire movement. . ."[60]

- In June 2005, five major unions showed their opposition toward many of these "changes" by disaffiliating from the AFL-CIO and forming the Change to Win Coalition, led by Andy Stern of the SEIU. For a movement that rose partly out of factionalism, it was no surprise that the new coalition was consumed with dissension. The Carpenters Union dropped out in 2009, the Laborers International Union (LIU) re-affiliated with the AFL-CIO in September, 2009, and two unions which merged to create UNITE-HERE went through a messy separation. While the SEIU has become one of the largest unions in the US, there was no significant change in union structure or strategy—certainly not to the Organizing Model.

Several of these unions, particularly the SEIU and the Carpenters, enforced significant internal structural changes, merging independent locals into megalocals, allegedly to expand the resources available for organizing. In one response, SEIU United Healthcare Workers West, comprised of 65,000 members, resisted some of the changes and a controversial strategy from

---

[60] Richard W. Hurd. "The Failure of Organizing, the New Unity Partnership and the Future of the Labor Movement." *Working USA*. Summer, 2004

the national office of accepting mediocre contracts in exchange for voluntary recognition. Accompanied by palace intrigue among the SEIU officers that resembled the Trump White House, the local was first pushed under trusteeship and then broke away to form the independent National Union of Healthcare Workers. Several of the unions returned to the AFL-CIO but the SEIU, along with the largest union in the country, the National Education Association (NEA) remain independent.

As the crisis deepens, especially in states where open shop legislation has been passed, structural challenges to the union leadership are more volatile. In Michigan, for example, which became an open shop state in March, 2013, the largest state workers union was in chaos.

> "The vice president of Michigan's oldest state employee union said today he has resigned over an ongoing dispute about the direction of an organization many members say is in a state of chaos, especially in dealing with the staff union. Brent Heyer, who has accused Michigan State Employees Association President Ken Moore of attempted union busting and otherwise abusing his position, told the Free Press he resigned Wednesday. Heyer said he and some other leaders of the union can't find out how much of members' dues are being spent on protracted legal disputes they fear could bankrupt the MSEA. . . . Among the issues is Moore's decision – later ratified by the board of the union in a divided vote – to appeal to the U.S. 6th Circuit Court of Appeals an August National Labor Relations Board ruling that said Moore and the MSEA broke federal labor laws in actions they took against their own employees, including illegal firings and discipline and refusals to turn over information.. . . 'It's incredible to see, the MSEA is actually crumbling right in front of our eyes,' said Michael Walker, who serves on the 14-member MSEA board as an alternate director for the Saginaw-Flint region."[61]

As the unions in the United States face the challenge, major structural changes have been happening in Canada. In January, 2018, the largest Canadian union, Unifor announced that it was leaving the Canadian Labor Congress, the equivalent to the AFL-CIO. Unifor was created when the Canadian Auto Workers separated from the UAW "when Canadian workers resisted the concessions that had been agreed to by the UAW in bargaining with the large American car makers on both sides of the border. Nationalism and a commitment to the creation of Canadian unions runs deep in Unifor culture." Even though "Union activists are deeply worried that fighting over already organized workers will waste resources and serves as a distraction from the movement's real task: organizing the unorganized." Unifor first tried to raid the ATU local in Toronto and then began working with dissident members of UNITE-HERE.

In response the CLC issued a statement: "Therefore, the CLC condemns, in the strongest possible terms, the decision and actions of the Unifor leadership to disaffiliate from the CLC and raid the members of UNITE HERE Local 75 in the Greater Toronto Area. Raiding a union is a deplorable act that is irreconcilable with the principles of solidarity on which our movement was

---

[61] Paul Egan. "Internal war raging at Michigan state employee union." *Detroit Free Press*. February 10, 2016.

founded. The actions of Unifor are made worse when they defend their raiding activities with nationalist justifications and wholesale attacks on international unions." [62]

At the same time, the UE is supporting a North American Solidarity project with Unifor. According to Peter Kennedy, now retired as the first Secretary-Treasurer of Unifor, and currently a participant in the UE-Unifor North American Solidarity Project Study Group. "Unions have to change in order to fight the corporate capitalist agenda," said Kennedy. "The labor movement has been talking a good fight for 30 years but haven't been doing anything about it. We either do things differently or we are writing our own obituary." He emphasized that "UE is an important part of what we have set out to do, which is to change the dynamic of the labor movement."[63]

* * * * * * * * * * * * * * * * * *

Another strategic problem that affects every level of the union movement is the refusal to ask for, or to share, best practices, even among union officers who realize that a crisis is here. As the *Friedrichs* catastrophe came closer in late 2015, some unions began to raise alarms. The president of AFSCME proclaimed that the union would devote 40% of its resources to internal organizing and proposed training sessions. There were already unions, like private sector unions in the 27 open shop states, and like the APWU and AFGE, and of course AFSCME in many states, which have always confronted open shops and have experience running campaigns and increasing membership, but there was almost no effort to learn about these practices and to try to apply them in other unions.

In one top-down initiative, the Organizing Institute of the AFL-CIO made an enormous step toward changing this dynamic with a National Organizers Workshop conference in March 2015, in Washington, DC. Proclaiming itself *Ready to Talk Shop and Dream Big*, the conference stressed "Movement Building," and hosted 51 different panels--a wonderful organizing buffet, including one specifically titled "Open Shop Organizing," presented by AFGE staff. The topics, presented by members of a wide range of organizations, ran a range from "Worker Mobilization and Multi-Union Cooperation" to sustaining "personal happiness while organizing," so the conference was a hopeful start.

Another longtime place to exchange strategies is the publication *Labor Notes*, which has always presented a rank-and-file perspective and focused more in the past year on organizing campaigns. The column NewsWatch is full of great news, and their biannual conferences attract hundreds of union activists.

One effort to share best practices using new technology is a web site called UnionBase, which was originally set up when one of the founders, Larry Williams, worked for the Teamsters. "When it came to technology, most unions were still living in the Dark Ages. At the Teamsters, Williams says, he found himself looking up colleagues' phone numbers in old-fashioned directories. 'We had paper stacked up to the ceiling,' he adds. . . . UnionBase has been enhanced with educational material on labor and other features. About 10,000 people have

---

[62] LabourStart.
[63] UE News Bulletin. February 6, 2018.

visited the site since 2015, he says." The site now claims to be "the world's first social platform for the labor movement with 30,000 union profiles, an expertly crafted user experience for union and non-union workers" and could be a new and unstructured way to trade Best Union Practices." [64]

A new method for exchanging strategies is the Labor Research and Action Network (https://lranetwork.org/), whose officers, a combination of union officers, labor studies instructors and community activists, promote it as an "exciting collaboration connecting academics and labor practitioners to build workplace and economic power for working people in this country. The project offers webinars and conferences to "examine methods of building worker power and advancing a new social movement in an economy where collective bargaining is imperiled, and where employer-employee relationships are increasingly fragmented."

Union Communication Union Services (UCS), now administered by The Worker Institute at Cornell, is also starting to offer open webinars, on topics like the challenges of being a new union officer and on internal organizing.

* * * * * * * * * * * * * * * * * * *

The dramatic changes in technology and in global ownership have stimulated the development of completely different forms of organization—alt-unions and worker centers. These organizations have adapted to the so-called "gig economy," where workers have such irregular conditions of employment that they almost seem like independent contractors. The difficulty is that these organizations often do not propose moving to become unions or to demand recognition and union contracts from employers, so the organizations could then support themselves by union dues.

One prominent alt-union is Restaurant Opportunities Center (ROC), which calculates that there are about 14 million workers in the restaurant industry and advocates as a solution "Engaging those who work in the restaurant industry through job training and placement (COLORS Restaurants and our CHOW job training program); leadership development and civic engagement; legal support and policy advocacy . . .and (2) Engaging employers through our 'high road' employer association RAISE, which provides: training, technical assistance, and a peer network of like-minded employers following the high road to profitability, which includes higher wages and working conditions for those employed at their restaurants; leadership development and civic engagement opportunities; research and communications work that documents the benefits for all three stakeholders of taking the high road and more."[65]

As union organizer Steve Early pointed out, however, "ROC now operates in twenty states, with a $4 million annual budget raised primarily from private philanthropies like the Ford Foundation. The organization reports having 10,000 'members' but their individual dues

---

[64] Rick Wartzman. " Meet the Millennial Who's Trying to Save the Labor Movement with a Facebook for Unions." Fast Company. September 1, 2017.

[65] http://rocunited.org/

payments fund only a small portion of the organization's total budget. . . . Collective bargaining is strangely missing from the author's 'recipes for change.' Yet that self-help mechanism is employed by hundreds of thousands of 'food chain' workers, including those who cook and serve meals in unionized hotels and casinos, airport restaurants and stadium concession stands, campus, corporate and government cafeterias."[66]

One potential Best Union Practice, combining union organizing and a shrewd political tactic, developed when 1,200 New York fast-food workers signed pledges to contribute $13.50 a month to financially support the group Fast Food Justice. "To the dismay of many business groups, New York City enacted an innovative law last year that many labor advocates hope will become a model to finance such organizations across the nation. Under the law, fast-food employees who want to contribute to a nonprofit, nonunion workers' group can insist on having the restaurant they work for deduct money from their pay and forward that money to the group. But before a group can receive these contributions, it must get 500 workers to pledge to contribute. . . . Fast Food Justice's leaders say they hope to get 5,000 workers to contribute by the end of 2018, and 10,000 by the end of 2020. (New York City has about 65,000 fast-food workers.) Contributions from 5,000 workers would mean revenue of more than $800,000 a year." Of course, the Restaurant Law Association, representing the franchise owners and the corporations, are challenging the deduction law in court.[67]

The history of the United Farmworkers is a great resource for organizing strategies. The movement among workers with the most irregular employment structure and anti-union employers, with extra challenges of language and immigrant status, started without even any legal protection. With the essential commitment that the workers themselves had to become the organizers, the officers, most prominently Cesar Chavez, Delores Huerta and Larry Itilong, created an early Leverage Diagram, spreading it internationally through consumer boycotts. One challenge for the farmworker union was that none of their work was covered by labor law but, as a model for us to follow, they turned challenge into an opportunity because they were not limited by labor law that generally prohibits "secondary boycotts." This union and unionism, became a highly visible *Causa* and consumer power was leverage. The famous grape and lettuce boycotts, and picketing stores that sold non-union produce, created a social movement that mobilized religious and community groups to support the demand for union recognition. The tangled history of the Farmworkers as it later became a "union" does not erase some of the great organizing strategies.

---

[66] Steve Early. "No Unions Behind The Kitchen Door? *Review of Saru Jayaraman's Behind The Kitchen Door.*" *Labor Studies Journal*, Fall, 2013
[67] Steven Greenhouse. "Fast-Food Workers Claim Victory in a New York Labor Effort." *The New York Times.* January 9, 2018.

One alternate structure of unionism that would bring disaster is a "members only association." Union organizer Chris Brooks describes this failed strategy:

"If an open-shop future is inevitable, argues labor lawyer Thomas Geoghegan in *Only One Thing Can Save Us*, then unions should abandon representation elections for members-only bargaining, in which only union members are covered by a union contract, and 'represent' only the people— be it 40 percent, or 30 percent, or fewer—who sign up, take the oath, and pay the dues, and for- get everyone else" (emphasis in original). Likewise, Shaun Richman, a former director at the American Federation of Teachers, argues that unions in open-shop states should pursue a legal strategy through the courts that will establish members-only bargaining so unions can 'cede exclusive representation to kick out the scabs.' Law professors Catherine Fisk and Benjamin Sachs join Geoghegan and Richman in arguing not only that exclusive representation should be dropped in open-shop environments through members-only bargaining, but that the results of doing so could ultimately be beneficial for unions that will now be forced to win over workers through securing strong contracts or offering superior union services."

Employers would love to see unions voluntarily represent a minority of workers, allowing the bosses to establish separate pay and benefit schedules—one in the "contract," and the other like a non-union workplace. It is fantasy to think that with a minority of the workforce as members, a union would have any bargaining power to negotiate or to enforce a contract. In the 1930's unions fought for exclusive representation as the way to build bargaining power after campaigns by the employers to encourage multiple unions in the same workplace.

Brooks provides an excellent evaluation of the situation in the state of Tennessee, where one legislator denounced ""collective, socialistic bargaining," and a law passed in 2011 eliminated exclusive representation for the union and created a "multi-organizational form of negotiations." New groups, "coalition of independent education associations" (IEAs) appeared . . . to provide a mixture of liability insurance, ongoing professional development, and legal representation —all at a cheaper rate than typical union dues. IEAs also attempt to set themselves apart from unions by publicly denouncing 'unprofessional' tactics like strikes and pickets . . . and support right-to-work legislative packages." Financially tied to right-wing groups like the Koch Brothers' American Legislative Exchange Council (ALEC),[68] it is clear that the movement to revive company unions is one strategy that the employers are supporting.

At the same time, some of these new organizations can be exciting. One great movement came early in the Trump administration, showing how quickly, effective and almost spontaneously, thanks to social media, workers can organize and how a work stoppage can generate enormous community support. Playing to his anti-immigration supporters, Trump proclaimed an Executive Order on January 27, 2017 "Executive Order Protecting the Nation from Foreign Terrorist Entry into the United States," suspending refugees from entering the U.S.

---

[68] Chris Brooks. "The Cure Worse than the Disease: Expelling Freeloaders in an Open-Shop State." *New Labor Forum*. August 24, 2017.

for 120 days, with Syrian refugees indefinitely. It also barred travelers from six other Muslim-majority countries for 90 days, including those with visas, green cards, or legal residential status.

In a turbulent day, unionized taxi drivers in New York City went on a work stoppage, refusing to pick up passengers. In a tweet, the Alliance stated late in the afternoon of January 28: "Our 19,000-member strong union stands firmly opposed to Donald Trump's Muslim ban. As an organization whose membership is largely Muslim, a workforce that's almost universally immigrant, and a working-class movement that is rooted in defense of the oppressed, we say no to this inhumane and unconstitutional ban." The NY Taxi Workers Alliance called for all drivers to avoid JFK Airport on Saturday [January 28, 2017] in order to facilitate protests against the Executive Order.

When it appeared that Uber was encouraging drivers to go to the airport to scab on the strike, people began deleting the Uber app, so the company slightly reversed itself. Uber CEO Travis Kalanick sent an email to employees announcing his plan to help Uber drivers who might be overseas and unable to re-enter the country because of Trump's travel ban, which he called "unjust." Kalanick said Uber will provide lawyers and immigration experts to drivers banned from entering the country using a $3 million company-created legal defense fund. Drivers will also be compensated for lost wages. Kalanick was among 19 business executives appointed to a panel to provide economic advice to President Trump.[69]

Kalanick was one of the first to resign from this panel, as the Trump administration came under attack from the very wealthy individuals it represents and was subsequently ousted as an executive at the company for alleged sexual harassment and not for this concerted activity.

* * * * * * * * * * * * * * * * * * * *

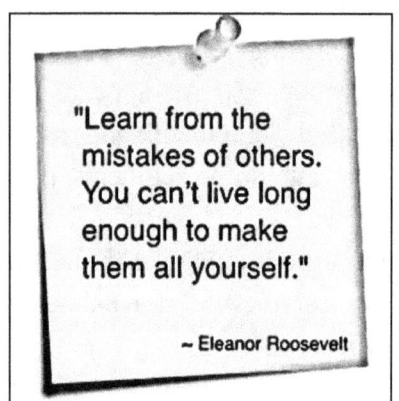

"Learn from the mistakes of others. You can't live long enough to make them all yourself."
~ Eleanor Roosevelt

The world's economy is moving so fast, and changing so dramatically, that almost every organization is responding so union officers and members need to study organizational strategies from other areas to evaluate Best Practices. Yes, unions are different, with different values, but if we share a goal of building our organizations, then we can, and should, and must, learn from them. Not imitate them but begin to *think organizationally*.

We have seen from the failures of major industries—the steel industry and General Motors to mention two from my experience—what happens when an organization simply repeats what has been successful in the past, following the Old Joe tradition and promoting from within with no new ideas or strategies. In relation to the "real world" and in relation to the advancement of individuals within the organizations, these dutiful executives fail and the companies or industries fail along with them.

---

[69] Ashley Lutz. "Furious customers are deleting the Uber app after drivers went to JFK airport during a protest and strike." *Business Insider*. January 29, 2017.

At General Electric and UnderArmour, the chief executives were eased out when the companies underperformed and "in 2015, 17 percent of the largest 2500 public companies in the world changed their CEO, more than in any of the previous 16 years of the CEO Success Study from Strategy&, PwC's strategy consulting business.[70]

The NAACP, "energized by liberal activists," dismissed its president, Cornell Brooks after only two years in office, "in order to confront President Trump more vigorously, just weeks after Brooks was arrested outside the office of Senator Jeff Sessions. "The group, which has been eclipsed in many ways by the more youthful Black Lives matter movement and the broader opposition to Mr. Trump, is embarking on a national listening tour of cities across the country to get ideas about how it can remain relevant," with one officer insisting that the organization has to figure out "are we the right fit for the current reality."[71]

What about our unions? As one AFSCME rep stated: "I'm done with the trades. Fuck them. The quicker a formal split happens the better. Let's just do SEIU aft Afscme nea CWA and some other unions who aren't racist shit heads. The trades are EAGER to bash from POC/leftist/ women heads. They are useless idiots who will actively help trump with his repression. Brain dead. I got 'in trouble' today on a big org director call for saying that it was a real error not going to members with a clear trump message. That he wants to destroy our union and members deserve to know that. That 2020 will not be free and fair elections and we might as well fight now when we still have power. And that it was a real mistake not to have a plan for inauguration. Evidently, the natl exec board has considered all these things. As I was told. We are gonna be living in an authoritarian theocracy very soon."

As an example of the challenges to the union structure, the confrontation in Charlottesville, VA in August opened an enormous social issue, and the discussion and responses could almost become a separate chapter. While several union officers distributed letters opposing the KKK and the Nazis, Local 10 of the ILWU declared a one-day work stoppage for August 26: "Therefore, ILWU Local 10 in the best tradition of our union that fought these right-wingers in the Big Strike of 1934, will not work on that day and instead march to Crissy Field to stop the racist, fascist intimidation in our hometown and invite all unions and antiracist and antifascist organizations to join us defending unions, racial minorities, immigrants, LGBTQ people, women and all the oppressed."

Did other unions show a similar commitment? These "social movements" are a wonderful opportunity for unions to become proactive and visible and to reflect the

---

[70] Strategy&. "CEO Turnover at a Record High Globally, With More Companies Planning for New Chiefs from Outside the Company." April 19, 2016.
[71] Yamiche Alcindor. N.A.A.C.P., Energized by Liberal Activists, Dismisses Its President." *New York Times*. May 20, 2017

resources we already have. Obviously, there are challenges before "The Union" can participate because of the diversity of opinions among our members but discussions and debates, and votes, on important issues are exactly what is necessary to break out of the isolation. Union members, and the unions they support, live in a very real and very complicated world and we must welcome the challenges, and not try to avoid them.

* * * * * * * * * * * * * * * * * *

Changes in technology have opened up huge new avenues for communications—from the officers to the members, among the members, and between us and our communities. No one demonstrated this skill more vividly than Donald Trump when he systematically cut down more than a dozen opponents in the Republican primaries and then got elected. His use of social media—his obsessive use of social media—is so successful in keeping him as the center of attention that we need to learn from it.

Technology could be important for unions, but increasing membership—and non-member—participation is often seen as a threat to the officers who have already administer the union's technology. In the old days, it was the official union newspaper or leaflets posted on a bulletin board, behind a locked glass, in the work place. Now web sites or communications are effectively top-down, whose content controlled with no method for input from our members to express themselves to the top officers of their unions about strategies and concerns. As you saw in the discussions about the internal organizing campaign in the BMWED or in Quebec, the officers used a survey and interviews but a combination of new technology and Best Practices displays other possibilities.

In early August, 2017, Google fired a software engineer named James Damore for posting a 10-page paper that claimed there are fewer women software engineers because the male and female brains are configured differently. Leaving aside the substance of this debate, look at a process called Memegen, an employee-only version of the social media service Google Plus, where Damore posted his opinions. There are "about 87,000 Google groups — essentially email lists formed around a central theme — and more than 8,000 discussion groups like "misc" — short for miscellaneous — where employees debate and disagree on topics ranging from the optimal temperature in the office to the brand of laundry detergent the company should use for washing employee towels."

This system was so swamped with comments that Sundar Pichai, Google's Chief Executive, cancelled a planned meeting. ""In recognition of Googlers' concerns, we need to step back and create a better set of conditions for us to have the discussion,' Mr. Pichai wrote."[72]

What an enormous capacity for expanding communications among all members, staff and officers of a union, a great way to share Best Practices. A steward in San Diego finds a new interpretation of the union contract, exactly what a steward in New Jersey was looking for. A local in Rapid City creates an internal organizing plan to sign up non-members, exactly what the

---

[72] Daisuke Wakabayashi. "A Crisis Forces Google to Uphold Its Values While Fostering Debate. *New York Times*. August 11, 2017.

officers in Miami were considering. What if a rep in Los Angeles created a labor history course that an steward in Bangor could use? The possibilities are, literally, unlimited. This process is one example of borrowing best practices from other organizations and adapting them to union use.

New technology can make it very easy to share strategies among unions. In one on-line forum, a basic union question was posted: "Does anyone know of contract language which provides for either on-line membership sign-up and/or voice authorization sign-up as an alternative to the traditional written sign-up approach?" This is a challenge that so many union officers and reps are facing that a sharing of strategies will be of huge value.

Some locals have set up closed Facebook sites, where members—and only members admitted by the site's moderator—can exchange strategies and experiences. One ATU local president streamed himself live during a hurricane with information about work schedules for the members that they could not get from management. Several locals have even created apps, so that news about the local can be instantly distributed. In every case, the union is established as a credible source of information, building loyalty and encouraging non-members to join. If Trump can do it, we can—and he's not even credible. The advantages of sharing this information are enormous and would enhance the status of someone who is "just a member," and can obviously be adapted by members who want to run for office.

The two-way discussions between members and officers are an essential component of the Organizing Model of Unionism and a "listening tour"—even an electronic one-- by the officers can build up a union. The failure, or refusal, of Hillary Clinton to engage in one has been listed as a cause for her campaign failure. Now technology has made it easy and cheap for every member to express an opinion anyway, often on a Facebook site or through private Twitter accounts.

With a huge expansion of social media, opinions and topics will be openly debated. In August, 2017, for example, a displaced steelworker in Baltimore posted on his Facebook page, a defense of the white supremacists and Nazi demonstrators in Virginia, with dozens of comments. It was like a debate at the union hall, except their union hall doesn't exist anymore, but anyone across the country could speak up in a debate that is so important.

What would an internal discussion board like this do for your union? Would the top officers fear that the members would soon share evaluations of the officers and staff reps? Of course, but now technology has made it easy and cheap for every member to express an opinion anyway, on a Facebook site or through private Twitter accounts. Yes, there would be hot topics—like contract negotiations or the ability of the union officers—but these are discussions that go on in every workplace. Letting members participate, especially the younger and more tech savvy ones, will build up the union. After all, differences of opinion, especially on union strategies, are fundamental to our organizations so we need to be able to share them. Selfishly speaking, incumbent officers who adapt these new communication strategies and visibility also expand their chances for re-election.

* * * * * * * * * * * * * * * * * * *

Another controversial area of union structure is the support—or not—for diversity in the workplace. Donald Trump clearly seized upon the opposition among many union members in targeted geographic areas to turn the increasing diversity of the country into a major political attack. After all, doesn't *Making America Great Again* mean restoring the dominance of white males who think the ozone layer is doing fine? And white males, many of whom are union officers and members? It became clear at the rally in Charlottesville, VA, on August 12, 2017, that this white supremacy is serious, and illustrated by KKK members and—more importantly—Nazi flags, certainly challenging the strong patriotism of the white male conservative base. As we talk about our union movement becoming global, we unfortunately have to recognize that the white supremacists movement is also expanding to many other countries, wrapped in an anti-immigrant hatred.

The issue of diversity is enormous within many locals. In Fairfax County, VA, a suburb of Washington, DC, the superintendent of schools was discussing the hiring and retention of teachers and stated that there are "143 cultural groups" in the county, and therefore in the schools.[73] This astonishing breadth of culture is, and increasingly will be, in the workplaces and therefore in our unions and organizing campaigns.

Some union officers loudly support tight limits on immigration. "We applaud the three executive orders he has issued to date and are confident they will make America safer and more prosperous. Morale amongst our agents and officers has increased exponentially since the signing of the orders," said a joint statement from the National Border Patrol Council and National ICE Council, a division of AFGE. "The men and women of ICE and Border Patrol will work tirelessly to keep criminals, terrorists, and public safety threats out of this country, which remains the number one target in the world – and President Trump's actions now empower us to fulfill this life saving mission, and it will indeed save thousands of lives and billions of dollars," it added.[74]

Some locals, on the other hand, have moved boldly to celebrate diversity and to build a movement that defends all of their members and their families. In language that resembles the defiance of abolitionists who publicly challenged The Fugitive Slave Laws of the 1850's, locals are declaring themselves to be "Sanctuary Locals." As described by Tim Goulet about Teamsters Local 810 in New York City,

> "The 'sanctuary union' resolution was inspired by similar resolutions by the National Union of Healthcare Workers (NUHW) in California and the National Education Association (NEA) in Washington, DC. The resolution was proposed in a general membership meeting in front of a large group of truck drivers and building mechanics—not the sort of crowd you usually associate with radicalism. Yet the resolution, along with an argument tying together the attack on immigrants with possible national right-to-work legislation and the rest of Trump's multi-front offensive on the

---

[73] WAMU-FM. The Kojo Naambi Show. May 15, 2017.
[74] Paul Bedard. "Unions of Border Patrol, ICE agents cheer Trump actions." *Washington Examiner*. January 28, 2017.

working class, resonated with the membership, in a way that I don't think was possible only a couple of years ago. The resolution commits Local 810 to not cooperating with federal agents in the prosecution or attempted deportation of members. It also means we will mobilize our forces to protest raids by ICE and resist employer collaboration, which is nothing but a clear-cut method of union-busting. The resolution also declares support for the continuation and strengthening of DACA and DAPA (Deferred Action for Parents of Americans) programs for immigrants. Moving forward, members are planning to present the 'Sanctuary Resolution' to other Teamster locals, and next month, it will be taken to Teamsters Joint Council 16 in New York City for possible ratification."[75]

In another surprising movement, Kenneth E. Rigmaiden, the General President of the International Union of Painters and Allied Trades (IUPAT) began a public campaign to defend two members in California who were picked up by ICE officers at work and detained, even though their petitions for asylum were being considered. Combining unionism with protection for immigrants, Ringmaiden announced: "Most of our union members move between states, cities, and towns; going from job to job building a better future for themselves and their families. That's what we do; we go where the opportunities are. Hugo and Rodrigo moved from their home countries for similar reasons. We will continue to stand by our union brothers Hugo and Rodrigo, the same way we have stood by other union members before them; be it when they have been exploited by an employer on the job or while experiencing extreme hardship of any kind. We will not let a broken immigration system take our brothers away from us without a fight."[76]

At the same time, on the other side, on January 29, 2017, U.S. Customs and Border Protection (CBP) agents at the Los Angeles and Washington, DC airports-- obviously having read up on civil disobedience-- continued trying to deport travelers from blacklisted Muslim-majority countries, despite a federal court order in Brooklyn halting the practice. President Trump's Executive Order suspended refugees from entering the U.S. for 120 days, with Syrian refugees indefinitely. It also barred travelers from six other Muslim-majority countries for 90 days, including those with visas, green cards, or legal residential status. On the following day (January 28), a federal court in Brooklyn issued an emergency stay for the forced deportations. This federal order halting deportations entitles detainees to see an attorney, but reports indicated that CBP Protection agents were also defying that provision.

* * * * * * * * * * * * * * * * * * *

Another area of change for union structure is a new emphasis on union visibility. Over time, as unions grew, there were union halls and union functions so that everyone knew about us. Now unions are almost invisible—very few Labor Day Parades or community activities, no more public appearances and media blasts.

In the late 1930's, the second-most quoted person in the US newspapers, after President Franklin D. Roosevelt, (who could have taught Donald Trump a thing or two about media

---

[75] Tim Goulet. "We Are A Sanctuary Union." *Socialist Worker*. Portside June 28, 2017.
[76] IUPAT. July 10, 2017

control) was John L. Lewis, the President of the Congress of Industrial Organizations (CIO). While John L was so visible, most union officers today are invisible. When was the last time you saw a union officer interviewed on commercial media? Or heard a strong public statement about a key issue?   While it is not difficult to see why most media—now owned by increasingly large right-wing corporations—wants to block us out, we still should make public appearances. Even better, we can create our own media—through Facebook videos that can be sent to every member, through podcasts or even by individual Twitter messages.

In Washington, DC, there is a radio program "Your Rights at Work," hosted by a central Labor Council staff person, that is on the air for an hour every week and which takes calls from listeners. The show features interview with workers about their unions, some labor songs and a weekly section on labor history, prepared by Union Communication Services. Using new technology, all of the shows are available for podcast, with an inventory that goes back to 2014.[77] One international union, the ATU, purchased an hour of commercial radio time every week on a Baltimore AM station for a program—Lunch With Labor-- hosted by the local ATU president to discuss union issues and to interview other union officers.

One exceptional example of union visibility is the on-line newspaper, WorkDay Minnesota, which has posted stories about union activities across the state for almost 20 years. The DC Central Labor Council also posts a news site Union City Union City (streetheat@dclabor.org) with news of union activity and an extensive labor history section.

If you disagree with this point about visibility, do an experiment: go into work tomorrow and take a survey of your union brothers and sisters. Ask them to identify

1. Their union steward
2. Their union Chief Steward
3. Their local union president
4. Their state or district union president
5. The international union president
6. The president of the Central Labor Council
7. The president of the state federation
8. And, as a bonus, the present of the national AFL-CIO.

My experience is that most of our members can answer the first three but fall abruptly after that.

There are many ways to expand union visibility and it can start at work: CWA members who work for Verizon have the union insignia on the sleeves of their work jackets while many ATU locals negotiate for drivers to wear a union patch (even paid for by the employer) on their uniforms. On our own, we should all wear union pins, or have union decals on our hard hats to prove our pride.

Each of us needs to spread union visibility into our communities. Do you wear your union insignia outside your workplace? When you go to the grocery store, or on vacation, do you wear a union cap or T-shirt? How about bumper stickers on your car? A local union that really

---

[77] http://www.dclabor.org/union-city-radio/your-rights-at-work-january-18

wanted to stress visibility could purchase yard signs, with a banner like" A Proud Union Family Lives here," with the union logo, so everyone can see it.

Finally, look at some old-fashioned visibility—make your union hall a center of activities, for your members, their families and for the community. As unions developed, the hall was a center of activity for members and their families, partly because the workers couldn't afford any other entertainment and often lived within walking distance of the hall. There were union dances and parties, holiday parties for the children, education classes, athletic leagues at nearby fields and a general sense that the union was very important to the lives of the members, their families and the communities.

Have social events, like parties and dances, or children's holiday parties or retirees card games. As members participate in these activities, it's a great way to overcome racial or ethnic or age or cultural differences so everyone understands that we are all just union brothers and sisters.

Or just make the hall a hanging-out place. As one officer in the ATU posted on the local's Facebook site:

If you're not doing anything now stop by the union office for a little social and let's strategize on our business.

This casual invitation changes the structure of the union hall and, most importantly, encourages members to stop by and to strategize on how to make the union stronger.

NOW GO DO IT

1. **Create a Membership Participation Chart to see how many of your members have participated in a union activity in the past 3 months.**
2. **If you are in an open shop state, how many workers are not members? What kind of issues keep them from joining?**
3. **What kind of internal organizing campaign have you tried?**
4. **Do a survey of your members to evaluate union support and loyalty—not to particular officers but to the union itself.**
5. **Do a "listening tour" in your department—ask members how they feel and what improvements should be made. Get together with officers or staff from another union—maybe even a different industry—and have the same discussion.**
6. **How about regular meetings to discuss the future of the local?**

HOW ONE UNION DID IT
Establishing a Communication Action Team (CAT)
By Gene Bruskin
Brotherhood of Maintenance of Way

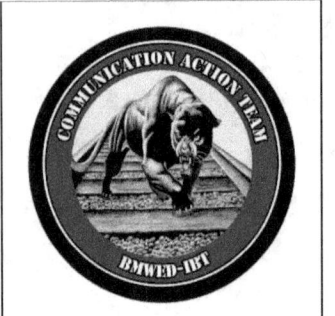

The BMWED (Brotherhood of Maintenance of Way Division/IBT)) is a national union, founded in 1887, representing the 35,000 workers who build and maintain the tracks, bridges, buildings and other structures on the railroads of the United States, including Amtrak and other regional commuter rail. The BMWE created a Communication Action Team (CAT) in 2015 after member surveys, polls and conversations done in early 2014 showed BMWE members, especially young ones, felt disconnected from the union for a variety of reasons.

The union recognized the hostile anti-union political climate posed the potential threat that the 2016 Presidential elections could create a Republican "Trifecta" that could pull the Union security clause from the Railroad Labor Act (RLA). Meanwhile, national bargaining with the freight carrier was reopening and concessionary proposals were expected from the employers.

All of this called for a program to increase member involvement.

The national president, Fred Simpson, with other officers and leaders, held an initial meeting in Dec 2014 with 25 mostly younger members from a variety of railroad employers and geographies, to seek honest input and ideas concerning shortcomings in the unions and ways to strengthen the union.

This input led to the establishment of the Communication Action Team (CAT) to:
- Strengthen communications with members
- Promote member involvement in the union activities
- Build visible member support for national bargaining goals
- Build a culture of solidarity in the workplace to address worksite issues
- Create a deeper identification among members with their union

Rank and file RR workers were selected to become full time "Internal organizers (IOs)." Trade unionists with experience setting up member mobilization program were brought in to assist in the training of the new organizers and the design of the program. An experienced organizer from outside the union was hired to do the day to day national coordination. The VPs initially were concerned but then accompanied the trainers on visits to the job site and helped identify rank-and-filers to be trained as Front Line Communicators.

Over two years the number of IOs grew from 4-10 to be able to thoroughly reach out to the members who work for all the carriers and in all regions of the country.

In the first stage of the program, a survey was designed to get people's ideas and priorities for upcoming bargaining. *Importantly*, the survey was intended to be completed as part of one-on-one conversations with other workers and Internal Organizers.

<u>Structure and Principles of the CAT program</u>

- The members of the CAT team were called Front Line Communicators (FLCs) and would be solicited from the ranks among interested and motivated workers, with local officer input, for one day trainings. These FLCs came out of the trade so they knew the work and the lingo and met other members on the worksites, not at lodge meetings. The VPs initially were concerned but then accompanied the trainers out of the job.
- The trainings would focus on building one-on-one communication skills, providing information and resources to rank and filers, explaining the threat of Right to Work initiatives, and encouraging participants' growth and activity as member-leaders and activists. "Popular education" techniques were used in the training with the participants actively involved in all aspects of the program: doing one-on-one role plays, meeting in groups, sharing ideas and information, etc.
- The outreach focus would be based on the concept of "Bring the bell to the people," namely going to worksites. The BMWE members often move in "work gangs" to locations around the country, wherever track needs to be laid or repaired.
- Internal Organizers were trained to visit worksites regularly, find and recruit FLCs, and educate members about the national bargaining and how to actively support the efforts at the bargaining table.
- At the trainings FLCs were initially given surveys and other materials to share with all the members at their worksites. All surveys were to be completed as part of one-on-one conversations and each conversation should include gathering updated contact information-email and cell numbers.
- FLCS are trained to be communicators and mobilizers but not to handle grievances—the internal structure of the BMWE was called in for any worksite complaints and contract enforcement issues that arose.
- Union Chairmen and Vice-chairmen of RR systems and Federations are encouraged to be present at trainings and accompany IOs in the site visits.
- Social media is an important *supplemental* part of the program since members are often on the road and attendance at lodge meetings is often difficult, but all members have phones. The unions national FB page grew substantially and more localized or company specific sites were set up, some private and public. Accurate email and cell numbers collected facilitated other forms of electronic communications.
- The program has strong support from the national President and the national leadership as well as most regional and local leaders and adequate resources are provided for including trainings, travel, computers, printing materials etc.

- Diversity of membership is seriously considered in hiring IOs, recruiting FLCs, printing materials in Spanish and Navajo and, in one case, doing training on a reservation with translations for Navaho workers.

Evolution of the program

· Over 9,000 surveys were collected in the first phase and they showed that healthcare was overwhelmingly the main concern of members. The employers proposed concessions in healthcare at the bargaining table.

· The process unfolded using the "Three M's": Message- Healthcare Not Wealthcare (coming from the members); Method-member to member organizing; and Movement- escalation of member activity and tactics.

· Ninety trainings have taken place and close to 1,300 FLCs have been trained.

· The IOs conducted more than 1,500 worksite visits

· The national union's FB page now has close to 10,000 members and local and regional FB pages are also active.

· Nationally coordinated escalated actions have taken place in more than 300 worksites, led by FLCs, building from leafletting, to national sticker days with ((Healthcare Not Wealthcare stickers), national call-ins to the Freight operators CEOs; rail yard gate rallies and cross craft/inter-union outreach.

· Members were brought together with other unions and allies. Allied groups (JwJ, Sierra club, other unions) were invited to rallies and FLCs and IOs participated in Labor For Single Payer, Climate Change, Right to Work and other campaigns outside of the worksites, including 2016 electoral work.

· The national president and other leaders give regular "town hall" bargaining and member mobilization reports to members using You-Tube technology, with more than 10,000 typically tuning in.

Overall the CAT program has begun having a transformative effect on the BMWE, with members who were previously considered apathetic becoming active, rank and file leaders coming forward and the union culture of solidarity building significantly.

The Job Description for the CAT Team:

"The CAT (Communication Action Team) is expanding its reach. The BMWED is seeking applicants for an additional full time Internal Organizer to help organize fellow BMWED Brothers and Sisters as we struggle with the Carriers for a just National Agreement. The Internal Organizer will work with BMWED National Division leadership to promote a culture of solidarity through workshops, worksite visits, and various union related activities. The organizer will engage with BMWED members at their work reporting locations, hotels, worksites, lodge meetings, local headquarter points, and any other locations where members gather."

CHAPTER 4—NEGOTIATIONS

"We shall defend our Island, whatever the cost may be, we shall fight on the beaches, we shall fight on the landing grounds, we shall fight in the fields and in the streets, we shall fight in the hills; we shall never surrender . . ."
Winston Churchill   June 4, 1940

We have discussed both individual changes and changes in the structure of our unions, so now it is important to see how we can change the union's basic functions, especially since the global economy has been so dramatically transformed. Each of the next four chapters, discussing the basic functions of a union, could be expanded into a full book, or longer, but a brief summary will cover some of the important points about new attitudes and strategies. The numbers—in union membership, in lousy contracts, in the general rise of anti-unionism politically—also tell us we cannot simply keep doing what we have always done.

If dealing with your employer is a war, then negotiations are the pitched battles and grievances are the daily skirmishes waged on many fronts. Many of the negative changes for unionism come into vivid focus when you sit down with the management to work on a new CBA. Negotiating this contract establishes one framework for dealing with management, both in the private and public sectors, and is a moment when all the members—and non-members--take great interest in what "The Union" is doing.

Labor historian Mark McColloch once described labor relations since 1945 as "a kind of trench warfare" because each side had settled into permanent positions and faced each other directly across the table. In "normal" times, contract negotiations were like a mating dance, with accustomed positions, posturing and pronouncements. This structure of "collective bargaining" perfectly reflected The Servicing Model of Unionism, with two entrenched forces locked in ritual conflict. With minimal preparation, a small group from the union met with a familiar management, usually agreeing to a blackout on

negotiations so that nothing could escape to rouse the membership. A ratification meeting, often with an imperfect or incomplete compilation of any changes in the contract, was rushed to the members for a vote. Basic workplace procedures, like layoffs, were repeated, almost routine or cyclical, and were thought to be "normal." The boss acted in a predictable manner and the union responded with an equal lack of imagination.

In The Servicing Model, "The Union" took credit for all the good contracts and the support usually spilled over as support for incumbent officers. The only involvement of the membership was to show up at the meeting to vote *yea* or *nay* on the contract and go back to work, their lives uninterrupted. Most importantly, union members were totally disconnected from the process, so they thought "The Union"—not them-- was negotiating.

It worked—for a while! Starting in 1945, union members gained a decent standard of living, as US industries dominated the world and the social contract accepted unionism as part of the package. Those times are gone—and even Donald Trump cannot bring them back. The environment for negotiations has been drastically changed—for the worse--by changes in work processes, driven by new technology and new work schedules, and by new management structures and attitudes.

While many union officers suddenly fear both Trump and the open shop movement, in reality very few unions can claim real success in negotiations over the past 40 years—too many contracts with two-tier systems and fulltime "part-time" workers, no defined benefit pensions, increasing health insurance co-pays, broader Management Rights clauses. More importantly, our negotiations have been almost exclusively defensive—trying to keep our employers from taking away money and benefits and our power in the workplace. If negotiations went sour, "The Union" was responsible and got the blame, creating a lot of the bad feeling toward unionism that moved so many union members to vote for Trump.

Contract negotiations are now the flash point where extraordinary demands from the boss demand daring strategies and imaginative organization from the union, including total membership and community involvement. Even though the situation is threatening, most unions have not yet voluntarily started rethinking the old Servicing Model.

As one union officer stated: "Organized labor's legislative strategy since the 1950s—restoring the old model of union bargaining—is unlikely to prevail in the 21st century. That model thrived in an era of standardized industrial production, long-term or even lifelong employment in an industry or firm, and the relative geographic immobility of both workers and capital."[78]

Since contract negotiations is the one moment when all members—and non-members—are passionately interested in what their union is going to be able to do, it is an opportunity for building the union. There is also a danger because divisions within the membership are intensified, just as they were during the presidential campaign of 2016. As contract proposals are formulated, you will see these differences, especially if managements demand significant concessions from some of the unit and if the membership believes that the only choice is between a lousy contract and going on a long strike. Will long-seniority members strike, for

---

[78] David Rolf. "Toward a 21st-Century Labor Movement." *The American Prospect*. Spring, 2016.

example, to eliminate a two-tier structure that limits the wages and benefits of younger workers? How much bargaining power will your members be willing to spend for insurance coverage for same-sex partners or retirees or for Muslim religious holidays? And the Big Question: if we ask for "too much," will it jeopardize our jobs?

Though the relentless attacks by our bosses, and through their control of the two major parties and the political system, major management decisions that affect us are blocked from any negotiations—plants moving or closing, the subcontracting of work, companies' being sold to shadow investment companies. Yeah, we can by law negotiate the *effects* of these decisions but not the crucial decision *itself* so unions are marginalized and the areas for "negotiations" are very narrow. Is it any wonder that members drop out in open shop states, angrily trashing "The Union" for all the problems?

* * * * * * * * * * * * * * * * * *

As we figure out how to change union strategies, we first have to recognize that there has been a structural change on the other side: how management is organized, in both private and public sectors. In the past, the owner was usually a corporation which could be clearly identified and pressured, and which owned the business with a long-term view and continued relations with the community and the industry. In fact, some of the most contentious issues were over pensions, because the boss objected to "mortgaging the long-term future of the company" and to paying people who were no longer working

Examining the company's finances was relatively easy. It you were dealing with a public corporation, you could buy a few shares of stock and get all of the information necessary—executive salaries, questionable consulting fees-- to block management's whining about their poverty. A private company, often small and family-owned, showed up in Dun and Bradstreet reports.

The rise of vulture capitalism, with more than 2,000 private equity firms headquartered in the U.S. backing more than 14,000 companies, has changed everything so "trench warfare" is gone. What a difference from an isolated bargaining committee, dealing with one owner on one contract!

Unions are now negotiating with "owners" they never see, and can barely track down, symbolized by Trump himself. *The Art of the Deal* means The Trump Organization, the collective name of approximately 500 different business entities of which Donald Trump is the sole or principal owner.

In the 1980's, there was a dramatic shift in corporate philosophy as "corporate raiders," led by T. Boone Pickens, Carl Icahn and Michael Milken, took small shares in public companies and then demanded that they slash expenses and return money to investors, an obsession dramatically illustrated by Gordon Gecko and "Greed is Good" in the movie *Wall Street*. "That philosophy now shapes the investment decisions of big institutional investors and shareholder activists alike."[79]

The "owners" are frantic to cut every cost and to pull in as much profit as possible, as quickly as possible. Phrases like "long-term planning" and "employee welfare" are obsolete so sharks like Warren Buffet, Mitt Romney, Wilbur Ross or Donald Trump take companies private—and secret. Companies without ruthless management are described as "undervalued," and executives are challenged by the "activist investors" to move up or to move out. This class has also gained enormous political power. Appointing Ross, promoted as "an investor in distressed assets," to be Secretary of Commerce continues a pattern established by Bill Clinton, who turned over the direction of the economy in 1992 to financial manipulators like Robert Rubin, a board member at Goldman Sachs who started the "risk-arb" desk in the complex world of high finance.

At the highest levels of management training, this enormous shift has brought a vicious new approach to negotiations. A book on the Harvard Business School, which has 76,000 living M.B.A. alumni, claims that the school "has contributed pretty much every bad thing that has happened in American business and the economy in the last century." A retired professor named Michael Jensen "bears responsibility for the rapacious hostile takeovers and the obsession with stock prices and short-term results that led to the Enron and World-Com scandals, as well as for the emergence of outlandishly high executive pay. . . . Jensen advocated an 'agency' theory of management in which management's sole duty was to maximize shareholder value. This upended the 'shareholder' model, in which management was seen as having broader obligations to a corporation's workers, customers and communities."[80]

As an example of the dramatically changing economy over the past several decades, an article compared two women who worked as custodians: Gail Evans at Kodak and Marta Ramos at Apple.

> "In the 35 years between their jobs as janitors, corporations across America have flocked to a new management theory: Focus on core competence and outsource the rest. The approach has made companies more nimble and more productive, and delivered huge profits for shareholders. It has also fueled inequality and helps explain why many working-class Americans are struggling even in an ostensibly healthy economy. The $16.60 per hour Ms. Ramos earns as a janitor at Apple works out to about the same in inflation-adjusted terms as what Ms. Evans earned 35 years ago. But that's where the similarities end. Ms. Evans was a full-time employee of Kodak. She received more than

---

[79] David Gelles. "Texas-Size Tycoon Calls It Quits." *New York Times*. January 21, 2018.
[80] James B. Stewart. "Profit or Loss. How Harvard Business School has reshaped American capitalism." *New York Times*. April 30, 2017.

four weeks of paid vacation per year, reimbursement of some tuition costs to go to college part time, and a bonus payment every March. When the facility she cleaned was shut down, the company found another job for her: cutting film. Ms. Ramos is an employee of a contractor that Apple uses to keep its facilities clean. She hasn't taken a vacation in years, because she can't afford the lost wages. Going back to school is similarly out of reach. There are certainly no bonuses, nor even a remote possibility of being transferred to some other role at Apple. . . . But Kodak also created enough working-class jobs to help create two generations of middle-class wealth in Rochester. The Harvard economist Larry Summers has often pointed at this difference, arguing that it helps explain rising inequality and declining social mobility.

"'Think about the contrast between George Eastman, who pioneered fundamental innovations in photography, and Steve Jobs,' Mr. Summers wrote in 2014. 'While Eastman's innovations and their dissemination through the Eastman Kodak Co. provided a foundation for a prosperous middle class in Rochester for generations, no comparable impact has been created by Jobs' innovations' at Apple."[81]

New management comes in, slices and dices the company's assets and the workforce, selling off, or subcontracting, important parts of the company and demanding significant concessions in negotiations, while collecting enormous fees. Their goal is the next quarter and workers and the union contract be damned.

The news about Burger King in early 2017 symbolized this dramatic change. Sold in 2010 for "$3.3 billion, minting over a billion dollars in profits and a five-fold gain for exiting investors including Bain Capital, TPG and Goldman Sachs, . . . Burger King's new owners have made over $14 billion, surely one of the greatest investment scores in history. Following the money on this cash-cow burger chain reveals a dramatic post-crisis shift in the balance of power on Wall Street." While most union members figure this may be another world since Burger King workers are non-union, a new player is 3G Capital, which does have unionized companies, like Kraft Heinz and Anheuser-Busch.[82] Warren Buffet, that genial mogul who endorsed an HBO program describing him as "one of the world's most open-hearted philanthropists," owns 43 different companies in dozens of different industries, everything from paint companies to Dairy Queen. There is now even a "Brazilian Warren Buffet," a man named Jorge Paulo Lemann, who runs 3G Capital, whose company owns Kraft Heinz and offered $143 billion to buy Unilever (based in the Netherlands).

---

[81] Neil Irwin. "To Understand Rising Inequality, Consider the Janitors at Two Top Companies, Then and Now." *New York Times*. September 3, 2017.
[82] Antoine Gara. "The rebirth of Burger King Has Made 3G Capital, Bill Ackman and Warren Buffet Over $14billion." *Forbes*. February 21, 2017.

While these figures may seem too large to calculate for the average union members, or to non-union workers at one of the companies, every dollar they take is one that could have been paid out in wage increases, benefit improvements and better working conditions. The businesses we negotiate with are now huge and global so union members have to see themselves, not as separate or isolated in one country, but as part of a global workforce. We have to begin to create a global workers movement, with consistent global solidarity, so that unions everywhere can deal with these owners, no matter what country they operate in.

The same changes have affected the "public" sector, which is now financed at every level by sales of bonds and certificates to private investors, who demand maximum return on their loans, with guarantees that they will be first in line for payment from shrinking tax revenues. As corporate welfare grows, with tax rebate incentives for investors of every kind, public budgets shrink, making public sector negotiations as complicated as the private sector because these investors are a dominant presence at the negotiating table, even though we cannot see them.

* * * * * * * * * * * * * * * * * * * *

We have responsibility to show the members how to protect themselves in these turbulent and complicated times. In the process, members will see that their union contract is such an important protection that they will get motivated to build unionism and increase membership participation. Instead of blaming "The Union" for failures in negotiations in tough times, members should create a whole new approach to negotiations to block the pattern of concessions. The tired phrase "No More Business as Usual" has never been more accurate than it is today.

The most important aspect of contract negotiation is leverage—forcing the boss to pay more than he wants to pay and helping us take back the control of the workplace. In the past, unions threatened a strike as leverage and negotiations became a simple choice: either we get what we want or we walk out. In the public sector, some agencies have an arbitration process so the responsibility for the proposed settlement was shifted from the union to a third-party. The changes in ownership structure, and the shift of public employment, means the old solutions may not longer work so we have to develop new attitudes and new strategies to get what we deserve.

Union officers and staff also need to get off the Excuse Express—in too many cases, they accept concessions in negotiations by stating that all of the other unions are taking them, so "there is nothing we can do." It was not so many years ago, for example, that it was considered "normal" for a boss to pay for a worker's family health insurance, with no co-pays out of our checks. Multi-tier wage scales were unknown. Once the decline began, however, a "new normal" came to be accepted—yeah, everyone pays something for their health insurance or a two-tier system was the best we could get.

Unions at every level—officers, staff and members—need to be smarter about preparing for negotiations, with a proactive attitude and a range of new strategies to meet the modern economy. The danger of our times leads to the opportunity for this new thinking, for fresh ideas and, quite honestly, for extreme measures.

Planning for negotiations should start at least a year before the two sides sit down at the table. One important part of your preparation is to figure out who really makes the decisions in negotiations. Many of us who negotiated contracts with a division of a corporation know the drill: when we make a proposal, the personnel people on the other side of the table respond "We will have to check with corporate." Now the corporate structures are infinitely more complicated so we have to be able to know who, and how, to pressure them to get the contracts we deserve.

Research shows who your "boss" really is and which other corporations it owns, especially if some of them around the world are unionized Some unions, like UNITE-HERE, have created expanded research departments to track down the power within an employer since the hospitality industry is controlled by private capital. The UNITE-HERE research program, occasionally advertised as "Research for Radicals," includes enormous lists of resources: company databases, litigation, political contributions, and corporate subsidies—in short, a full picture of how the employer operates and who might be able to influence management decisions.

Another new series of webinars and discussion groups is sponsored by the AFL-CIO Economic Power & Growth Hub, which provides an online Research Webinar Library at https://sites.google.com/a/aflcio.org/training-videos/. One topic was "Engaging Members and Workers in Campaign Research," presented as a webinar in November by a rep from the IUOE and the presentations are stored in a library for later access. A staff rep at the AFL-CIO stated "Hundreds of researchers and organizers from dozens of unions use the webinar library. We just don't advertise it to the public."

Union research needs to look at every possible method for gaining leverage, finding good examples from the past without just blindly trying to duplicate a campaign that worked well for one employer at one time. If there was ever an example of rethinking campaign tactics, Donald Trump is it, so we have to be as resourceful. The growth and diversification of corporations looks like a disadvantage for us but by creating complicated supply chains, and by using just-in-time manufacturing strategies, companies can actually be more vulnerable because there are so many points along the chain where they can be disrupted.

A union has to understand *kyusho,* a martial arts term for "pressure point," because forcing management to negotiate requires understanding how a company, especially a vulture capital firm, operates and where in the chain of production it could be vulnerable.

After this research, the union needs to create a Leverage Diagram—a poster calculating exactly where the pressure points on the boss are. With a chart, members visualize the power that they need, and the power that they have, and what power must be added. The same Leverage Diagram is important for public sector negotiations because public officials are often physically at the table while decisions are made somewhere else, and the union must account for all of the potential pressure points.

As part of the research, calculate who your potential allies might be---community groups, other organizations, churches or fraternal groups, elected officials (or candidates) and, of course, other unions. Using the backward calendar, make an investment in Solidarity-- after all, if you want to get Solidarity, you first have to give it. Proactively reach out to these groups, offering help and support so that when your union needs backup, you have already established strong relationships. Building Solidarity is one important way to involve every one of your members by checking to see who belongs to different groups that might help the union. Groups are much more likely to respond helpfully when asked by one of their own members.

The officers and staff need to be active with other unions in a proactive way, not just sitting through some Central Labor Council meeting or playing in a union golf tournament. See what unions have contracts coming up and offer to help out, even sharing this new strategy.

Many memorable photos from labor history show unions marching together, to support each other in negotiations or during a strike. Social conditions were different: workers lived near their workplaces, and knew members of other unions so that there was a union community. As unions developed strength in the 1950's and 60's, as workers migrated to the suburbs, and unions became protective of their own interests, this sense of movement disappeared. Union negotiations in the past, even in the public sector, were conducted in isolation—that is, one union felt it was negotiating only for itself, and by itself. There was no attempt to create a movement—*La Causa*-- where other unions would help and the community would be involved.

Negotiations should be developed as an organizing campaign. As part of a global workforce, we have to begin to create a global worker movement-- joining with other unions, in different industries or even in different countries, to find the pressure points that will cripple these global corporations, so that unions everywhere can deal with these owners, no matter what country they operate in. It is so important for every member to see that our local union is no longer an island—one union dealing with one boss.

One excellent source to study this Leverage Diagram is the book *Ravenswood: The Steelworkers' Victory and the Revival of American Labor*, by Tom Juravich and Kate Bronfenbrenner, which describes bitter negotiations in 1990 between the USWA and an aluminum company in West Virginia. The company had been owned for decades by the same company but was sold to vulture capitalist Marc Rich, once described as "the wealthiest fugitive in the world." Rich—yes, the one pardoned by President Bill Clinton—locked out 1,700 workers and hired scabs. The book shows that the ownership of Ravenswood continued a pattern of relentless anti-unionism, symbolized by the firing of the PATCO strikers in 1981, but most importantly, showed that the union eventually developed all new strategies to deal with both the change in ownership and in attitude.

One lesson of *Ravenswood* is that the USWA was totally unprepared for these changes. Even while the company was advertising in newspapers for scabs and building a fence around the factory, the union committee was happily driving to Pittsburgh for "normal" negotiations, only to find itself abruptly locked out. The Best Practice? Unions going into negotiations today need to bulk up, both strategically and financially, preparing not for trench warfare but for a management *blitzkrieg*.

In *Ravenswood*, one important lesson was leverage--tracking down exactly who the owner of the company was. It took the union almost a year, with trips to Switzerland, to uncover Marc Rich and to begin to try to pressure him directly. Planning and preparation could have speeded up the process and shortened—or avoided-- the strike.

Looking at organizing campaigns that develop leverage is very helpful. As one example in the south, "The question has to be: what will it take to force the company into making an agreement with the union that recognizes the organizing rights of workers? At Smithfield, we won that agreement by going after the company in a variety of ways. We took the campaign to all of the outlets where their products were being sold and marketed. We talked about how Smithfield pork is packaged with abuse. The company was spending millions on their brand and we were damaging it by simply telling the truth. We did that internationally as well. In the end we got an agreement for an NLRB supervised election but with additional protections against company abuses. It was those additional rules that made it possible for us to win."[83]

One early moment in *kyusho* in negotiations was the corporate campaign developed by Ray Rogers for the JP Stevens strike of 1970. As labor reporter A.H. Raskin noted at the time, "Pressure on giant banks and insurance companies and other Wall Street pillars, all aimed at isolating Stevens from the financial community helped generate a momentum. . .that could not be achieved through the 1976-1980 worldwide boycott of Stevens products or through more conventional uses of union muscle such as strikes and mass picketing." Raskin quoted Ray Rogers that" we took their strength and made it a weakness."[84]

It is possible to develop a Leverage Diagram to create these pressures for every situation. Even though a high level of worker involvement has not been seen in the US in decades, making the tactics sound like fantasies, plan them anyway—if you don't visualize victory, you won't get it. Keeping the power in the hands of the workers is critical and they must understand that Someone Else will not settle the contract.

Here's one example of how a Leverage Diagram might help. On September 5, 2017, Frederick Kunkle, the principal officer of the Washington-Baltimore Newspaper Guild at the *Washington Post,* got a written warning for writing an Op Ed for HuffPost, on September 1, attacking the newspaper owner, Jeff Bezos for being tough in contract negotiations. Kunkle attacked "Bezos' rollback of employee retirement benefits and planned overhaul of the

---

[83] Chris Brooks and Gene Bruskin. "Labor's Southern Strategy." *Dollars and Sense*. September 3, 2017.
[84] Ray Rogers. "How A Corporate Campaign Defeated JP Stevens." *The Labor Educator*. April, 1999

company's severance policy, and complained that 'One of the wealthiest men in the world is thinking of ways to give back... But he's still taking from the very people who helped him build his fortune.'" Kunkle's Op Ed went on to detail Bezos' efforts to knuckle down the newspaper's union over workers' rights and benefits.[85]

The discussion veered off into Kunkle's right to publish an opinion, and whether it is a "concerted activity," but let's look at how we could settle this contract.

- What if there were nationwide boycotts of Amazon—people stopped buying from it and stopped using its services and credit cards until the Guild got its contract?
- What if other union members—like the Teamsters at UPS or the Postal Workers or even FedEx drivers—declared Amazon packages to be "hot cargo" and refused to deliver them until the Guild got its contract?
- What if community groups began picketing Whole Foods, recently bought by Bezos, urging a boycott until the Guild got its contract with the Post?

Attacking Bezos—originally a hedge fund guy with a net worth of about $ 100 billion—in every area of his empire could turn his power into vulnerability.

Obviously, a campaign like this would require enormous organizational resources but we have seen the power of social media in forcing company executives from big firms like Merck, Under Armour, Intel, 3M, and Campbell Soup to change their policies. All of them resigned from Trump's Manufacturing Council & Strategy & Policy Forum, over his positions on the Charlottesville rally, so there is power that can make the owners come around.

Social media has enormous potential for leverage, as word can be spread, and any employer involved in consumer sales can be pressured. In December, 2017, John Schnatter, the founder and CEO of Papa John's Pizza, was forced to step down after he criticized NFL players, especially Colin Kaepernick, for kneeling before games as a protest. A consumer boycott sprang up, zipped around social media and "Shares of Papa John's are down about 13 percent since the day before the NFL comments were made, reducing the value of Schnatter's stake in the company by nearly $84 million."[86]

That's a lot of money. That's a lot of leverage!

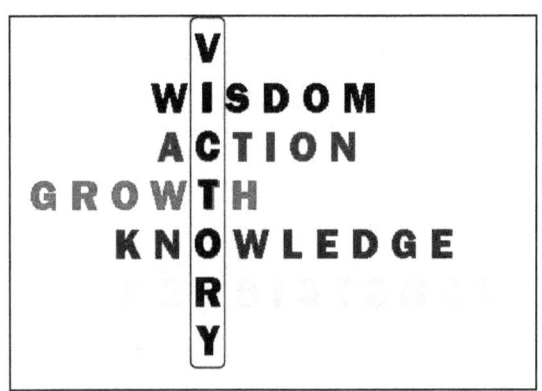

Don't get caught up in the idea that quick fingers on social media are all you need to get a contract. Beyond the research and planning, the organizing campaign must increase membership participation, so a lot of the organizing is good, old-fashioned one-on-one discussions. The members need to be directly involved in the negotiations from the beginning, even if there is reluctance from the officers and staff over this increased participation.

---

[85] Daniel Marans.** Did The Washington Post Break A Law When It Disciplined A Reporter Over A Jeff Bezos Op-Ed?" *HuffPost.* September 15, 2017.
[86] "Papa John's Schnatter Out as CEO." *MoneyWatch.* December 22, 2017.

Yes, it will be very different and yes, there could be disagreements but that's the nature of a collective campaign. Contract negotiations are the one time when every member wants to participate in the union--membership meetings are packed and everyone talks about the new contract. More importantly, it is the best opportunity to sign up non-members, who may resent having to pay dues but who are certainly eager to get a good contract.

Open bargaining is a great tactic, both for generating leverage and for building your union. Instead of a small committee meeting in private with the boss, let all of your members attend. Create a communications structure—e-mail, text, apps--for reporting back on every session to anyone whom cannot attend., a kind of electronic listening tour. Plan with your members that they can sit in and caucus with the committee. This tactic, incidentally, appeared so extreme that one union officer asked me whether such a strategy was a violation of the union's international constitution!

Most importantly, all of our strategies are *proactive*—we take the initiative, we look for the best times to pressure our management, we decide what actions will be most effective. Proactive planning, and a backward calendar of at least one year before negotiations start, gives the union time to diagram the employer and to organize all of the forces that can contribute to building this leverage. If we fully examine the corporate structure of the individual property we are dealing with, new opportunities for leverage appear. How many of the companies have union contracts, with dozens of different locals? How many of these unions have ever proposed coordinated bargaining?

We should also look to other unions for best practices—what has worked for another union in similar circumstances? Obviously, every negotiations is different and unique so we cannot duplicate another union's strategies but we should observe them and learn from them and use what we can in our own situations. Union locals—officers, staff and members—in the same union, or in the same geographic area, need to get together to share best practices and new strategies.

Let's also look at other movements to develop leverage.

"After months of wincing in the face of negative ads funded by the industrialists David and Charles Koch, Democrats believe they have finally found a way to fight back: attacking the brothers' sprawling business conglomerate as callous and indifferent to the lives of ordinary people while pursuing profit and power. By drawing public attention to layoffs by subsidiaries of Koch Industries across the country — a chemical plant in North Carolina, an oil refinery in Alaska, a lumber operation in Arkansas — Democrats are seeking to make villains of the reclusive billionaires, whose political organizations have spent more than $30 million on ads so far to help Republicans win control of the Senate. The approach should seem familiar. President Obama and his allies ran against Mitt Romney in 2012 by painting a dark picture of Bain Capital, the firm Mr. Romney founded, as a company that cut jobs and prized the bottom line over the well-being of its employees. Senator Mark Begich, Democrat of Alaska, has called out the Kochs — whose combined net worth is estimated to be $100 billion — in his latest ads. In one, which features a picture of the brothers grinning, one of them wearing a tuxedo, Alaskans look directly into the camera and unload. 'They come into our town, buy our refinery,' says one. 'Just running it into the ground,' says another. 'A lot of Alaskans are losing jobs, and I'm definitely concerned about the drinking water,' says a young woman holding a baby."[87]

Even the attempts by the Trump administration to challenge the policies of the North Korean government are a *Kyusho* campaign. Da President is threatening military attacks but is also trying to cut off the North Korea's finances, imports and commerce, also proposing—in a classic secondary boycott—to cut off any financial institution that does business with North Korea.

We also need to emphasize that negotiations are about more than just money. The Trump campaign and administration has created huge movements over "social" issues and these must be included in our negotiations. Emphasizing contract language is one way to move all of the demonstrations about "social" issues into a union framework, showing how they are common in our workplaces and how strengthening our unions will block them. Having strong language in your contract to protect equal pay for comparable work—protecting all workers on the basis or sex, race, age, or any other category—is also the best advertisement for new organizing. It illustrates that workers have the power through an organized campaign to gain and protect this equality, regardless of the support, or not, of government.

A critical proposal—the "social issue" of equality-- in negotiations is eliminating all discriminatory contract provisions: the two-tier wage system, the blocking of all workers from a pension plan, the continuation of "temporary" or "probationary" workers for years with no benefits. Yes, our membership is divided so the permanent workers may not want to spend their leverage on these second-class citizens but preparations for a new contract should challenge this selfishness and prejudice, just as we demonstrate against the Trump administration.

More importantly, how about reviving some demands in negotiations that could benefit all workers but which have been dropped as unions went on the defensive for the past 70 years? How about a shorter work day at no reduction in pay? Unions struck in the 1880's for the 8-hour day, the 40-hour week was recognized in the Fair Labor Standards Act of 1937—and we still have it today! Workers' productivity has soared, and we are not sharing in the benefit.

---

[87] Jeremy W. Peters and Carl Hulse. "To Strike at Kochs, Democrats Revive Tactic That Hurt Romney." New York Times. April 6, 2014.

As a comparison, "Germany's biggest union, IG-Metall is proposing to reduce the workweek from 35 hours to 28 with a 6% pay increase. "The union argues that workers in the metals and electrical sectors should benefit from steady growth and a booming economy."[88] In early February, according to the IG Metall trade union, assembly lines were shut down at 97 companies, with around 304,000 employees. Overall, more than 500,000 workers participated in the 24-hour strike that began on January 31. A complicating factor was the willingness of union officers of IG Metall to back down on the demand for a 25-hour work week and a 6% pay increase and settle for an extension of the 35-hour week with a 3.6% raise but the workers organized to oppose any concession, showing the militancy of the workers is a challenge to the structure of the union.

On February 6, 2018, the union announced that it had won the demand for a shorter work week with a substantial pay raise 'after six rounds of often bruising talks and a series of 24-hour strikes," winning a 4.3 per cent wage increase and the right to a 28-hour working week "in a landmark deal that will be seen as a benchmark for other sectors." "It envisages a 4.3 per cent wage raise from April, and other payments spread over 27 months. Workers will be allowed to reduce their working week from the standard 35 hours to 28 while preserving the right to return to full-time work. "The wage settlement is a milestone on the path to a modern, self-determined world of work," said Jörg Hofmann, IG Metall's chairman.[89]

Why not?

How about full retirement at age 55? Or 50? Once again, we need to make all workers see that our causes are their causes. The Op Ed [Appendix 5] looks at the issue of major social changes to compensate for technology and corporate changes.

One unique challenge to traditional patterns in negotiations was a strike in September, 2017, by General Motors workers in Ingersoll, Ontario, who made keeping their plant open and fully-staffed was the most important demand. After several days on strike, Dan Borthwick, president of Unifor Local 88, told *Automotive News Canada* that the union would come back into negotiations only "if GM Canada says it will designate the plant the automaker's lead producer of the Chevrolet Equinox to ensure production and jobs aren't shifted to Mexico. . . . Job security has become more of an issue for the union since GM shifted production of its Terrain SUV from the plant to Mexico earlier this year at a loss of more than 600 positions at CAMI. About 200 people took early retirement or buyouts.

"'Our members realize the necessity of obtaining a job security document. Without that, GM can take the Equinox away just as easily as they took the Terrain away. And then, you'd have 2,800 people on layoff instead of on strike,' Borthwick told *Automotive News*. 'We believe this is the time to do it. We need contract language that secures our future. This is the time to make a statement and fight.'"

---

[88]NewsWatch. *Labor Notes*. December, 2017.
[89] Guy Chazen. "German Unions Wins 28-hour work week and 4.3% pay raise." Financial Times. February 6, 2018.

The leverage that a union gets from the just-in-time production model was illustrated as parts and transmission plants that supply GM announced layoffs, increasing the impact and the union's bargaining power as the owners of these secondary plants can pressure GM to settle.[90]

And the Canadians didn't even have Trump.

Think of the power if all of the GM workers—US, Canada and Mexico—overcame nationalism and were bargaining on a master contract.

Unions have to be bold and imaginative in negotiations—picking new issues and new power. Management—or more properly, mismanagement--has lost credibility in virtually every case so the union can and should assert new power and new authority. This is a huge shift in attitude and approach for the union but, as we have said many times, these are new and desperate times which call for new and desperate measures.

There is really no choice. It's change or go the way of the dinosaur. The newspapers are filled with stories of companies—like General Motors—being forced to "reinvent" themselves. Unions are facing the same challenge.

* * * * * * * * * * * * * * * * * *

One of the formulas for developing leverage in traditional negotiations in the private sector was "settle or strike." Some strikes, like the 116-day strike by steelworkers in 1959, the 10-year strike at the Congress Hotel in Chicago, the Postal Strike of 1970, and the Teamsters strike against UPS in 1997, have risen to mythical status.

As you develop your Leverage Diagram, you have to evaluate whether a strike is the most effective pressure tactic. There is an expression called *congruence*, in which you get only two choices and both are bad. In negotiations, the choice used to be either take a crappy contract or go out on strike. As you evaluate your employer, and calculate pressure points, you may find that a strike is not the strongest pressure you can exert.

Many unions have dropped a strike as a leverage tactic. According to the Bureau of Labor Statistics, there were only 15 major work stoppages in 2016 involving 99,000 workers. The total days idle for major work stoppages in effect in 2016 was 1.54 million. The average number of major work stoppages by decade has declined over 95 percent since 1947. The period from 2007 to 2016 was the lowest decade on record, averaging approximately 14 major work stoppages per year."[91]

These figures, combined with the endless succession of lousy contracts, have provoked some commentators to urge a revival of more strikes, as if a strike were the only leverage that a union can develop. A book by Joe Burns, *Reviving the Strike: How Working People Can Regain Power and Transform America*, states "In many ways, the tactics of the 1930's were developed to fight against exactly the same problems facing trade unions today, namely an employer determined to continue production, with no shortage of scabs to take strikers' jobs. If one

---

[90] Greg Layson. "GM invited to resume negotiations with striking Canadian union." *Automotive News*. September 21, 2017.
[91] Bureau of Labor Statistics. News Release. "Major Work Stoppages in 2016." February 9, 2017.

believes that the unions of the 1930's were justified in stopping production, then there is no basis to say that today's labor movement is not equally justified in utilizing similar tactics."

Burns, however, is smart enough to recognize that we no longer live in the 1930's.

"The contemporary labor movement needs a strike based on labor's economics, not those of management; based on labor's values, not management's. Like the trade unionists of the 1930s, today's labor movement must prioritize developing effective strike tactics which hold the promise of improving workers' lives. To be clear, unionists cannot simply import traditional union tactics into today's world, as much has changed since the 1930s: workers are no longer concentrated in dense urban centers, the labor left in this country is weak, and unionists face a transformed economy dominated by massive global corporations. However, trade unionists have always had to adapt to constantly changing conditions and shifting employer strategies. The main problem is not that trade unionists have been unable to overcome these obstacles and create an effective strike in the past. The problem is that today, they are not even trying."[92]

The strike can be one of the most powerful weapons that workers have because it can bring operations to a halt, and profits suddenly drop to zero. Money is actually lost as inventory sits on the loading docks while the boss still has to pay the bills. But new corporate structures make it easier to shift production to blunt the power of a strike, moving work to other non-union subsidiaries or even to other countries. In preparation for negotiations, then, union research must focus on the total company—where it is vulnerable to pressure? From producers, from suppliers, from lenders?

Of course, a strike is tough on the members and their families but planning ahead can develop leverage. As unions develop new strategies for involving the membership, management will let us know what moves have been effective in building leverage. An interesting posting on the ATU Local 11997 (Jacksonville, FL) Facebook page:

"Today our Union President was approached by Management with the concerns of a statement he had made to our local about putting away some money for this upcoming contract!!!!! They said one of our coworkers had mentioned it to them and they had some concerns about our intent's for the contract (a strike really is what they are concerned about) and I was happy to hear our President tell management that he did tell our body to start putting away money for the upcoming contract,' I wouldn't be a good leader if I was not preparing them, never know how this contract will play out.'"

As a comment, the posting member then remarked: "To the individual that's taking information back to the company just know you are cutting your own throat and I hope we can find you and get you kicked out our local ...... just wishful thinking!!!!"[93]

As you plan to develop leverage for negotiations, having the participation of community groups can be helpful in another way, as was illustrated by the United Farmworkers. One of the most effective tactics for early unions was the "secondary boycott"—that is, if you have a strike

---

[92] Joe Burns. *Reviving the Strike: How Working People Can Regain Power and Transform America.*
[93] Dwayne Russell. March 6, 2017

at your employer, you could also picket or strike the suppliers or customers as well to increase your leverage. It is a rule of unionism that when we develop a sharp strategy, the bosses will make it illegal and so secondary boycotts are now prohibited by part of the infamous Taft-Hartley Act of 1947. As the National Labor Relations Board describes it, the federal law "prohibits certain kinds of 'secondary' conduct - that is, conduct aimed at a 'secondary' employer (or secondary employees) in order to exert pressure on a 'primary" employer.'" Outside groups can propose and support a boycott, however, giving indirect leverage to your union so go out and help others and make friends, who can then help you when you need it.

As we look at negotiating strategies, and the rise of anti-unionism, it is important to recognize the increasing imposition of lockouts as a company leverage tactic. "In recent years, the federal courts and the National Labor Relations Board (NLRB) have expanded the permissible use of lockouts by management to the point that they now represent a significant portion of work stoppages. . . . Analysis of all work stoppages from 2010-14 reveals that the vast majority of recent lockouts occur in three industries: manufacturing; arts, entertainment, and recreation; and utilities. These three industries account for approximately 70 percent of all lockouts during this four-year period. Similarly, lockouts clustered around a few unions. The United Steelworkers and the International Brotherhood of Teamsters each experienced approximately 20 percent of all lockouts, while musicians' unions combined experienced almost 10 percent of all lockouts."[94]

To reinforce the power of companies to lock out workers, the new General Counsel of the NLRB, Peter Robb, cancelled a pending trial against Honeywell Aerospace Division, which locked out 260 UAW members at its airplane components factories in South Bend, IN and Green Island, NY for 9 months. After the NLRB issued a complaint—with a potential backpay settlement of more than $20 million—and scheduled the trial for May, 2018, Robb announced in January, 2018, that the case would be dropped.[95]

* * * * * * * * * * * * * * * * * * *

The same challenges confront public sector unions, reflecting both the change in attitude and the changes in structure—like privatization--that have devastated private sector negotiations. Public sector unions must now become more aggressive and stop playing the same defensive game over the past 40 years. Take the crisis as an opportunity.

Public sector unions have a more complicated challenge because public employment has been a steady position—maybe not extravagantly paid but secure, with great benefits and a solid retirement plan. In states with collective bargaining laws, or in the federal government, workers could expect a lifetime of employment and a predictable retirement. Members found a kind of

---

[94] Moshe Marvit. "Is It Times for the Courts to end Labor Lockouts?" The Century Foundation. June 30, 2016.
[95] William Rogers. "Union Disappointed in NLRB's Decision to Drop Honeywell Case." *Left Labor Reporter*. January 11, 2018.

comfort level and it has been hard in many cases to rouse them into militant action. Unions negotiated "agency fee" clauses in their contracts, so that free riders had to pay a service fee to the union, generating a reliable revenue stream.

How this has changed?

The word "Public" has been transformed from a positive word into an obscenity. All "public" services—like public school systems, public health, public housing and public transportation, public recreation and even prisons—have been drastically cut or privatized. As wages drop, of course, the need for these public agencies increases. This ideological shift has been a carefully calculated campaign, depriving public institutions of financial resources and political support.

Our failure to develop a strategy to enforce higher tax rates for wealthy individuals, making funding available for public institutions and for public workers, has been a problem for decades. As local government shifted to various giveaways or to Tax Incentive Financing (TIF) that helped large developers avoid property taxes, public budgets were thrown into a crisis mode that affected contract negotiations in a terrible way.

As a current example of this distortion, the proposal by Amazon to locate a second corporate headquarters has created frenzy among competing cities to throw public funds at the feet of one of the richest individuals in the world. Amazon has already sopped up various public subsidies around the country, totaling $ 613 million for 40 of the 77 warehouses it built between 2005-2014. According to a report from the Institute for Local Self-Reliance, additional subsidies for Amazon data centers were about $ 147 million. The personal wealth of Amazon owner Jeff Bezos is estimated to be more than $ 100 billion—yes, billion—so he certainly needs and deserves public assistance.[96]

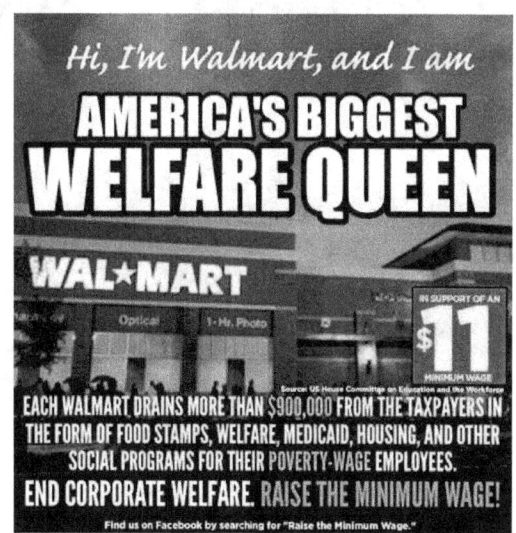

As late as the mid-1960's, the top tax rate for wealthy individuals was at the 90 percent rate—that is, (on paper at least) the wealthiest individuals paid 90 percent of their income in federal taxes. Starting in 1966, the rates were decreased, not only on paper but with a wider range of deductions for wealthy people, until today, when a wealthy person—who was recently elected President of the United States and who claims to be worth "millions, millions"—has not paid personal income tax in years. The new Trump tax bill, passed in January, 2018, will make this bad situation even worse by cutting tax rates on the wealthiest Americans.

Just as organizers look for a "tipping point," when a campaign suddenly become important, anti-unionism seized on the recession in 2008 as the opportunity to shred public sector

---

[96] Olivia LaVecchia. "How Amazon's Tightening Grip on the Economy is Stifling Competition, Eroding Jobs and Threatening Communities." *Independent Business*. November 16, 2016

unions. "The recent assault on public sector unionism occurred as a result of the Great Recession of 2007 to 2009, which was worsened by the fall 2008 financial crisis. Plummeting tax revenues, high levels of unemployment and also the perception that government spending had been exorbitant led radio and television commentators, magazines and newspaper to denounce public employee unions as the cause for this alleged uncontrolled government spending. The title of an article, supporting public employees, which appeared in *The New Republic*, summed up this negative attitude toward government employees: 'Why Public Employees Are The New Welfare Queens.'"[97]

In every case, public workers were portrayed—like the $70/hour auto workers of 2008—as the cause of the financial crisis and not as its victims. Most public sector workers had really not seen the attacks coming, even though there were warning signs up for several years. In the years 2007-2010, the private sector unions like the UAW were shredded while the public sector unions sat by and watched. As the attacks expand into the public sector, union members in every industry have to pick up the pieces, to become leaders and not victims. Workers need to understand that the attacks on public sector workers represent a social attack on the standards of living for *all* workers: decent wages, an early and secure retirement, leisure time, health care, housing, education and recreation.

Many governors and state legislatures ferociously attacked public sector unionism in the first months of 2011, after the unfortunate success of anti-union candidates across the country in the elections of 2010. Governor Scott Walker of Wisconsin got thar fustest with the mostest, going to the legislature with drastic proposals to basically eradicate public sector unionism. Over the next months, it became also clear that Walker was the leader of a well-organized and well-financed national movement to eliminate public sector unions, using financial situations as the excuse, another shining example of the Shock Doctrine.

Astute politicians like Walker and Illinois governor Bruce Rauner used the normal contract proposals of the unions as an opportunity to curtail bargaining rights over issues like pensions and retiree health care and to also campaign for the open shop. These politicians cleverly presented themselves as the defenders of the taxpayers against exorbitant demands by the overpaid public worker unions and claimed to stand alone between us—the citizens—and enormous tax increases, while also supporting legal challenges to fair share laws. Scott Walker, in particular, outrageously presented himself as the representative of the "have-nots" against union demands.

---

[97] Victor G. Devinatz. "Right-to-Work Laws, the Southernization of the U.S. Labor Relations and the U.S Trade Union Movement's Decline." *Labor Studies Journal*. December, 2015. p. 305

In Vermont, Governor Phil Scott "pushed a highly controversial proposal to shift negotiations over teachers' health care from the local collective bargaining process into a single, state-level negotiation. Although educators have been accepting concessionary contracts for many years, legislators believe that school boards have not adequately cut costs on health care. Scott's solution to the impasse was simply to strip educators of their right to direct bargaining over health care. Scott's governing mantra is 'Make Vermont More Affordable,' which in reality means cutting public-sector spending--in this case, by attacking union health care benefits--and insulating the wealthy from all demands for progressive taxation, while pretending be on the side of working-class property owners paying regressive property taxes."[98]

Even in Canada, the strong anti-union movement against public workers appears in proposed legislation. "The increases in salaries will be consistent with the Public Services Sustainability Act (PSSA), a bill introduced in the provincial legislature in March of this year, which aims to 'protect the sustainability of public services' in Manitoba by imposing wage freezes on public sector employees as expired employment contracts come up for renegotiation."[99]

The attacks on the contracts of public sector workers are both a danger and an opportunity. The danger is obvious—where's the opportunity?

One bright side to the struggle in Wisconsin over Scott Walker's attacks on public sector bargaining was the sudden flurry of information about tax policies—the exposure of a gross system of "taxation" that has pushed an increasing burden off the corporations and on to workers. Our whole tax structure has been tipped to provide huge subsidies for the wealthy, both corporations, developers and individuals, so that there is a desperate shortage of funding both for public  workers and for public services. Public workers are being hit twice: as workers, they have been hammered, losing benefits and pay while also seeing the public services they offer being chopped into little pieces.

The Philadelphia Teachers Union, for example, went four years without a new contract—and without raises for the members—until ratifying a new agreement in June, 2017. Without political organizing, however, the school budget could not absorb the raises—or make up the back pay-- so layoffs may start and teachers will now have to contribute to their health insurance, and principals will be allowed to hire teachers without considering seniority.[100]

---

[98] Nolan Rampy. "High stakes in Burlington's schools showdown." *Socialistworker.org* September 11, 2017.
[99] Imreet Kaur. "Faculty Ratifies Four-Year Agreement Under "Duress." *The Manitoban*. September 13, 2017.
[100] Liana Loewus. "Philadelphia Teachers to Get Raises After Four Years Without a Contract." *Education Week*. June 20, 2017.

"The union has not had a contract for nearly four years; teachers have gone without a raise for nearly five. . . . The school system projects a deficit of hundreds of millions of dollars in the next few years." Teachers staged a one-day protest walkout, without the endorsement of the officers of the Philadelphia Federation of Teachers and some of the teachers are threatening to leave the system and find work elsewhere. A caucus within the union, the Caucus of Working Educators, organized what they call "a coordinated teacher absence" as a protest.[101]

In Baltimore, the public school system administrators dramatically announced in the spring, 2017, a deficit of $129 million and threatened to lay off 1,000 teachers, after 171 support staff were laid off in 2016. Eventually, with some state aid, the layoffs were reduced to 32 people who work in the district headquarters and 83 people in the schools. Among them were 13 classroom teachers, 21 librarians or school counselors, and 24 assistant principals, administrators said.[102] The Baltimore Teachers Union (BTU) contract is now almost a full year past expiration with no apparent resolution in sight but the union officers have created no political campaign to support their negotiations. At the same time, the newspapers in January, 2018, were filled with photos of school children in Baltimore, huddled in their classrooms with their coats on during a cold spell in because the school system had not maintained heating systems in dozens of schools.

The historical working-class community, where workers lived near their jobs and where they could exert some political power, has disappeared, in many ways a reflection of union success. When unionized public workers in major cities move up into the have-a-little class, they move out geographically. In the BTU, 75% of its members live outside the city where they work and cannot "elect" their bosses. The Baltimore City administration proposed giving local police officers, firefighters and sheriff's deputies a property tax break of $2,500 a year if they own a home in the city. Numbers show that only to 19.5 percent of police officers lived in Baltimore City at the end of 2016, down from 21.4 percent the year before. In contrast, almost 90 percent of Chicago officers live in the city and in Philadelphia the figure is almost 85 percent.[103] (There are obviously other possible consequences for a city like Baltimore which has seen several years of confrontations between African-American residents and the police, who are sometimes described as an "occupying force," hardly the basis for community support in negotiations.)

Since so many other workers—mostly non-union—are dramatically affected by the availability of public services, public sector unions can build an impressive coalition including
- public workers,
- the "clients" they serve--whether it be park and library users, individuals with disabilities, mass transit riders, homeowners worried about police and fire protection, public school children and parents, or individuals who receive direct public financial assistance—and

---

[101] Kristen A. Graham. "1,000 Philly Teachers Call Out to Protest Lack of Contract." *Philadelphia Daily News*. May 1, 2017.
[102] Tim Prudente. Amid Baltimore school layoffs, tears and disbelief." *The Baltimore Sun*. June 1, 2017
[103] Ian Duncan. "Baltimore plans to offer $2,500 a year property tax discount for police and firefighters." *The Baltimore Sun*. September 11, 2017

- other unions which have been so far paralyzed by the recession.

This movement could attack both the short-term financial disputes in union contracts while proposing a kind of "Peoples Budget," with new priorities and significant structural changes, reversing the last 40 years of divisive social policies that have penalized and impoverished workers in the US.

Just as in the private sector, public sector unions need to carefully research the financial position and power structure of their employers. It is not always easy. One officer of SEIU Local 1021 in San Francisco said to me when I did a training that the city budget for her area was 4 inches thick and that nobody could understand it, while another member said public financing "was way-y-y-y complicated." This tangle of money from multiple sources is a challenge that we have to take up, however, to unravel the mysteries of public financing.

Some of the figures are difficult to get and to understand and some appear almost every day in various media. The research is, of course, critical every union, at some level, has specialists who know how to dig out the data and crunch the numbers. The focus on leverage must be clear so the information can be "translated" for your members and the affected communities. Simply sponsoring demonstrations with the slogan "No Cuts" is just not good enough.

One exciting project which should increase membership participation is creating a kind of "clipping service of the whole membership" so that everyone is paying attention, often for the first time, to the stream of information that appears in the media and to the bits that can be retrieved from the wastebaskets—real or electronic--in public offices. It would be an activity for all the workers in one department to get together at lunch time and swap their articles and discuss the implications for their union. The local could create a web site/Facebook so all the material is easily available and could even offer a prize for the best discovery—almost like a company reward for the best money-saving idea in the suggestion box. The point is to both do the numbers and get the members alert and active.

A second target for public workers is spending in the area of benefits, like health insurance and pensions, which are proclaimed to be major causes of public deficits and which are major issues in every union negotiation. Health care is a total mess in the US. In fact, if there were an example of the total failure of "free market" economics, the US health care system is #1 with a bullet and can be calculated at a state or local level, which may make the figures seem more immediate to union members.

Workers in almost every industry now pay part of the premiums, so the cost of health insurance and the percentage of total income that US workers pay is far beyond anything paid in other industrialized countries—all of which have some sort of national health care. In every negotiations, health insurance, and especially health insurance for retired workers, is a major issue. A single-payer plan—so frightening to the health insurance industry (not to be confused with a "health care" industry) would save billions of dollars every year.

Want to talk pensions? They are another favorite target and one which, in both private and public sectors, has been slowly growing for decades because the pension funds need to be, uh, funded. Corporations and public agencies have relied instead on the paper growth of the stock market and very lax enforcement of requirements to postpone the day of reckoning. Let's be clear about one area: workers deserve early and economically secure retirements—we earned them, despite the attacks from the wealthy, who have been basically retired since the day they were born. Regaining control of public income at all levels will leave sufficient funds for pensions.

In Pennsylvania, "Two years ago, Gov. Wolf vetoed a Republican pension bill that moved all new state and public school employees into a 401(k)-style plan. Wolf said the bill 'provides no immediate cost savings to taxpayers and does not maximize long-term savings for taxpayers.' But his veto didn't solve the problem. The state's public-sector pension liability is $74 billion and growing by $172 a second. About half of every new dollar in education spending pays for pension benefits. The pension shortfall is due to several factors, including people living longer and investment losses during the recession."[104]

In New Jersey, under the benevolent guidance of former Governor Chris Christie, "New Jersey's $73 billion pension fund for 769,000 active and retired public workers is composed of seven underlying plans, including the Police and Firemen's Retirement System. New Jersey's pension system is the worst-funded in the nation, according to Bloomberg. As of 2015, it had 37.5 cents for each dollar in future benefits owed to retirees, the worst in the country, according to an analysis by Pew Charitable Trusts."[105]

How about our favorite public sector topic—privatization? Over the years, the issue has been framed that cutting public workers is a benefit to the taxpayers because the contractors—usually non-union—are "cheaper." In fact, the costs are shifted—non-union contractors get no health insurance so the public has to pay for their care. Services decline and there is very little accountability and, in the end, careful research will prove that there is no net savings to public funds, only favors done for political cronies who dump money into what Huey Long called "the deduct box." Huge industries—like private prisons, for example—grow by directing public policy to punishment (and reimbursement) rather than to crime prevention. The area of privatization is one in which all public sector workers can enthusiastically participate in gathering information, focusing the discussion and widely spreading the information, especially because their jobs could be next on the chopping block.

The list of structural expenses goes on but you get the point. For the sake of agitation among our neighbors, however, looking for juicy—or even lurid—public expenditures helps to fan the flames of discontent. Every level of government has gradually shifted tax obligations and tax benefits to devastate workers but the local tax structure is right in front of our members and our neighbors and the examples seem so much more vivid than federal problems. All of the records are public so we just have to dig them out, add up the numbers and translate them—in terms of increased taxes or lost public services-- for our neighbors. For our members in

---

[104] Philadelphia Inquirer. May 7, 2017
[105] Andrew Seidman. "Using veto, Christie clashes with Police, Fire Unions." *Philadelphia Inquirer*. May 8, 2017

negotiations, simple calculations work: what wage increases, benefit improvements or additional staffing could have been—and should be—paid for instead of tax breaks.

A final preparation for negotiations in the public sector is *kyushu*—applying pressure and researching exactly whom should be the target. As we plan negotiations we need to know who makes the decisions in our negotiations: each public sector is different, especially when functions have been subcontracted to a private vendor. So many public agencies are now fragmented—there is an allegedly independent agency, but there are subcontracted functions and complicated political chains. There are the political figures that control the agencies and make the strategic and financial decisions that appear in our negotiations. Negotiating with the private subcontractor puts the union into a different legal framework and with different options for leverage. We may also find the same shadowy vulture capital companies involved, as they have bought up billions of dollars of public bonds and want to make sure they get their profits.

One real challenge is the threat of a public sector strike. While there have been sporadic strikes by public sector workers, like SEIU Local 721 in Riverside (CA) County, a public sector strike can create more opposition than supporters since the services to the public are shut down. A union can plan a systematic organizing campaign to convince "the public" that a strike is the only recourse but cutting off essential services can be dangerous. The same concerns exist in the health care industry, where a possible strike by nurses, for example, might turn patients and their families into union opponents. Despite the abundance of articles glorifying a strike as the only solution to a boss's intransigence, unions need to look at diverse methods for getting leverage, constantly calculating whether their tactics will increase solidarity.

In Chapter 7, we will discuss union political action, a particularly controversial topic after the 2016 presidential election. As one way to gain leverage, it is essential for public sector unions to elect their own bosses—and even to have their own members get elected. In too many cases, unions spend large amounts of money, and the members expend large amounts of time, energy, and shoe leather, supporting candidates, usually Democrats, who then refuse to support union issues.

* * * * * * * * * * * * * * * * * * * *

There is one other aspect to negotiations that is often overlooked by unions, and it's called *Bargaining Between Contracts*. When the employer makes a change in the workplace the union usually reacts by filing a grievance, plodding through the steps and maybe going to arbitration. Here the boss—both private owner and public agency-- insists that the Management Rights clause of the contract gives the power to act unilaterally, without "obstruction" from the union. This expansion of control of the workplace has been going on for almost 100 years and is as important as money to a boss. A big problem is that most union members accept this power and look only to specific clauses of the union contract for some restrictions. After all, the boss owns the business and should be able to run the show, right?

Wrong.

Unions today need to challenge this management power and authority every day. In fact, the Recognition Clause of the union contract [Appendix 7] gives the union the right to bargain over "all terms and conditions of employment," any changes in, around or related to the workplace. Demanding to bargain is proactive, and the officers should expand negotiations in the same way they do for a contract battle. Since contracts are often negotiated only every three, or four, or more, years, bargaining over current issues creates excitement and enthusiasm among the members—and non-members. Union officers should use the same strategies—open bargaining, workplace demonstrations, community support—as they do for negotiating the full contract. Obviously, some of the issues may not affect as many members but as employers move aggressively, there will be important issues which the employer expected would not be challenged.

The union should make it clear—and loudly and publicly--that no changes in the workplace will be accepted at any time, even mid-contract, without extensive negotiations so that the contractual, legal and social rights of every member are protected. What do we mean by "social rights?" In "normal" times, for example, it's consider the unchallenged right of management to do as it pleases with its workers—such a laying them off, subject to the limits of the contract. Most importantly, negotiations require the union to be PROACTIVE, so even negotiations on a change in working conditions shifts the momentum, and should be coordinated with the regular program to sign up any non-members, especially if, or when, *Janus v AFSCME* gets the Supreme Court stamp of approval.

NOW GO DO IT

1. How successful has your union been in the most recent negotiations? How many of the members participated in these negotiations? Do a power analysis of your employer to figure out who makes decision in negotiations?
2. Create a Leverage Diagram, getting help from the union's Research Department if necessary. Evaluate all of the possible tactics to pressure your boss.
3. Create a Leverage Diagram, getting help from the union's Research Department if necessary. Evaluate all of the possible tactics to pressure your boss.
4. Evaluate all of the possible tactics to pressure your boss.
5. What other unions in your area have been successful in negotiations? What did they do to get what they wanted?
6. What can you learn from them?

CHAPTER 5—GRIEVANCES

> "It is common sense to take a method and try it; if it fails, admit it frankly and try another. But above all, try something."
> Franklin D. Roosevelt (1933)

One of the fundamental obligations of the union is defending the union contract. If contract negotiations are the wars between us and our bosses, grievances are the daily skirmishes, so important for building membership strength and loyalty. While Donald Trump rants on about "world problems," the day-to-day issues for our members at work—where they spend the majority of their waking hours--can be a main focus for making our unions great again. A steward should understand that—now more than ever—the boss regards the union contract, with its protections and procedures, as a major obstacle. The union is the only organization strong enough to challenge the authority of management to wreak havoc. Defending the contract is defending the union and the way it is handled can increase the participation and loyalty of the members—or can suffocate it.

The Grievance Procedure provides one framework but the practices which have endured for 40 years no longer work and need to be changed. During this, union stewards who handled grievances have followed the routine, learned from Old Joe and Old Jane, and passed down from one generation to the next: wait for a member to complain, do a brief reactive investigation of the case, file a grievance, looking carefully at the language of the contract, and kick it up through the steps to arbitration.

If it ever really worked, the "normal" grievance procedure, where issues were decided on the merits of a case, is broken, blocked by supervisors who don't have time to meet, or who have a rubber stamp for GRIEVANCE DENIED. The standard response from Personnel Persons is that the Management Rights clause lets them do any damn thing they desire. They may even denounce a grievance as Fake News!

The apparent restrictions in the contract, the wider Management Rights clause and the aggressive approach by management, have frustrated union members at every level—officer, staff and members—while opening opportunities for anti-union organizers to encourage members to drop out because they are not being forcefully represented. Since there is no organizing strategy involved, the process leaves out most of the members, who could help develop leverage to settle the case.

In most cases, there is no report to the members about what grievances are being processed or, more importantly, why the grievances are important to every member. Most stewards look at a grievance as a defense of an individual member, and not as a defense of the contract that protects all of us, including the non-members.

The Organizing Model opens many new ways of protecting our conditions. Union stewards, or the local officers in a large bargaining unit, will be forced to adapt to new conditions and to learn new skills and attitudes to confront increasingly hostile employers. In the first place, everything in, around or related to the workplace that members don't like can be a grievance. The Recognition Clause of your contract—which was the only language that early unions had—gives the union the right to represent workers for "wages, hours and all terms and conditions of employment." While this clause opens the possibility of bargaining over every condition, it also opens up everything is up for grieving. [See Appendix 7]

Get your members—and non-members—involved in every grievance. File group grievances, hold demonstrations at work over important issues, be loud and be visible. You should borrow strategies from organizing campaigns. Organizer Gene Bruskin described an important tactic in the campaign at Smithfield Foods: "In any union drive, anyone who is not a 'yes' is a 'no.' Action is the best measure of support, better than signing cards. If you try to organize an action on an issue in a department and only three people out of 25 in the department participate, then you probably have only three 'yes' votes and everyone else is a 'no.' Someone's chances of voting for the union are pretty good if they are willing to sign their name on a petition to demand workplace changes and is then willing to march on the boss during their lunch break with 24 other workers to present that petition. If a worker does that, then the chances are really good that they will vote yes, especially if that action results in a win. The results are far better than if they just signed a card."[106]

Try to persuade your members that there are collective actions, and solutions, through the union, even when the employer looks shaky—threats of plant closure or of subcontracting public-sector work. We have seen how concession bargaining has become so common, as workers calculate that if they give in to management of economic issues, they can collectively protect their jobs. The worst thing—almost inevitable, unfortunately—is that desperate members think "every man for himself" and will try any trick to hang on their jobs. In grievances, it is individuals who scramble. Low-seniority workers, for example, may demand that "ability" replace contract language as the basis for a layoff, frantically hoping to find some way, as individuals, to keep their places.

A steward needs to be proactive and look for any violations of the contract. Most members don't know the contract and miss opportunities to support grievances. Even worse, individuals are intimidated and are afraid of the consequences if they are called out as a "troublemaker" for demanding that the contract be enforced. Instead of waiting for a member to come to you, go out around your members—it's like a "listening tour" -- to see what issues are bothering them. This is also a great chance to increase union visibility and to check in with non-members as well. If they see union activities that will personally benefit them, they are more likely to join up.

---

[106] Chris Brooks and Gene Bruskin. "Labor's Southern Strategy." *Dollars and Sense*. September 3, 2017.

It is perfectly legal to make such rounds, even though your supervisor learned at a management training to try to block you by warning—truth be damned-- that "soliciting grievances is illegal and could get you into trouble." The consultants fear any proactive moves by a union steward because they know how you can strengthen your union—and they are paid huge dollars to try to prevent this improvement. And, most importantly, now your members know who the steward is and have personal relationships.

Make a list to see how many members complain about a situation and if these problems appear in different areas of your workplace, then go through your contract to mark all the clauses that support your case. If nothing fits, use the Recognition Clause.

Immediately create a communications network for the workers you represent. Develop an electronic list—e-mail/Twitter or app—so you can zip out information to all your members. Finding out the facts and getting them to your members is critical because rumors are an enemy of unionism. Plan regular meetings—daily, if necessary—to report back on negotiations or grievances on the economic situation. Even in locals where getting a quorum at a membership meeting has been difficult, you will be surprised at how eager members are to have accurate information about their situation. There is, once again, opportunity in this crisis.

Stewards now have to also respond to the racial and ethnic hatred that Trump is supporting because incidents at work can lead to very complicated and divisive grievances. A listening tour will quickly expose any individuals, or groups, who support the alt-right and who could direct their hated at co-workers. Proactively challenging these attitudes is Good Union Practice but also prevents discipline if the situations—language or actions—get out of hand the management starts disciplining members.

* * * * * * * * * * * * * * * * * *

A major challenge is the dangerous economy, with layoffs or subcontracting all around us. In the past, a layoff was generally temporary so processing the paperwork under the contract was routine, almost drudgery. In many cases, members were glad to get some time off, especially if the union contract provided SUB pay. In the public sector, there had been virtually no layoffs and one of the difficulties for public sector unions was that members almost felt too secure. Public agencies simply decreased the workforce gradually by not filling jobs that became vacant due to retirements or quits, or by hiring "temps" that could be dismissed without cause. Now stewards and officers in public-sector unions are dealing with new situations, as agencies propose layoffs or subcontracting.

After an official announcement from management about an economic nuclear strike—a plant closure, massive layoffs--chaos may follow, almost like a barroom brawl. We saw the results in the 2016 election when desperate workers voted for a Strong Man who promised to miraculously return their jobs. The political weakness of US unions, described in Chapter 7, makes it tough because workers want to blame someone—anyone—for their desperate situations. Rather than shifting the blame around, raise the importance of positive action—political, social economic—to change the economy.

Instead of giving workers greater power, the union could collapse, with all the protections and procedures dominated by aggressive management. Stewards accustomed to a "good working relationship" with management will suddenly find themselves facing desperate and abusive bosses. The union steward's skills will be severely tested because there are now two areas of concern. One is within the workplace, with the wide range of contract issues. The other is for the members who are pushed out of their jobs and scattered around the landscape. A member is still a "member," even when on layoff and may need to help and support of the union even more, as will be described in Chapter 8.

- In the midst of the chaos, efforts should be made to sign up non-members in the open shop states. Obviously, they are affected by contractual interpretations and need the information that will be provided at union meetings, so these free riders may finally—if belatedly—see the light. Odd as it may sound, these tough times can be a time for building unionism and increasing membership so signing up the free riders is simply one part of a union's proactive plan.
- Know your contact, every clause of it, so that the rights of every member are protected. If there is language pertaining to layoffs in which the company might be required to justify a reduction in force, jump on it. Don't simply accept "the right" of the employer to get rid of your coworkers. Workers have "rights" as well, but only if they organize themselves to demand that these rights are recognized and respected. Challenge every attempt by the boss to lay people off.
- A steward should be continuously vigilant when the boss tries to cut corners. Most union contracts, for example, have language to prevent subcontracting if it results in the loss of bargaining unit work but mere words are a small obstacle when money is involved. This is a great time to implement your "thousand eyes" strategy—after explaining to your members the contract language on subcontracting, for example, they must be constantly looking around for new faces and be ready to report in immediately to a steward. Not only does this campaign help protect your work but it also builds an internal organizing program that every member should be eager to join. While some employers like to subcontract to an outside company, at least one major telecommunications corporation had a slick alternative: hiring union retirees as "contractors," hoping that friendships will discourage a grievance. The CWA, representing these workers, stepped up forcefully and got an agreement so that when one of these friendly contractors left, the job would be filled by a fulltime bargaining unit member.
- Learn the details of The Worker Adjustment and Retraining Notification Act (WARN) (http://www.doleta.gov/programs/factsht/warn.htm) which requires that in case of "mass layoffs," a 60-day notice is required. If your employer is determined to lay off, your coworkers should get as much notice, or payment, as possible. The calculations for coverage and for the definition of "mass layoff" can be a little tricky, so union officers and staff need to be alert and knowledgeable.

- While the WARN Act does not cover public workers, there is a real need for state legislation to extend the same protections to public workers. In the past, public-sector unions—never contemplating such an economic collapse—have been negligent about pushing for such laws, but now's the time. The Maurice and Jane Sugar Law Center for Economic and Social Justice (www.sugarlaw.org) provides great information on pending state legislation about advance notification and has drafted model legislation for unions to propose.
- As public agencies look at either mass layoffs or major subcontracting, public sector workers need the same guarantees on advance notification as their neighbors who work in the private sector. Unions should gear up politically to support the expansion of the private sector laws, hopefully before the crisis hits.

If it looks like the union cannot delay or prevent significant layoffs, a steward then must use all of the procedures in the contract to make sure that every member is treated fairly. Here are some of the basic points to look out for.

- If there is bumping language in the contract, the steward has to be knowledgeable about all of the complicated procedures to make sure that company pets are not somehow protected beyond the contract. In a scramble for a dwindling number of jobs, it's almost like musical chairs, without the music. Individual workers will explore every possible resource to hang on to their paychecks. If there are challenges from members about the bumping procedures, a steward should deal tactfully with each one because these conflicts are among members, each of whom is desperately trying to hang on to a job. Be fair, be reasonable and set aside your personal friendships to simply demand that everyone live by the terms of the union contract. Proposed grievances will be extremely divisive because a remedy for one worker who objects to a layoff is that another worker will walk the plank instead.
- It is also important to appreciate the super-seniority provisions in some union contracts, negotiated to protect a steward in case of a layoff so that there should hopefully be experienced union representation in a difficult time. Members who are being laid off may suddenly discover that a steward with lesser seniority is staying on the job so the displaced member may become a zealous defender of strict seniority. Hold your ground that the contract cannot be changed and that there are good reasons for protecting the union structure.
- It is generally a good rule to support the position that the contract should not be broken, or even bent, in this crisis. Management has often tried to create a "herd mentality," trying to stampede workers into informal concessions and givebacks at the workplace level, using the financial crisis as an excuse.
- If workers are being laid off, therefore, a steward must beware the Monty Hall syndrome—let's make a deal! The boss—especially one that has dealt with a particular steward over a long period of time--will often ask the steward to relax enforcement of some contract articles, saying "Don't be so tough on us when times are bad." Hang tough

on enforcement and beware the rumors—or the facts—that some steward has been bribed to overlook violations.

- At an extreme, the union itself can be blamed for the layoffs. In some discussions, the major companies and their political retainers step right up to blame various provisions in union contracts for the companies' failures. The battle for the hearts and minds of your members, their families and their communities about the importance of unionism is one that a steward needs to take on.
- Often a contract will have some relaxed standards for bumping—a worker can be trained for 30 days, for example, but the boss will boohoo that now is not the time for such an expense. The union must insist that every contractual protection be observed and that all members, even the ones affected by the layoff—and admittedly this can be a tough sell—understand the importance of the procedures. Beware the end-around: when the boss comes to the union to renegotiate some of the crucial contract language, using the crisis as the opportunity.
- If there is a layoff, it is crucial for a steward to make certain that all contract protections are strictly enforced. Many contracts allow continuation of employer health insurance and, if it runs out, COBRA allows workers to buy coverage at a much cheaper group rate for up to 18 months. How about accrued vacations or holidays? Make sure that the boss settles up in full before your member goes out the door. One sharp steelworker steward was able to get two extra Christmas holidays at the end of 2008 for workers on short-time, simply by really knowing the contract.
- And of course a good steward keeps up the pressure on the employer to recall workers, even a few at a time. It is easy for a shrewd employer to shift work around so that fewer workers are putting out the same production. Don't let this happen or the workers on layoff will never come back.
- One of the most difficult issues for a steward is dealing with overtime assigned when members are laid off. Even the self-proclaimed "union heroes" may waver when OT is available, neglecting to recognize that they are taking work that could bring a recall. The union should inform management that no overtime will be worked while existing positions are vacant, increasing pressure both to bring back members from layoff and cut back on additional workloads for active workers.

Most importantly, do not simply concede to your boss the right to dispose of workers. Fight in negotiations to revive one of the oldest union demands—a shorter work day with no reduction in pay. We started fighting in 1884 for the 8-hour day. As we saw in the Republic Window sit-in in Chicago, where workers simply took over the factory rather than accept layoffs, workers will respond with determination and imagination to protect their rights, if properly organized.[107]

---

[107] Kari Lydersen. *"Revolt on Goose Island: The Chicago Factory Takeover, and What it Says About the Economic Crisis."* (2009).

The continuing crisis will be a major test for every union and every steward but unionism has survived tough times before. Officers and stewards must offer leadership to show that the tougher the times, the greater the need for workers to pull together.

NOW GO DO IT

1. Create a list of all of the union's grievances over the past 6 months?
2. How many members were directly affected by these grievances?
3. How successful has your union been at winning grievances?
4. What leverage did the union develop to try to force management to resolve the grievances?
5. Educate your members about the contract—have a break time meeting and cover one article each day until you get through the whole contract.
6. Take a "listening tour" to see what problems your members have—and make sure they know who their steward is.
7. Prepare with your members for the worst—layoffs, subcontracting, workplace closure—and plan dramatic responses. Be proactive.
8. What has your union done to strengthen protections in case of an economic recession or major technology changes by your employer?
9. How has your union blocked subcontracting?
10. Has your union ever filed a grievance using the Recognition Clause?

CHAPTER 6—ORGANIZING

"When you're at the bottom, you have no place to go but up—if you want to go up."

Both new organizing and internal organizing are crucial areas for us to capture to avoid being Trumped. The dismal numbers for union membership, and the geographic clustering of our locals, show both the dangers we face and the opportunities we have. It seems so *d'oh*: we are losing members so we need to grow and every union campaign has to have one basic goal: bring in more members.

Even though the BLS report for 2017 showed the increase of 282,000 new members, unionism in the United States has failed to build and to sustain new organizing programs. Our numbers have continued to drop and the consistent decline is an unfortunate arc, bending toward the bottom, that will have oblivion as the last stop.

Clearly, the elimination of unionism in the US is a goal for many right-wing groups but do we have to be their enablers? This drop is not due to Trump but has been continuing for almost 60 years, with little response from union officers who set strategies and control resources. The blame game excuses have multiplied: it's the Labor Board, it's the union busters, it's the moving of work—you name it, there's an excuse, except that unionism has confronted this same opposition for hundreds of years and was able to organize.

When we restructure our unions, it is essential to make organizing the first priority so that every project can be evaluated on how many new members it will bring us. We need them to join our unions and to work politically for important advances—to benefit all of our members and all of them. When we expand our numbers, we build our bargaining power and visibility, as well as our financial resources and political potential. We must look at how to appeal to non-union workers, now the huge majority of our country and encourage workers to look to themselves to make things better, and not to a self-proclaimed Savior like Trump.

A much larger percentage of union dues is spent on servicing than on organizing, the obvious me-first argument --members pay dues to get a service, not to recruit workers who are not covered by a contract. We have repeatedly talked about attitude and strategy. New and internal organizing emphasize PROACTIVE but we must convince our members that new organizing is also a "servicing campaign," to build bargaining power in their organized workplaces.

While the process of organizing is covered in detail in another book,[108] we can describe the outlines of an organizing strategy. The campaign for new organizing has several parts: first,

---
[108] Bill Barry. *From First Contact to First Contract: An Organizer's Handbook.* [shameless self-promotion]

to convince our members that organizing is so important that spending dues money and shifting staff will be supported. Then create an organizing program, with experienced organizers, to encourage non-union workers to overcome the fear and the threats that bosses routinely use to block organizing campaigns.

We need to talk with our members about new organizing as a basic selfish interest. Some organizers try to persuade members about the importance of "the movement," but I prefer telling them that organizing more workers, especially in their industry or with their same employer, is more money in their pockets and more job security. The low percentage of union members is a threat to every clause of our contract. New organizing raises the wages and benefits of competitors, improves conditions in our geographic area and reduces the threats of companies moving to low wage geographic areas. Self-interest works, doesn't it? Just look at Trump.

Any union member who has been through negotiations is the past 25 years knows the song: we can't pay because our competitors won't. Non-unionism has replaced unionism as the new "normal." I can remember in the 1980's when non-union companies no longer feared the threat of an organizing campaign, and began to cut benefits for their workers: no daily overtime, no wage scales, no fully-paid health insurance, no pensions, as well as horrible health and safety conditions. Isolated as the have-a-littles, union members did not budge—until they came for us. Now these non-union conditions are "normal" in every work place, a lesson we should have learned but did not.

Over and over, the news is about employers using the threat of non-union workers to force concessions in unionized contracts. As one example, "Seattle's Boeing workers had their pensions frozen and suffered huge increases in their health care costs. Boeing, the largest and most profitable airplane manufacturer in the country, was able to force concessions on 30,000 workers in Seattle, the Machinists' largest bargaining unit, by whipsawing them against thousands of non-union workers in South Carolina."[109] Same company, same work—but the non-union workers became the leverage for Boeing to pull concessions from the unionized work force.

Members of the UE in Erie, PA, began demonstrating in the fall, 2017, because General Electric proposed taking 570 jobs and moving them to the non-union plant in Dallas, a "southern strategy" at GE, and many other companies, for almost 100 years.

Since new organizing is a benefit for every member, it is a challenge that has to be accepted by each of us, and not just a few paid organizers. As staff is shifted from servicing to organizing, stewards will absorb more responsibility, handing grievances instead of just telling a member to call the rep, or to call the 1-888-grievance hotline. Members need to volunteer their time to support a very expensive organizing program with no guarantees of immediate success. Every time members get together, formally—at local meetings, for example—or informally—in the break room or at social events—new organizing must be emphasized.

When members get involved in the campaigns, they get excited and really understand that the conditions we have taken for granted are denied to most of the workforce. Often, our

---

[109] Chris Brooks and Gene Bruskin. "Labor's Southern Strategy." *Dollars and Sense*. September 3, 2017.

members forget what it is like working non-union but hearing the horror stories during an organizing campaign certainly makes the point, building their loyalty to their union.

There must be a sense of urgency today when we talk about "the culture of organizing," with clear objectives and strategies, skilled organizers, and full funding. Many unions, even at the international level, do not have Organizing Directors, and at many union functions, like local meetings, district conferences or international conventions, the phrase "new organizing" is never mentioned.

At the best of times, most unions do not choose to spend the money to set up a successful organizing program. Union officers, who set the strategies and control the union's resources, simply avoid any discussion about the decline in numbers, as if ignoring this very dangerous situation would simply make it go away. Officers usually come up through the servicing structure—as stewards, Business Agents or local officers-- and do not understand organizing, which requires both a different set of union skills and a different personality. If "organizers" are hired, it is often a patronage appointment and the organizer, no matter how eager or committed, simply has no instructions on how to be successful.

According to organizers, in some locals with geographically "white" areas, racial and ethnic prejudices discourage the organizing of a subcontractor or competitor with large numbers of minority or immigrant workers.

In addition, some officers too concerned about the potential impact that new members will have on local union elections—more specifically, on their own chances for re-election. Answering this obstacle in 2004, while setting a goal of increasing membership by 10 percent every year, ATU International Vice-President Mike Siano stated: "What we need to do is identify new targets and put a plan in place. And, to those who believe that new units will affect their Local's political balance, I say, take the risk. You are stronger when our members are stronger, and good leaders will not shy away from these efforts."[110]

When John Sweeney challenged Tom Donohue for the presidency of the AFL-CIO in 1995, Sweeny's "New Voice" campaign proposed changes based on the premise that "the most critical challenge facing unions today is organizing," and called upon national unions to "organize at a pace and scale that is unprecedented." With organizing at the top of the agenda, the subsequent victory of Sweeney's slate was widely interpreted as an endorsement of this priority.

In 1996 the AFL-CIO released "Organizing for Change, Changing to Organize," a report that called upon union officers to take risks and make the dramatic changes necessary to succeed at organizing. It identified four keys to winning:
- Devote more resources to organizing.
- Develop a strong organizing staff.
- Devise and implement a strategic plan.
- Mobilize your membership around organizing.

---

[110] *In Transit*. December, 2017.

As the AFL-CIO began to push new organizing, "Some CLCs have used the AFL-CIO's MEMO training-Membership Education and Mobilization for Organizing. This approach says that rather than unions simply assigning staffers to organize, members should be involved. And the federation is using moral suasion to get locals and internationals to commit thirty percent of their budgets to recruitment. At the Washington State Labor Council convention in September 1996, for example, stickers reading '30% by the year 2000' were distributed. Delegates signed a petition endorsing Sweeney's call for thirty percent across the board. In Sweeney's old union, SEIU, if locals commit certain percentages of their budgets to organizing, they receive a dues rebate."[111]

In a similar move, the officers of The Amalgamated Clothing & Textile Workers (ACTWU) changed the union constitution to require that every division commit a fixed percentage of revenue to new organizing. If a district failed to do so, the International would take the money and send to a more aggressive region that was organizing.

In 1989, the AFL-CIO founded the Organizing Institute (OI) to train both union members and college recruits in organizing skills. By the mid-1990's, hundreds of new organizers, many of them recruited from outside the u8nion movement, had been trained and placed into campaigns.

To promote acceptance of the challenges associated with Changing to Organize, the Organizing Department set as an objective for 1998 to: "lead an expanded Changing to Organize program and provide technical assistance to unions on crafting strategic plans to support a greatly increased organizing focus…," and to "help unions move the Changing to Organize message deeper and broader among local union leaders." Sweeney decided to operationalize the call to shift resources by asking all unions to move toward a goal of devoting 30% of their budgets to recruitment. Unfortunately, there was "quiet resistance" to the commitment of 30% of resources for recruitment, which was viewed by most unions as excessive, and new organizing disappeared as a priority, even as our numbers continue to decline.

This whole movement flopped in the face of resistance from international union officers. ". . . [U]nion leaders at all levels are cautious. Even if they agree that recruitment is important they will pull back if they sense resistance from union members. This is especially a problem at the local level and in those instances where the leader has no personal expertise in organizing. Union staff also may be recalcitrant; though few will openly challenge leaders that promote organizing, those assigned to representation express pessimism and resent the increased workload that typically accompanies resource reallocation."[112]

In 2000, Sweeney persuaded the AFL-CIO Executive Council to commit to organizing one million new members every year. We must revive this commitment of resources today, even as union treasuries are shrinking. This means union officers and members have to create a list of targets, with a schedule, staff, skills and financing.

---

[111] Jane Slaughter. "John Sweeney's New-Old AFL-CIO." *Solidarity*. March-April, 1997.
[112] Richard Hurd. "The Failure of Organizing, the New Unity Partnership and the Future of the Labor Movement." Cornell University, 2004.

* * * * * * * * * * * * * * * * * *

One basic element of organizing is the Leverage Diagram that the union develops for negotiations and for grievances. When you figure out who makes the decisions that affect your workplace, and how they can be pressured, you will also see a beautiful list of logical organizing targets—non-union workers at your own work site, non-union workers in a duplicate facility or who work for a direct competitor, or who work for another company owned by your investors.

Your union should create some brief organizing materials—a list of your benefits and protections, how the union compares to the wages and benefits in non-union targets, and some videos from members who have grievances settled. Here's a great example (that also encourages your own members):

Kroger shop steward wins $250 in back pay for coworker: For years now, Kristy Vance has seen managers, management trainees and loss prevention staff stocking shelves at her store, Kroger #402 in Blacksburg, VA. This not only violates the Kroger-Roanoke contract, which specifies that only bargaining unit members can stock shelves, but it also reduces the number of hours Local 400 members are scheduled to work. Kristy wasn't going to tolerate it. This fall, she took photos and documented 24 hours of management doing shelf-stocking. She sent the photos and evidence to her representative, Mark Collins, and filed a grievance against Kroger. The company could not dispute what happened and Local 400 won a back pay award for part-time associate Alex Taylor. He was the most senior part-timer and had only worked 16 hours during the week in question, so he received a check for $250, covering the extra hours he should have been assigned. "I'm really pleased we got results because this has been a long time coming," Kristy said.

DC Union City November, 2017

It is important that your organizing materials expand beyond the money issues to include areas like "just cause," with stories of workers who have gotten their jobs back, or unfair suspensions lifted, because of the union contract and its enforcement by a strong steward system.

The members also need to be surveyed to find first contacts. Ask them if they have family or friends working in a non-union workplace and see how these leads fit your Leverage Diagram. You could pass along the leads to organizers from other union, if they are in a different industry or location, but an organizing *movement* will start and the members will participate.

Emphasizing union visibility is another support for organizing—and it doesn't cost your members any time or any effort to wear their union caps and shirts when they are away from work. Anything to create a sense of a union *movement* to attract non-union workers.

One controversy that can arise when we do a survey for organizing contacts is that many of the members' non-union contacts work in industries that your union does not represent—yet. An important strategy decision is whether your will expand your membership to take in workers of a different industry, especially if they work for a common "owner," like a hedge fund or vulture capital firm, to expand your leverage. For craft unions, or for unions that have traditionally limited themselves to a particular industry or type of work, this decision may be difficult. You may also be able to work with another union in the different industry to start an organizing campaign, a relationship that will require that your staff share organizing leads and strategies with other unions. These are challenges that can be overcome if you keep your eye on the prize: leverage is money in our pockets, and the more workers organized, the more we have.

One strategy to deal with this challenge is the web site UnionBase, where an article emphasized that, for Larry Williams, "His long-term aim is for those who'd like to be unionized at most any employer anywhere in America to sign on to UnionBase and reach out to organizers at one of 30,000 locals who, in turn, can assist them in successfully petitioning for a representation election at their workplace–and ultimately winning."[113]

* * * * * * * * * * * * * * * * * *

The fundamental question is: how can the conditions for non-union workers be improved? Since World War II, they have ridden, like corks on a wave, on the "normal" employment conditions that strong unions negotiated. As importantly, since the New Deal of the 1930's, non-union workers have depended upon government action, usually at the federal level, to make their situations better. Paid poorly? Raise the minimum wage? Have no retirement? Expand Social Security. Need health insurance because your boss doesn't provide it? Enact Medicaid. Don't earn enough to feed your children? Have free breakfasts in public schools. A sense of entitlement developed over the past 75 years, as if good working conditions were a Constitutional right. The whole tradition of self-help, of workers organizing to make things better, has been lost, consciously erased as a culture, and, as recommended, by Lewis Powell, from schools and textbooks.

If you can believe surveys, there is a huge opportunity for new organizing because a solid majority of Americans "approve" of labor unions, despite all the expensive propaganda against us that floods the media. While this survey does not mean that every worker is willing to sign a card and be threatened by his/her boss for supporting a union, it does show a hopeful "mainstreaming" of unionism—that is, a wide acceptance of our movement and principles, despite the efforts of anti-union consultants to portray us as thugs and losers.

---

[113] Rick Wartzman. "Meet The Millennial Who's Trying To Save The Labor Movement With A Facebook For Unions." *Fast Company*. September 1, 2017.

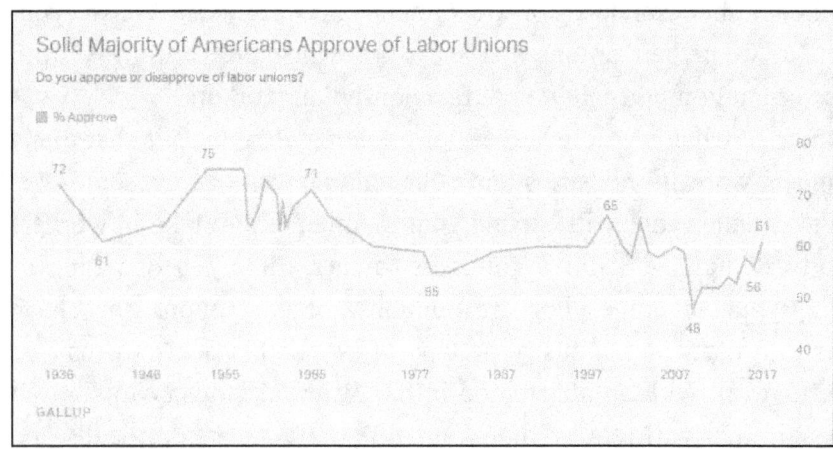
The challenge of "mainstreaming" in the United States is also "an abiding fixation of the far right, whose members are well aware of the problems their movement has had with attracting young people in recent decades. . . . Colin Robertson, a far-right YouTube personality who goes by the name Millennial Woes, explained to an older extremist the importance of putting forward a friendly, accessible face: 'If we don't appear like angry misfits, then we will end up making friendships with people who don't agree with us," he said.'"[114]

One of the arguments for a high unionized percentage of the workforce is that the conditions we negotiate are passed along to the non-union workers to block organizing campaigns, "doing right voluntarily," as Lemuel Boulware described one of the first anti-union programs in the 1940's. For decades, as unions were strong and had some political power, legal protections were extended to the non-union workforce. The balance is now tipping in the other, and very dangerous direction—not only are non-union workers threatened with losing legal protections but companies want to push non-union conditions on unionized workers.

As we set up our organizing strategies, it is important to recognize that the times are ripe for organizing—people are riled up, employers are even bolder and the minimal legal protections at both state and federal levels for non-union workers are being drastically cut. There is no more "normal" for many workers but the trick is to focus this anger on our bosses, with organizing as a solution, rather than allowing a self-proclaimed savior like Donald Trump to capture this resentment.

And the world of work is dramatically changing. "Recent studies indicate that freelancing, independent contracting and temp work are on the rise, although most Americans still hold traditional, full-time employment. In July, 'temporary help services' workers made up just over 2 percent of all non-farm jobs in the country, federal data show. What is noteworthy remains the prevalence of such temp workers across a range of industries. No longer are they merely office workers answering phones — they're packing boxes and operating machinery in warehouses, and employed as security guards, janitors and nursing assistants. A 2016 study by Harvard and Princeton researchers dug into federal employment numbers and found something striking: '94 percent of the net employment growth in the U.S. economy from 2005 to 2015

---

[114] Jesse Singal. "Undercover with the Far Right." *The New York Times*. September 19, 2017.

appears to have occurred in alternative work,' which includes temp workers, on-call workers, independent contractors and freelancers.'"[115]

"Since 2001, department stores alone have lost half a million jobs. The coal industry by comparison has lost about 22,000 jobs in the same time period. . .. According to government data, general merchandise stores like Macy's and Sears have bled more jobs since October [2016] — about 89,000 total — than the total number of people employed by the entire US coal industry . . . The job exodus in the retail industry, which still employs about one out of every 10 American workers, is only expected to continue. . . . More than 3,200 retailers have announced store closures so far this year, and Credit Suisse analysts expect that number to grow to more than 8,600 before the end of the year. 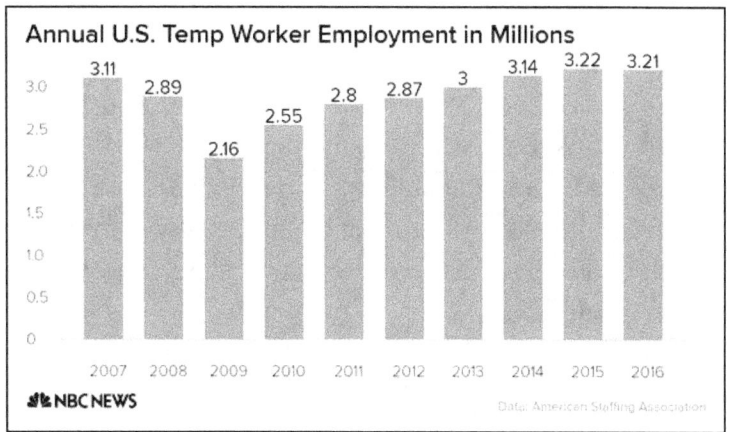 For comparison, 6,163 stores shut down in 2008 — the worst year for closures on record. . . . A worker at a Sears store in La Jolla, California said part-time workers at his store have had their hours cut by 70%. Employees that previously worked 20 hours per week are working about 3 hours per week now, or not being scheduled at all, he said."[116]

"Children are no longer living better than their parents did. In the eight years since the recession, the Wilshire Total Market valuation has more than TRIPLED, rising from a little over $8 trillion to nearly $25 trillion. The great majority of it has gone to the very richest Americans. In 2016 alone, the richest 1% effectively shifted nearly $4 trillion in wealth away from the rest of the nation to themselves, with nearly half of the wealth transfer ($1.94 trillion) coming from the nation's poorest 90% -- the middle and lower classes. That's over $17,000 in housing and savings per lower-to-middle-class household lost to the super-rich." [117]

Another structural change has been the shift from public programs and public ownership to private business, a gradual transformation that has been going on for many years. Public housing projects are gradually being replaced by Section 8 vouchers, which enrich private landlords. Once Medicaid assisted poor workers with medical bills but Congress is now considering a system of vouchers to be paid to private insurance carriers, and not to providers of medical services. There are even regular attempts at the federal level to privatize Social Security, throwing all the older workers into some sort of private equity pool. And, of course, there is Betsy Devos . . .

---

[115] Jake Heller and Erik Ortiz. "Temp Work Now a Permanent Fixture, Creating Problems for 'Invisible' Workforce." NBC News. August 31, 2017.
[116] Hayley Peterson. "An American Jobs Threat Worse than Coal is Coming to your Home Town." *Business Insider.* May 2, 2017.
[117] Paul Bucheit. "Now Five Men Own Almost as Much Wealth as Half the World's Population." BuzzFlash. June 12, 2017.

The challenge for unionized workers at every level of the union is to reach out to non-union workers, both to organize and to get active politically in our own self-defense. Once again, it is in our self-interest because conditions for all workers will either rise, because union push by organizing and political action, or will fall, and we will all be screwed.

The opportunities for unionism to organize as government protections drop is obvious. Almost every day, the Trump administration cancels workplace protections—for discrimination, for class actions suits against an employer, for overtime pay—as part of a systematic plan to restore the workplace swamp. The nomination of Andrew F. Puzder was certainly one of the most outrageous and insulting proposals for workers. Puzder would have been the first Secretary of Labor who advocated eliminating labor from a workplace, replacing fast food workers with machines. Puzder proclaimed: "They're always polite, they always upsell, they never take a vacation, they never show up late, there's never a slip-and-fall, or an age, sex or race discrimination case."

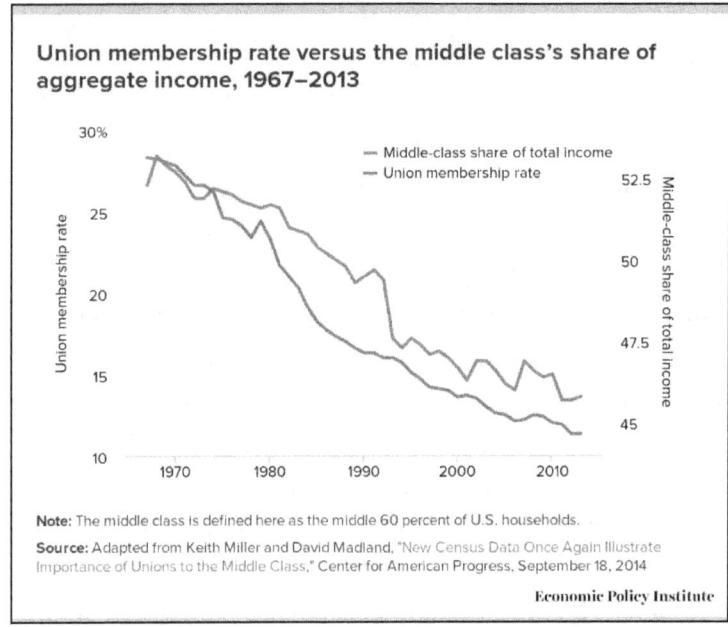

"Putting one of the worst fast-food CEOs in charge of national labor policy sends a signal to workers that the Trump years are going to be about low pay, wage theft, sexual harassment and racial discrimination," reads a statement from the organization Fight for $15. The group attributes the statement to Carl's Jr. cook Rogelio Hernandez and Hardee's cashier Lacretia Jones. "Puzder is against unions, calls the minimum wage and overtime 'restrictions' and employees 'extra cost,' and even said he wants to fire workers like us and replace us with machines that can't take vacations or sue their employers when they break the law," the statement said.[118]

This at a time when wage theft, and "tip theft," for hospitality workers has reached astonishing depths. "Tip theft and other forms of wage theft is already a serious problem, according to the left-leaning Economic Policy Institute. It estimated workers **lost more than $50 billion a year** in wage theft in 2014, or far more than the cost of robberies, burglaries and other property crimes. About $1 billion in stolen wages and tips were recovered for workers in 2012, thanks to federal or state agencies and private lawyers. Wage theft ranges from failing to pay for overtime to skimming tips that should go to tipped workers."[119]

---

[118] Tonya Garcia. "Trump labor secretary pick Andy Puzder talked about replacing workers with robots." MarketWatch. December 10, 2016.
[119] Aimee Picchi. " Who owns a tip? Trump may shift it to restaurant owners." CBS News. October 31, 2017.

The most recent estimate on the theft of tips was so large that the senior officials in the Department of Labor ordered staff "to revise the data methodology to lessen the expected impact . . . .Although later calculations showed progressively reduced tip losses, Labor Secretary Alexander Acosta and his team are said to have been uncomfortable with including the data in the proposal." [120]

Talk about fake news!

The Trump administration revoked many of these protections. As an example, on March 27, 2017, "Trump revoked the 2014 Fair Pay and Safe Workplaces order that then-President Barack Obama put in place to ensure that companies with federal contracts comply with 14 labor and civil rights laws. The Fair Pay order was put in place after a 2010 Government Accountability Office investigation showed that companies with rampant violations were being awarded millions in federal contracts. To try to keep the worst violators from receiving taxpayer dollars, the Fair Pay order included two rules that impacted women workers: paycheck transparency and a ban on forced arbitration clauses for sexual harassment, sexual assault or discrimination claims.

"Noreen Farrell, director of the anti-sex discrimination law firm Equal Rights Advocates, said Trump went 'on the attack against workers and taxpayers. We have an executive order that essentially forces women to pay to keep companies in business that discriminate against them, with their own tax dollars,' said Farrell. 'It's an outrage.' Out of the 50 worst wage theft violators that GAO examined between 2005-2009, 60 percent had been awarded federal contracts after being penalized by the Department of Labor's Wage and Hour Division. Similar violation rates were tracked through the Occupational Safety and Health Administration (OSHA) and the National Labor Relations Board."[121]

One current Supreme Court case, a consolidation of *Epic Systems v. Lewis, Ernst & Young LLP* and *NLRB v. Murphy Oil USA, Inc*, is another legal attack on the rights of workers. This case challenges the requirement "where workers were required to sign an agreement that any legal claims against the employer would be subject to arbitration, and that in no circumstances could two or more workers combine their claims in the same case." At one point in the argument, Justice Breyer said that the only way the employers could win would be by 'undermining and radically changing the understandings that have gone back to the New Deal (though actually the Norris-LaGuardia Act predates the New Deal). It seems obvious that an agreement requiring workers to waive their rights under the NLRA would be unenforceable. We'll know in a few months whether that I still the case."[122]

Look at workplace safety and health—certainly a "social" issue, right? According to the U.S. Bureau of Labor Statistics, 5,190 people were killed on the job in 2016, the most since

---

[120] Ben Penn. "Labor Dept. Ditches Data Showing Bosses Could Skim Waiters' Tips" Bloomberg News. February 1, 2018.
[121] Mary Emily O'Hara. "Trump Pulls Back Obama-Era Protections For Women Workers." NBC News. April 4, 2017
[122] Andrew Strom. "The *Epic Systems* Oral Argument Did Not Go Well for the Employers (Though it May Not Matter)." *On Labor*. October 4, 2017.

2008. The rate of fatal injuries for full-time workers rose to 3.6 per 100,000, the highest since 2010. The annual number of serious on-the-job injuries suffered by US workers is estimated at approximately 3 million. "These figures do not take into account the number of chronic and repetitive-stress injuries and sicknesses incurred without immediate physical harm that may become a lifelong burden to workers. It is estimated by the Department of Labor that 50,000 workers annually succumb to long term occupational illnesses, often the result of exposure to hazardous substances. These moves come under conditions where OSHA resources are already stretched dangerously thin—with, currently, a ratio of one OSHA inspector for every 59,000 workers—and in which inconsequential slap-on-the-wrist fines for violations convince corporations that it is more profitable to forgo safety measures."[123] Without accustomed legal protections, non-union workers now have to become self-reliant, which means organizing-- it literally could be the difference between life and death. Unions have to provide the resources and strategies to support these campaigns.

* * * * * * * * * * * * * * * * * *

One of the fundamental principles of The Servicing Model is officers' relying upon the union lawyers to set strategy but as judicial and administrative agencies like the Labor Board have become more conservative, this approach has failed. Many of the organizing practices that unions have used, like filing with the NLRB for a representation election, are more of a challenge than an advantage. While the Obama administration improved conditions slightly—speeding up representation elections, for example—the new Board is clearly so tilted toward protecting the power of the bosses that new and threatening precedents may become "law." The popular media focuses on Trump's twitter bloviating, but his administration is drastically changing the administrative procedures at the Labor Board, with the new appointments, especially anti-union lawyers William Emanuel and Marvin Kaplan. The new General Counsel, Peter Robb, is especially notorious for acting as the lead lawyer for the Federal Aviation Administration when 13,000 air traffic controllers were fired by the Reagan administration in 1981, so that there will be a dramatic, and negative, shift in NLRB decisions.

The New Labor Press listed five areas that are once again threatened by bad NLRB decisions:
- **No more legal delays to union elections** It's already a stacked deck: Employers can require workers to attend anti-union meetings, while excluding union organizers from the property. Under those conditions, delaying a union election gives employers more time to bust a union campaign. So employers used legal technicalities to delay elections. Then in 2015 the NLRB decided it would hold the elections first, and resolve employer legal challenges later. Business groups howled in protest at what they called the "ambush election" rule. It used to take 40-45 days to schedule a union election. Now it takes an average of 25 days.

---

[123] Steve Filips. "Workers killed on the job near Rochester, New York." World Socialist Web Site. February 1, 2017.

- **Joint employers are still employers** Employers sometimes try to get out of the obligation to bargain with a union by dividing control between two entities, like a company and an outside staffing agency. But in 2015, in a case involving Browning-Ferris Industries, the NLRB made it clearer that when two or more businesses share control over a worker's terms of employment, they're "joint employers" and still must deal with the union. In December, 2017, however, the Board ruled 3-2 to revoke the standard.
- **Grad students can be workers too** Colleges increasingly rely on low-paid grad students for teaching and research, while saying they're students, not employees. But in 2016 the NLRB said they can indeed be employees, and therefore have the right to unionize.
- **No more employee handbooks that deny workers' rights** Even nonunion workers have rights under the NLRA, such as the right to talk with coworkers about conditions, and to take collective action. To protect those rights, the NLRB has been cracking down on employers for employee handbooks that say workers can't tell coworkers how much they're paid, or that ask workers to give up their right to class action suits.
- **Email and Facebook are the new water cooler** If workers have the right to talk with each other about pay and conditions, that means they can talk about them on email or Facebook too, the NLRB has ruled. So employer rules barring those things are illegal.[124]

As an example of the new employer belligerence, Harvard University, with an endowment of $36 billion, challenged a NLRB policy known to every organizer as "The Excelsior List." This policy, so-named because it involved a campaign by the Textile Workers against the Excelsior Underwear Company in 1966, required an employer to provide to the union a complete list of names and addresses for every worker in a bargaining unit when the union filed for a representation election. It has been a helpful and a long-settled NLRB policy. Confronted with an election petition from the Harvard Graduate Students Union-UAW, however, Harvard provided an incomplete list in October, 2016. The UAW lost this election with 1,456 "no" votes against 1,272 "yes," with  an additional 314 challenge ballots for the most exploited academic workers. The union appealed on the basis of the lousy list, claiming that "some eligible students who were omitted from the voter list (the "*Excelsior* List") may have been prevented from participating in the election." John J. Walsh, Jr., Regional Director of the National Labor Relations Board, wrote in his July 7, 2017, decision that a list of eligible voters generated by Harvard before the election 'interfered with the employees' exercise of a free and reasoned choice' in the vote, according to a Facebook post by union organizers."

---

[124] https://nwlaborpress.org/2017/10/u-s-senate-confirms-trump-nominees-to-the-nlrb/ (October 3, 2017).

Harvard president, historian Drew Gilpin-Faust, whose total compensation for 2016 was $ 969,830[125] and who has been an outspoken opponent of Confederate idolatry, challenged this long-established precedent and opposed the union's demand for a new election.[126] In December, 2017, the NLRB surprisingly rejected Harvard's appeal and scheduled a new election but Harvard was willing to fight unionism, and to overturn a longstanding NLRB precedent in the process.

One persistent fantasy is that somehow Congress will improve on labor law protections. "To bring more Americans into unions would probably take some significant changes in labor law. For example, the Employee Free Choice Act, defeated by the threat of a Republican filibuster in 2007, would let workers form a union simply by signing up a majority of the workplace up. That would have circumvented the long election process that makes it easier for employers to mount a diapers-in-the-breakroom-style intimidation campaign."[127]

"Our labor law holds businesses accountable only to the workers whom they 'employ' in an old-fashioned, contractual sense. That too made sense in the industrial era, when leading companies had millions of employees. But today, janitors, Amazon delivery drivers and warehouse workers are often employed by subcontractors who have little real power over their livelihoods. And Uber and Lyft drivers are misclassified as independent contractors. As a result, these workers don't have clear rights to bargain with the companies that actually set the rules. And these workers are subject to big restrictions on striking or picketing against such "third party" companies. . . . A few simple but bold legal reforms would make a world of difference. First, Congress could pass laws to promote multi-employer bargaining, or even bargaining among all companies in an industry. If all hotel brands, all fast-food brands, all grocers or all local delivery companies bargained together, none would be placed at a competitive disadvantage as a result of unionization, which is often the main reason employers resist it so fiercely. Second, Congress could ensure that organized workers can bargain with the companies that actually profit from their work by expanding the legal definition of employment to cover more categories of workers."[128]

It's almost like believing in Santa Claus—because we are good little boys and girls, somehow a Congress that is bought and paid for will enact legislation to support campaigns to increase union membership.

* * * * * * * * * * * * * * * * * *

---

[125] Kaitlin Mulhere. "Only 3 of the 25 Highest-Paid Private College Presidents Are Women." *Chronicle of Higher Education*. December 4, 2016.
[126] Caroline S. Englemayer. "NLRB To Consider Election Objections In Feb. 22 Hearing." *Harvard Crimson*. February 14, 2017.
[127] Livia Gershon. "Unions Aren't Obsolete: They're Being Crushed by Right-Wing Politics." Vice. September 11, 2017.
[128] William E. Forbath and Brishen Rogers. "A New Type of Labor Law for a New Type of Worker." *New York Times*. September 4, 2017.

The strategies for organizing are endless and we need to look at all of them. Two campaigns in the newspaper industry, both involving the vulture capital firm called Tronc, illustrate some very different possibilities. In October, 2017, the reporters at the *Los Angeles Times* announced an organizing campaign with NewsGuild-Communications Workers of America after more than 130 years of being non-union, responding to the unpleasant changes in the workplaces. In a model of economic change, The *Los Angeles Times* is now owned by Tronc, which absorbed the Tribune Corporation, which had taken over the Times-Mirror Corporation and was in turn taken over by vulture capitalist Sam Zell and run into bankruptcy. *The Times'* drastic cost-cutting measures, including sweeping layoffs, agitated the staff. Last year, Tronc instituted an abrupt change to the vacation policy that effectively eliminated accrued vacation days, and in August, 2017, fired some of the top managers. A letter from the Los Angeles Times Guild listed many items for negotiation, including "1) Keep the benefits and working conditions we like, and codify them in a legally binding document so Tronc can't change them unilaterally. 2) Get a better deal on the things we don't like" also said "a majority of the newsroom" had signed union cards. [129]

The success of this campaign, with a union majority of 248-44 was helped by the kind of research discussed in Chapter 4. When management claimed that there would be no money for raises, the reporters did what reporters do—investigated. "The organizing campaign conducted some investigative reporting and found that Tronc had more than enough money to improve pay and working conditions, but instead of doing so, Tronc's top executives were lavishing themselves with excessive pay and expensive perks. 'Executive compensation (at Tronc) shot up by 80 percent last year,' reported the organizing committee. Tronc's CEO Justin Dearborn in 2016 was paid $8.1 million in total compensation, 'substantially more than his counterparts at the New York Times Co., Gannett Corp, Dow Jones/Wall Street Journal, and McClatchy.' Tronc's Chairman Michael Ferro traveled in a private jet that cost Tronc $4.6 million between February 2016 and September 2017."[130]

As a contrasting organizing strategy in the same industry, ST Acquisition Holdings LLC, which includes the Chicago Federation of Labor and other local labor unions bought the *Chicago Sun-Times*—outbidding Tronc—from Wrapports Holdings, yet another product of private equity adventure. "'Our investors include more than half a million hardworking people around Chicago, and you can bet we'll be talking with a voice that resonates with the working class,' [Edwin] Eisendrath said."[131]

Not only did the sale block another media monopoly, since Tronc already owned the *Chicago Tribune*, but a variant on a worker-owned co-op is a response to the triumph of Trumpism. "A worker cooperative directly connected to the labor movement . . .is the most beautiful version of democracy in the economy that I can imagine,' said Casey Amadon, Apple

---

[129] Sydney Ember. "Los Angeles Times Newsroom, Challenging Tronc, Goes Public With Union Push." *New York Times*. October 4, 2017. Also https://latguild.com/ for the union program.
[130] William Rogers. "Landslide Union Victory at LA Times." *Left Labor Reporter*. January 22, 2018
[131] Mitchell Armentrout. "Union group led by Eisendrath outduels Trib owner to acquire Sun-Times,." *Chicago Sun-Times*. July 12, 2017.

Street Market project manager at the Cincinnati Union Co-Op Initiative." In 2013, there were fewer than 300 worker cooperatives, with an average employment of eleven workers at each of them. One obvious question is raised: "Given that worker cooperatives offer higher employment stability, solidarity, opportunities for wealth accumulation, and other benefits relative to conventional firms, researchers have puzzled over their marginality in the U.S economy."[132]

The enormous possibilities of worker co-ops are seldom discussed as alternatives to the struggles we have with our employers (By god, that sounds like *socialism!!*) but, in the Time of Trump, every new strategy is important. Articles demonstrate, as does the Ohio Employee Ownership Center (http://www.oeockent.org/), which supports Employee Stock Ownership Plans (ESOPs), both the possibilities—obvious—and the difficulties, mostly funding, for starting worker-operated "businesses." The USW has a whole section on its web page about worker co-ops (https://www.usw.org/union/featured-projects). In 2009, the USW and the Mondragon federation of worker co-operatives in Spain signed a collaborative agreement. The agreement claims that unionization is a strategy to scale up the worker cooperative sector in North America. The Mondragon Corporation is comprised of over 100 separate worker-owned cooperative businesses in industrial, retail, finance and knowledge sectors, and was established in 1956 in Mondragon, Spain.

The challenge is, of course, money to operate—capital, like that provided by unions in purchasing the *Sun-Times* and in isolated financial support for cooperatives from unions like the USW and the UFCW. As companies close enormous facilities, in industries like steel, the operating expenses for the workers to run a mill would be enormous but it is an organizing vision that must be considered.

* * * * * * * * * * * * * * * * * * *

The opposition to new organizing is ferocious. As the president of Whole Foods, John Mackey stated in the early 1980's: "The union is like having herpes. It doesn't kill you, but it's unpleasant and inconvenient, and it stops a lot of people from becoming your lover."[133]

The bosses have the will, but they have also figured out the way—strategies to block union organizing and to cut down our numbers. Jake Rosenfeld, a sociologist at Washington University said that since the 1960's, companies have gotten really good at fighting unions. "Employers perfected the antiunion playbook in the United States in a way that they haven't in many other places."[134]

---

[132] Laura Hanson Schlacter. "Strong Together: The USW-Mondragon Union Co-op Model." *Labor Studies Journal*. June, 2017.
[133] Nick Paumgarten. "Food Fighter." *The New Yorker*. January 4, 2010.
[134] Livia Gershon. "Unions Aren't Obsolete: They're Being Crushed by Right-Wing Politics." Vice. September 11, 2017.

As a diagram for a non-union world, look at a comprehensive proposal from the Heritage Foundation, called *Blueprint for a New Administration: Priorities for the President*, part of its Mandate for Leadership series. This comprehensive attack, itemized by each federal jurisdiction, is frightening. Each item is cleverly presented as supposedly supporting expanded employment, making all workers happy. The proposal attack both union conditions as well as non-union ones.

As a political awareness note, the Blueprint was credited to almost 30 "scholars," affiliated with various foundations and organizations, an illustration of the focus and resources which the anti-union movement can deploy and of the availability of academic pimps, as Lewis Powell advocated.

For the Department of Labor, as one example, the Blueprint recommends "The Department of Labor (DOL) should focus on protecting workers from legitimate risks and dangers instead of administering ineffective and duplicative job-training programs and impeding job creation" and advocates repeal of the Davis-Bacon Act, which requires that all workers on public construction projects be paid "prevailing wages," or union scale. If this repeal cannot be achieved, the Blueprint claims "the President has authority to suspend its application. The President should declare America's national debt and underfunded entitlements a national emergency and suspend the DBA."

In another section, "Expand Union Transparency. Regulations promulgated between 2005–2008 under the 1959 Labor-Management Reporting and Disclosure Act required unions to disclose itemized spending to their members. The Obama Administration repealed many of these transparency requirements, including regulations extending transparency to union trust funds and local chapters of government unions. The DOL's Office of Labor-Management Standards (OLMS) should re-issue these rescinded transparency regulations."

Other proposals in the *Blueprint* include
- Moving the Occupational Safety and Health Administration (OSHA) from a penalty-based enforcement emphasis to more "voluntary compliance" by companies.
- "Protect the self-employed" by ending Obama's initiative to protect millions of workers, such as Uber drivers, domestic workers, and others commonly misclassified as "independent contractors" to evade employer responsibilities.
- "Rein in the NLRB" by ending National Labor Relations Board's efforts to speed up union elections, a change denounced as a "sneak attack." Obama's NLRB, the group grouses, had "cut the time frame for union elections in half."
- "Restrict Government Unions" by eliminating collective bargaining rights for public sector unions, which, Heritage claims, "organize against voters and taxpayers."[135]

"At the top of the Republican hit list are public sector workers—the most unionized portion of the workforce. Even before Trump took office, Republicans revived the Holman Rule, an 1876 measure enabling the government to summarily (and selectively) cut individual federal workers' pay to $1. As *The Washington Post* reported, 'Opponents and supporters agree that the work of 2.1 million civil servants, designed to be insulated from politics, is now vulnerable to the

---

[135] http://thf_media.s3.amazonaws.com/2016/BlueprintforaNewAdministration.pdf

whims of elected officials.' 'This is part of a very chilling theme that federal workers are seeing right now,' said Maureen Gilman, legislative director for the National Treasury Employees Union, which represents 150,000 federal employees."[136]

This ferocious opposition to unionism can be simply another excuse for not supporting an organizing program. Labor history teaches us, however, that the bosses have always fought us, so what else is new? When asked why unions can't, or won't, expand organizing programs, officers have no clear answers.

> "There are various reasons: It's more difficult to organize workers when they are dispersed in small shops and franchises than when they're crowded together in a large industrial plant; unionization drives now run up against a series of anti-labor laws and court decisions; and too much of the current labor leadership tends to be cautious and unimaginative. But the climate was far more anti-labor a century ago; back then even peaceful picketing was often met with injunctions and nightsticks. As for the union leadership, it's hard to imagine bureaucrats more hidebound than the gentlemen who headed the old American Federation of Labor at the start of the 1930s. And people forget that the garment shops of the early 1900s were small and scattered, and yet workers managed to organize -- without tools like the internet. In fact, the biggest impediment to service sector organizing today is just that we have been viewing it as some separate campaign off in a corner of the labor movement. We need to recognize that it's a crucial element in the broad struggle for social and economic justice."[137]

As Eric Robertson, an officer in Teamsters Local 728 in Georgia stated:

> "This type of organizing really forces unions to go 'back to basics' in terms of organizing and representation. Since striking in the public sector is illegal in Georgia, workers that want to organize have to actually change the laws at the local, county, or state level to achieve even basic rights like dues deduction. And even when you win, your options for recourse in disputes is much more limited and 'bargaining' for raises and improvements is actually 'lobbying,' whether that takes place in private, at public meetings, or in the streets. . . . Working people, youth, women, and people of color are now open to left, populist, and social-democratic ideas on an unprecedented level and are mobilizing and finding ways to fight back despite most of labor sitting on the sidelines. The old adage of crisis and opportunity coexisting together is profoundly true today, and what we do in this moment matters a great deal." [138]

One important aspect of new organizing is union visibility in social movements, which puts us on the street with many non-union workers. The support of some locals like the ILWU in San Francisco for protecting undocumented workers, and for supporting DACA, can provide countless contacts for organizing, especially if unions are willing to share, so a contact in a

---

[136] Christopher D. Cook. "Trumping Labor: The Republican Plan to Gut Workers' Rights." *The Progressive.* February 14, 2017

[137] David L. Wilson. "Labor Organizing in 2017: Looking Beyond Trump's Lies on Jobs." *Truthout.* January 22, 2017.

[138] Sarah Jaffe. "The New Operation Dixie." *Dissent.* Summer, 2017.

different industry that develops during a social movement can be passed along to the union that represents that industry.

As Eric Robertson emphasized, "For many unions these campaigns are multi-year projects, so many develop alternate ways of collecting dues and have to organize in often *very* hostile environments with no legal protection until they are officially recognized, and even then you aren't guaranteed protection from retaliation. What I learned from this is that workers in every circumstance want to organize, and it is our job to get outside our comfort zone and help them become part of a movement. This doesn't just apply to public workers, but also misclassified workers and others in the gig economy with jobs that are very different from the American workplaces traditionally organized through the NLRB process." [139]

> **Union organizing isn't about signing cards - it's about empowering people and changing lives**

According to Juan Miranda, a community organizer in North Carolina,
"we have organized workers around the idea that their power does not come from a law or a piece of paper but from their position as workers who do all the labor and therefore create all the wealth for the company. And that, especially in the South, where no rights are going to be handed to us, it is up to workers to come together to get what we want. The most effective strategies for us have consisted of bold demonstrations of power and public support—from call-ins and walk-ins and rallies with the support of community, labor, and clergy to more militant actions such as store shut downs and one-day strikes. We have been able to fight and win cases of racial discrimination, wage theft, retaliation, and sexual harassment by being able to show bosses that a) workers are not afraid to stand up for themselves and b) there is mass community support behind them."[140]

Organizer Gene Bruskin described the UFCW campaign at Smithfield, an organizing campaign is a social movement:

> "It's really important to figure out where the social groupings of workers are outside of the plant. Organizers can't step foot in the plant and it can be very difficult to find out where workers live. At Smithfield, workers lived in a 50-mile-radius of the plant, so we were very active in the church. We included big name preachers like the Rev. Jesse Jackson and William Barber to give the campaign moral authority, but we also focused on moving the campaign into the churches where the workers actually were, so their own preachers would be talking directly to the workers with the message 'we are behind you.' We went to the soccer clubs, where people played every Sunday morning. We also went to the Latino nightclubs. We built the union through communities that workers actually

---

[139] Ibid.
[140] Ibid.

participate in. Local institutions can play a big role as workers are taking risky actions in the plant. We had a full-time minister and a full-time community organizer focusing on just building support with local Black and Latino institutions around Smithfield."

Discussing the UAW campaign at Nissan in Canton, MS in August, 2017, Chris Brooks stated: "According to organizing committee members I spoke with there, the committee was too small, was not representative of every department and every shift, and only half the committee was very active. On top of that, they went to a vote without having a supermajority signed up on cards. Do you agree that a strong organizing committee is the best defense against an employer's anti-union campaign and that is a major reason for the UAW's failure?"[141]

One great organizing resource is the web site Union Busting Playbook, "The Playbook of Union-Busting Pros and Real Stories of Workers Who Beat Them." (https://unionbustingplaybook.com/#intro) which lays out many of the anti-union devices that consultants use to break an organizing campaign. With section like "The Plays: Eight Things Employers Do to Block Unions," and a Highlight Reel of workers running successful campaigns, with a promise to "keep updating these with the latest and greatest stories." While the Highlights are all CWA campaigns, the site is still a wonderful example of Best Union Practices that we can all share.

* * * * * * * * * * * * * * * * *

While the topic of "free riders"—signing up workers covered by a union contract who have not joined—has been covered in another book,[142] it is essential that every union include an internal organizing component into its strategies for rebuilding. Unions, especially in the private sector, have become almost pathetically dependent upon management to keep membership numbers up and the revenue stream from union dues steady. Negotiating a Union Security clause in a contract, usually accompanied by a checkoff agreement, is considered the most important agreement so union officers and staff have often sacrificed strength and benefits to keep this language. It has been considered "normal" in negotiations to trade a union shop and checkoff clause for a broad Management Rights clause and a severe No Strike clause, basically letting the boss hold on to more power and to limit the responses under the CBA that the workers can use to improve conditions.

A culture of dependency has developed so union officers and staff no longer have the attitudes or strategy to expand the Organizing Model of Unionism where the members become the organizers and the union can sustain itself without any concessions from management. The

---

[141] Chris Brooks and Gene Bruskin. "Labor's Southern Strategy." *Dollars and Sense*. September 3, 2017.
[142] Bill Barry. *Closing Up the Open Shop: A Guide to Internal Organizing* [second shameless self-promotion]

earliest union supporters in the US—who were considered criminals in the 1800's—found effective ways to shun non-members and to encourage participation. They even fined members who missed union meetings so the evolution into the necessity to get the employer to enforce union membership is a long and winding historical road.

For public sector unions, achieving an agency fee provision if a union shop is not legally or politically available carries the same importance but also leaves these unions as vulnerable as the private sector unions. As Scott Walker began to shred the public-sector unions in Wisconsin, officers of several public employees unions in Wisconsin agreed—without a vote of the membership—to accept benefit reductions if agency fee and checkoff could be maintained.

A more diabolical strategy was developed by Governor Paul LePage of Maine—divide and conquer-- to effectively split the membership of the two largest state unions, eventually persuading the members to "voluntarily" give up the agency fee clauses in their contracts.

As a kind of role model for Donald Trump, LePage has been described by various observers as "a crude buffoon," "the most ignorant, angry, racist, and buffoonish leader in America," and as "a terrible governor, a worse person, and he says something dumb nearly every single week. He's a never-ending source of stupidity." He told the Portland NAACP to "kiss my ass" when the civil rights group invited him to speak soon after his election in 2010 and demanded the removal of murals depicting Francis Perkins, the famous Secretary of Labor who had family roots in Maine. "The mural "sends a message that we're one-sided, and I don't want to send that message," said LePage.

LePage proclaimed his support for open shop legislation after his election in 2010 but was unable to get it passed in 2013. In 2015, the legislature once again voted against making Maine the 29th open shop state.

In the 2017 negotiations, LePage's administration proposed a choice to the Maine State Employees Association, Local 1989, with about 9,000 members, and to the AFSCME Council, with 900 corrections and mental health workers: get a two-year contract with 6 percent raises and eliminate agency fee clauses or keep the clauses and get a 1 percent raise. "MSEA-SEIU Local 1989 contract negotiators accepted the change in support of the pay increase in August, but negotiators for AFSCME rejected the proposal, recommending instead accepting only a 1 percent raise. But the 900 or so members of AFSCME rejected the negotiators' contract and voted to ratify LePage's offer, giving them the 6 percent wage increase while eliminating the mandatory fees for nonunion members."   While the president of the SEIU council proclaimed that "the union has "emerged stronger and more united" as a result," LePage clearly outorganized the officers of both unions.

The issue predictably raised on social media the discussion of the value of unions, with comments on the news article running from "As a dues-paying member of MSEA Local 1989, headline should be revised to read: 'State workers get greedy and lose sight of the bigger picture'" to "Umhuh. Lets see…'feed the family' or 'feed the union'. Workers chose their families. Correct choice" and "It's nice to see the Forced Unionism fees will no longer be required as a condition for those folks to keep their jobs" and "MSEA Local 1989 Union leadership - six figure salaries. Yikes. The salaried union organizers make more than who they represent. I'm sure they want mandatory dues so THEY get a paycheck" and ""Free riders? I'm not a free rider, I DON'T WANT A RIDE!! I can take care of myself thank you. If I don't do my job well, I will be fired, as it should be. I don't need a Union FORCING me to pay them for NOTHING! Jeez dude, you don't get it do you? The union makes nothing possible for me, I'm not a sheep" and finally, "Now, every single state employee should join the union. Remember as Labor Day approaches the 8 hour work day, the 40 hour work week, child labor laws, overtime pay, minimum wage, call-back rules, hazardous duty pay…you enjoy all because union workers fought and died for your rights."[143]

"Ramona Welton, the president of MSEA-SEIU Local 1989, said the concessions on mandatory fees were necessary to get better wages for workers," and claimed "she believed the union has "emerged stronger and more united" but the Director of MSEA, Rod Hiltz, resigned, explaining that 7 staff reps (approximately ¼ of total staff) were slated to be laid off, but with his resignation and resultant salary savings, there would be fewer losing their jobs.[144]

Complicating the situation even more was a report from a Maine staff rep that "during negotiations two years before, LePage made the same offer. The negotiating team, made of reps from each of the 4 units, voted not to inform the members of that offer so 3 units voted to accept the alternate offer of 1% per year, unaware of the 3% per year with loss of fair share offer. However, 1 unit, Operations & Maintenance, learned of the 3%...offer & so the members voted to reject the 1%. . . offer."

Some unions are beginning to focus on internal organizing, and to spread the Best Practices through on-line postings to other locals and members. The CWA, as one example, posted this new clip on-line as part of its CWA Strong:

"CWA Local 6139 in Beaumont, Tex. has been focusing on internal organizing for the past five+ years. The local represents bargained-for employees of AT&T Core, AT&T Mobility, and Helena Laboratories. At the two AT&T Mobility stores represented by the local, workers are 95% organized with only two non-members. Local President Marc LaRousse's strategy at the Mobility stores includes pointing out to new employees key articles in their contract that make their work lives better than they would be in unorganized workplaces.

"At Helena Labs, where 140 employees make and distribute medical supplies, the challenges are different. The turnover there is continual, so the local's best opportunity to sign up new members is at the new employee orientations occurring about once a month. Vice President Calvin Carter and District Steward Robert Millard talk with new employees for 15 minutes then ask them to join, and the vast majority say yes. This group has recently grown to 70% organized and now has six stewards."[145]

---

[143] Scott Thistle. "State workers drop mandatory union fees in favor of more pay." *Portland Press Herald*. August 31, 2017
[144] Steve Mistler. "Union Director Resigns, A Day After Maine State Employees Accept New Contract." Maine Public Radio.
[145] CWA Communications news@cwa-union.org July 6, 2017

Another CWA local, in Columbus, OH, with contracts at a wide range of public agencies, from Ohio State University to Pickaway County Jobs and Family Service, also has started an internal organizing program. The local represents about 2,200 workers, and about 500 workers were agency fee payers, just under 25 percent of total membership. Local 4501 President Kevin Kee said, "When our local and activists heard about efforts to limit the membership of our union, especially the *Friedrichs* case, it was a real wake up call." According to McKee:

> "We knew we had to do something. We started with a one-week organizing blitz in October 2014, dedicated to reducing the number of agency fee payers. Organizers from District 4 joined with Local 4501 members in making house calls and onsite visits. We exceeded our goal and actually got 158 new members to sign up that week. It was amazing, and it was the start of our program to make our local CWA Strong.
>
> Building on that first week, we knew we needed to continue to organize. We created spreadsheets and databases of every building at OSU where we represent workers, plus members' work shifts and contact information. It's a lot of work, but it's what is needed to reach out to members and engage in the one-on-one contact that is so effective.
>
> Over the last six weeks, we've stepped up our program, meeting with members and workers at worksites three times a week. With the help of a District 4 organizer, we've signed up another 167 people in just six weeks.
>
> We've learned that it's important to highlight what we're doing, if we've won a member benefit or made other gains, or when we're bargaining a new contract and know that the way to build strength at the bargaining table is by building strength in our numbers. That way, agency fee payers and non-members see what the union is doing. They recognize the value and say they need to sign up.
>
> We know that it's important to reach out to everyone. Sometimes, a university worker or county worker hasn't signed up just due to the fact that no one has reached out to them. That's all changed now. Our steady progress is becoming tremendous success."[146]

Another public sector union, anticipating a decision that will eliminate agency fee clauses, also proposed an internal organizing project. IBEW Local 1245 in Vacaville, CA, started a comprehensive Volunteer Organizing Committee (VOC) project.

> "IBEW 1245's Organizers have teamed up with our Public Sector Business Representatives and developed a fight back game plan for our 2,500 public sector members. IBEW 1245 Organizer Eileen Purcell laid out the twelve-month campaign, which aims to re-sign 100% of our current membership and build leadership and capacity. 'Volunteer Organizing Committees (VOCs) are the heartbeat of our campaign,' Purcell said. 'Our goal is to build leadership and capacity before, during and after the Supreme Court decision, so that we can re-sign our current membership as voluntary dues-paying members and reap the benefits of a fully engaged membership, no matter the

---

[146] CWA Communications news@cwa-union.org

threats we face. . . .' Connie Bibbs, a 31-year member of IBEW 1245, the Unit Chair at Sacramento Regional Transit (SRT) and a leader of the VOC reported on the progress that her committee has made so far. . . 'We held our first VOC meeting on July 17 at the Union Hall. On August 16, we held our second meeting. We doubled in size,' said Bibbs. 'Within 36 days, we'd held 98 face-to-face, 1-on-1 conversations, grown our VOC to 25 members, identified a point person in every one of our SRT departments, and collected 89 updated contact information cards (44% of our membership). Our next VOC meeting is September 20. We are ready to roll!'"[147]

So here is the challenge that workers confront: get organized and win these protections, and their enforcement, in a union contract or lament the loss as the federal government collapses. At the risk of preaching, workers have to act aggressively in their own interests, as workers have historically done in the US since the Philadelphia carpenters struck for the 10-hour day in 1791. Other unions are doing it today. How about you?

NOW GO DO IT

1. **Have a union workshop on organizing to explain the importance of building bargaining power for you and your co-workers.**
2. **Have a discussion with your members to find out any objections or opposition to organizing.**
3. **Set up organizing targets, stress the importance in involving every member, and emphasize the "selfish" goals: more money in your pockets.**
4. **Do a couple of workshops to teach organizing strategies and skills.**
5. **Create some organizing materials—leaflets about the benefits you have, videos of members talking about the value of a union, apps about organizing.**
6. **If you are in an open shop state, start an internal organizing campaign to sign up your free riders.**
7. **Develop a list on new organizing targets--non-union units for your employer or competitors or important contractors.**
8. **Look around in your community and among your friends. If any of them doesn't have a union, talk with them about organizing.**

---

[147] Eileen Purcell. "Defending Our House Against Anti-Union Attacks." *BeyondChron*. September 5, 2017.

CHAPTER 7--POLITICAL ACTION

"Just because you do not take an interest in politics doesn't mean politics won't take an interest in you."
- Pericles, 430 BC

For union members, the 2016 presidential election was possibly the worst in history. The two major parties ran millionaires against each other--for the Democrats, a Wall Street favorite and former member of the Wal-Mart Board of Directors, with a Vice-Presidential candidate who talked, as Governor of Virginia in 2006, about "Virginia's right-to-work law, a law I strongly support." For the Republicans—well, Donald Trump, who campaigned as a Working Class Hero, with a Vice-Presidential candidate who is "'100 percent right to work,'" according to Brett Voorhies, president of the Indiana State AFL-CIO.

It was the workers' votes that Trump wanted. "In a campaign speech in a small Pennsylvania town in June 2016, Trump noted that Pittsburgh's steel had built much of the nation. But 'our workers' loyalty was repaid with betrayal,' he said. 'Our politicians have aggressively pursued a policy of globalization—moving our jobs, our wealth and our factories to Mexico and overseas. Globalization has made the financial elite who donate to politicians very wealthy. But it has left millions of our workers with nothing but poverty and heartache.'"[148]

This is what union members, and displaced union members, wanted to hear!

In 2016, Hillary Clinton won union households by only 51 to 43 percent, with 6 percent of voters opting for a third-party, either the Libertarian or the Green Party (a large enough number that some Clinton loyalists blame Jill Stein of the Green Party for Clinton's loss). In the previous 7 presidential elections, the Democrat won union households by an average margin of 22 percent. As a family comparison, in 1992, Bill Clinton got votes 55 percent of union households, against George Bush who got 24 per cent and H. Ross Perot who got 21 percent.

Trump increased his party's share of union votes by 3 percent over Mitt Romney's total in 2012 while Hillary Clinton's share dropped by 10 percent, a 13-point shift since the 2012 election.

If 43 percent of union members voted for Donald Trump, despite the enormous support from most national officers, clearly there is such a disconnect that "staying the course" is not an option. A huge percentage of union members are unhappy and angry, both with the direction of their country and with the direction from their union officers. "The shift of Obama voters to President Trump was estimated at between 6.7 million and 9.2 million, heavily concentrated in the Midwest and other Rust Belt states. The biggest common denominator among Obama and Trump is their view that the political system is corrupt and does not work for people like them."[149]

---

[148] Theo Anderson." Move Over, Corporate Democrats. A New Wave of Left Populists is on the Rise." *In These Times*. January 4, 2017
[149] Perry L. Weed. "Democrats need to do more to win in the age of Trump." *Baltimore Sun*. September 27, 2017.

Discussing the recall election of Governor Scott Walker of Wisconsin in 2012, Kevin Drum noted that "in 2004, 38% of union members and 40% of voters in union households voted for George Bush. In 2008, 39% of union members and 38% of voters in union households voted for John McCain. In 2010, 37% of voters in union households nationwide voted for Republicans, and that's also the share of the union vote that Walker got in Wisconsin that year. . .' 'The union members, they'll support us,' said presidential candidate Mitt Romney during a campaign stop in Texas. 'Without the union members who support our campaign and support conservative principles — we wouldn't have Scott Walker win in Wisconsin if that weren't the case.'"[150]

The negative numbers for the union supporters of the Democratic Party are reflected not just in the high percentage of union votes for Donald Trump but, more generally, in the statistic than Hillary Clinton got 5 million fewer votes than Obama did in 2012 and 9.5 million fewer votes than he got in 2008. That's a lot of people staying home, despite the strong support for the Clinton campaign—and huge expenditures of PAC funds—from union officers.

"Now union leaders face a huge, embarrassing question: Why, after unions spent more than $100 million to defeat Donald J. Trump, did Mrs. Clinton win only narrowly among voters from union households, 51 percent to 43 percent, according to exit polls? In a further indication that union leaders were not on the same wavelength as the working-class whites who tipped the election to Mr. Trump, Mrs. Clinton lost among union households in Ohio, 49 percent to 44 percent."[151]

What's wrong with this picture?

Everything, and not just Donald Trump.

In 2017, the blame game for the Clinton debacle spread far and wide: third-parties, Russia, Bernie Sanders, misogyny and even Susan Sarandon but these are all FAKE NEWS. Like the boiling frog, this decline of support for the established Democratic Party by union members has been going on for years. Hoping to drain the swamp, union members voted in large numbers for George Wallace in 1968, for Ronald Reagan in 1980 and 1984, for Ross Perot in 1992, for the Contract with America in 1994, for Ralph Nader in 2000, for a Democratic surge in 2006, for the "outsider" candidate, Barack Obama in 2008, and for Bernie Sanders and Trump in 2016.

Even with the 2017 wins in the governor's races in Virginia and New Jersey, and in the controversial Alabama senatorial election, the Democrats are failing at the state level. In 2008, Democrats controlled both chambers of 27 state legislatures and had split control over 8 other

---

[150] Kevin Drum. "Did Unions Members Turn Against Unions on Tuesday?" *Mother Jones*. June 7, 2012.
[151] Steven Greenhouse. "What Unions Got Wrong About Trump." *New York Times*. November 26, 2016.

state legislatures, while Republicans controlled both chambers of 14 state legislatures. By 2015, the number of Democratically-controlled state legislators had plummeted to 11 while the Republicans' number increased to 30 state legislatures. By 2017, Democrats went from holding over 55 percent of all state legislative seats to just 43 percent in the last six years.

"A state trifecta control is when one political party holds majorities in both chambers of a state legislator and the governorship. According to the National Conference of State Legislatures, in early 2009 Democrats had 17 state trifectas while Republicans had nine. However, by 2016 the number of state trifectas the Democrats held was reduced to six: California, Delaware, Hawaii, Oregon, Rhode Island, and Washington State. Republicans now have 24, plus Nebraska's unicameral legislature and governorship. . . . In the 2016 election, Republicans were able to add four more state governments — Iowa, Kentucky, Missouri, and New Hampshire — to their list of state trifectas."[152] The Democrats control the governor's mansion and both legislative chambers in just six states, the lowest since the Civil War, and Democrats no longer control a single chamber in the entire South and in Kentucky, Republicans got control of the state House of Representatives for the first time in nearly 100 years.

"In 2009, according to the National Council of State Legislatures, there were 4,082 Democrats serving in state legislatures and 3,223 Republicans. By 2016, the numbers had reversed: 3,135 Democrats and 4,177 Republicans."[153]

"The prominent Democratic Party pollster Stan Greenberg concluded that the Democrats suffer a working-class problem. It started with the Great Recession and President Obama's bailout of wrong-doing financial elites while many, many Americans lost jobs, income, savings and homes. It was compounded by the Democrats' pursuit of multinational trade agreements and their favoring of Wall street and corporate interests."[154]

"Those who continue defending and advocating for the failed status quo are ignoring the people who suffer the most from its policies, as [Susan] Sarandon pointed out to [Chris]Hayes, . . Many voters turned to Trump out of desperation for an alternative to Clinton, who embodied the status quo. However, given the fact that the Democratic establishment has not taken responsibility for their failure in the election, pro-Clinton advocates will remain in their cyclical loop of praising those in power, rather than challenging them to take meaningful actions for working class, middle class, and low-income Americans."[155]

The political landscape has tilted so far away from us that Marco Rubio was identified by *The New York Times* as "a longtime champion of the working class," when he proclaimed about the tax bill "If you look at all the benefits that are flowing" to multinational corporations, "it was important to be able to go back to do more for working families. . . .Otherwise, the message what

---

[152] Michael Gryboski. "Why Democrats Have Lost Badly Since Barack Obama's Election." *The Christian Post*. November 18, 2016.
[153] Thomas B. Edsall. "Donald Trump Is the Godfather of a Democratic Renaissance." *New York Times*. August 10. 2017.
[154] Perry L. Weed. "Democrats need to do more to win in the age of Trump." *Baltimore Sun*. September 27, 2017.
[155] Michael Sainato. "Susan Sarandon Incites Meltdown of Clinton Supporters With Question About Corruption." *Observer*. February 16, 2017.

it has been for 25 years from both parties—that is, when push comes to shove, we want your vote but we are not that concerned about the working class."[156]

A great case study, a microcosm, of the Trump movement among unionized workers, was previewed in the industrial community of Dundalk, MD, where I worked for 15 years. The area grew up around the mammoth Sparrows Point steel mill, which employed 31,000 workers at the height in 1959 on a space of 2,100 acres of mills. Over the years, and for many controversial reasons, the company, and the American steel industry as a whole, declined until the mill closed permanently in August, 2012, leaving 2,100 active workers stranded. Prior to the final closure, the company had declared bankruptcy in 2002, dumped all pensions on The Pension Benefit Guaranty Corporation (PBGC) and cut off health care for all retirees (an estimated 14,300 just in Dundalk). It was a slow and very painful death, administered from 2003-2005 by Wilbur Ross, who was rewarded for his social engineering with the appointment as Secretary of Commerce in the Trump administration.

For decades, for generations, these steelworkers participated in the Servicing Model of Unionism, trusting their local officers and district staff to solve problems. Membership meetings were poorly attended and most of the members did not participate in any way in the activities of the union. When the mill closed, they thought it was a failure of "The Union"—which should have done something, anything, to keep it open—and of the politicians who did not lift a finger to keep the place open.

The anger of the workers was flammable and in 2014, in state and local elections, they tossed out every Democrat—"drained the swamp"-- for Republican candidates who were as surprised as Donald Trump at winning. Maryland, a state where Democratic Party registration holds a 2-1 margin over Republican registration, even elected a Republican governor. In social media, displaced workers boasted on Facebook about getting even—*"Alright people i did my duty and voted the basterds out. Everybody get out and vote, especially Brown and Kamenetz , vote them all out , never forget what happened to us. Make your voice heard and get maybe a little payback to those who hurt us. Never forget !!!!!!!!!!!!!!!"*

Another displaced worker posted *So many people lost their jobs . Do the politicians care " Hell no"!! They've got there's baby ... Screw you !!!*

At the monthly meeting of retired steelworkers, which usually attracts more than 250 old-timers every month, support for Trump—among the white retirees--in the fall of 2016 was open and loud.

---

[156] Sheryl Gay Stolberg. "Senator Found an Opening in Tight Negotiations." *New York Times*. December 16. 2017.

And Trump kept up his appeals, even after he was elected. In a speech on Missouri on November 29, 2017, he proclaimed: "Actually, the rich people don't like me, which is sort of interesting and that's fine. . . But really, the people that like me best are those people, the workers. They're the people I understand best. Those are the ones I grew up with. Those are the people I worked on construction sites with."

Talk about Fake News!

* * * * * * * * * * * * * * * * * * *

The Republicans have used their power in a consistent way: to directly attack unions, passing open shop laws and laws restricting public employee bargaining. Candidates at state and local levels who run on an openly anti-union platform are being elected (or re-elected in the case of Governor Scott Walker).

The right-wing National Review gloated:" Voters also rewarded right-to-work proponents. Wisconsin and West Virginia recently passed right-to-work laws. At the time, unions warned legislators would pay a price for crossing them. They didn't. Not a single Wisconsin legislator who voted for right-to-work lost. Instead Republicans gained seats. Every legislator who voted for the (vetoed) Missouri right-to-work bill won too. In West Virginia, Republicans lost a seat in the state house while gaining four in the state senate. What had been a narrow 18–16 senate majority has ballooned to 22-12. Voters returned almost everyone who voted for right-to-work."[157]

"In the presidential race, Trump early in his campaign endorsed the open shop. 'We've had great support from [union] workers, the people that work, the real workers, but I love the right to work,' Trump said. 'I like it better because it is lower. It is better for the people. You are not paying the big fees to the unions. The unions get big fees. A lot of people don't realize they have to pay a lot of fees. I am talking about the workers. They have to pay big fees to the union. I like it because it gives great flexibility to the people. It gives great flexibility to the companies.'"[158]

Another anti-union candidate who won, Bruce Rauner of Illinois, cited President Ronald Reagan's blow to the Air Traffic Controllers (PATCO) as inspiration for how to deal with the state's unionized workforce. Reagan permanently replaced 11,000 striking federal employees in 1981, in one of the most dramatic government acts of union-busting in U.S. history. "'I may have to take a strike and shut down the government for a few weeks and kind

---

[157] James Sherk. "Banner Night for right to Work." *National Review*. November 11, 2016.
[158] Sean Higgins. "Trump: 'I like right-to-work better'." Washington Examiner. February 23, 2016.

of redo everybody's contract,' Rauner told an audience of enthusiastic Republicans in a video that surfaced during his 2014 campaign. 'I will do it proudly.' His administration has also floated the possibility of deploying the Illinois National Guard to replace strikers."[159]

Even before Trump was inaugurated, political reporting from the states was like watching a horror show. Governor Matt Bevin of Kentucky signed on January 5, 2017, the state's new open shop law and proposed eliminating the prevailing wage law that is so important to building trades unions. He also supported new legislation to ban strikes by public sector workers. Kentucky AFL-CIO President Bill Londrigan called the right-to-work and prevailing wage measures "some of the most extreme anti-workers bills in the nation today, slashing wages and silencing working people across the Commonwealth"[160]

When Eric Greitens ran for governor of Missouri, a main page on his campaign web site proclaimed: "Missouri has lost countless good-paying jobs to more business friendly states, As Governor, I'll fight to improve Missouri's job climate with 'Right to Work legislation.'" As soon as he was inaugurated, Greitens pushed the open shop bill through the Republican-controlled state legislature and signed the bill into law on February 8, 2017 after only two weeks in office, making Missouri the 28th state to go open shop. "By signing the bill, Greitens fulfilled one of his major campaign pledges. Labor unions spent heavily to defeat Greitens last year based largely on his promise to enact right-to-work legislation. He also mentioned the idea in his State of the State address last month [January, 2017], saying that 'Missouri has to become a right-to-work state. . . Dan Mehan, president and CEO of the Missouri Chamber of Commerce and Industry, called the bill signing a 'historic accomplishment.'"

"Missouri AFL-CIO President Mike Louis and Missouri NAACP President Rod Chapel filed a petition for referendum with the secretary of state's office. They have until Aug. 28 — the day the right-to-work measure is scheduled to go into effect — to collect enough signatures to place the law on the ballot. If they succeed, right to work won't take effect until Missourians get the chance to have their say in 2018."[161]

And succeed they did!

By October, 2017, unions, working with the Sierra Club and Missouri Jobs for Justice in a coalition called We Are Missouri, got more than 310,000 signatures on petitions to call a

---

[159] Chris Brooks. "Illinois State Workers Authorize Strike Against Governor Who Invoked Legacy of PATCO." Labor Notes. February 23, 2017.
[160] Reid Wilson. "KY Governor signs Right-to-Work Law." *The Hill*. January 8, 2017
[161] Jason Hancock. "Gov. Eric Greitens signs Missouri right-to-work bill, but unions file referendum to overturn it." *Kansas City Star*. February 6, 2017.

referendum on the legislation, forcing a vote in November, 2018, and blocking implementation of the open shop law until this referendum. This campaign was a "flashback" to 1978 when unions blocked the attempt to put the open shop into the state constitution.[162]

In Iowa, the pattern from Wisconsin was duplicated when the state legislature passed on February 15, 2017, a severe new House File 291, with loud but ineffectual opposition.

> "Under the legislation, most public-sector union contract negotiations will be limited only to base wages. Unions will be banned from negotiating with their employers over issues such as health insurance, evaluation procedures, staff reduction and leaves of absence for political purposes. However, public safety workers such as police and firefighters will have a broader list of issues to be considered in contract talks. All unions will be barred from having union dues deducted from public employees' paychecks and unions would need to be recertified prior to every contract negotiation. The legislation also changes the arbitration process when contract talks reach an impasse. Currently, the union and management would make their best offers and an independent arbitrator would be required to choose the most reasonable of the two. The legislation requires an arbitrator to consider the employer's ability to finance any wage increase. It also puts a cap on how much an arbitrator can raise wages. The wage increase could not exceed whichever is lower: 3 percent or a percent equal to the cost of living increase outlined in the consumer price index."[163]

In Iowa, as in Missouri, unions were forced to take on a destructive challenge and responded with new organizing skills and energy. In the first round of union certification elections in September, 2017, all 13 locals of the Iowa State Education Association (ISEA) voted "by extraordinary margins" to keep the union. In a second round of balloting in October, 2017, only four out of 220 ISEA locals dropped representation, and new energies reverberated through the membership and building delegates.[164]

While the campaigns in Missouri and Iowa were impressive, union are still playing a zero-sum game, defending conditions that we already had, preventing a loss rather than gaining new benefits. Another defensive "victory" for unions was in Virginia, where a ballot issue to include the open shop in the state constitution was defeated—but open shop is still the law in Virginia.

Democratic candidates are not as strong about expanding unionism, reflecting the political feebleness of unions at the state level. When candidates fill out union questionnaires, there should be one central issue: "What will you do to help the union movement grow?" In open shop states, the first question must be "What will you do to repeal the open shop law and to implement full collective bargaining rights for public workers?" Too often, union officers feel intimidated or weakened and do not make these kinds of demands.

---

[162] Judy Ancel. "310,567 Signatures Block 'Right to Work.'" *Labor Notes*. October, 2017.
[163] William Petroski and Brianne Pfannenstiel. "Iowa House, Senate approve sweeping collective bargaining changes." *Des Moines Register*. February 16, 2017.
[164] Dave Kamper. "Iowans Stick to the Union." *Labor Notes*. December, 2017.

There also needs to be consequences for broken promises. In Baltimore City mayor's race in 2016, for example, machine Democrat candidate Catherine Pugh, who always had union backing for previous races, promised to support the kinda sorta $15 minimum wage (and it is "kinda sorta" because it would not reach $15 until 2022 and would not cover all workers in the city). After she was elected, and the City Council passed the bill, she vetoed it, later claiming that she "did not swear on a Bible" that she would sign the legislation.

What consequences did she face, not just for backing off an important issue but for flat out lying about it? A small demonstration but no open withdrawal of union support. In fact, one union political officer, offering a Teflon jacket, publicly advised her on how she could have made a better excuse for her actions. Sad!!

Another more hidden anti-union campaign, described in Chapter 4, can be seen in the dramatic shift, supported by both Democratic and Republican governors, to let corporations escape paying the taxes that fund public services—like the wages of public employees--as well as the public institutions, like schools, infrastructure and public transportation. An unfortunately typical tax giveaway is the campaign from more than 500 cities to lure the new Amazon corporate headquarters, a variation of "developer welfare." The state of California, for example, initially offered $300 million but the state legislature increased the offer to $1 billion. New Jersey Governor Chris Christie offered $ 3 billion. From 2005 to 2014, Amazon received at least $613 million in local government subsidies to build warehouses, according to a 2016 report by the Institute for Local Self-Reliance. The group, which pushes for local resources to be dedicated to community development, also found that Amazon received an additional $147 million in subsidies for its data centers.[165]

These are all dollars that are shifted from public treasury to private pockets, increasing social inequality and making public sector bargaining much more difficult. For public sector negotiations, the Leverage Diagram becomes more complicated as the allocation of tax dollars increasingly goes to private investment companies, which buy the public bonds that provide money—minus huge interest—for capital projects, like school construction or water systems. These investors are ruthless and demand to be the first paid, even if public services and public worker conditions suffer. A similar situation on a national level came when countries like Greece or Chile were so far in debt that they virtually declared bankruptcy—except the international lenders would not allow it. As public-sector negotiations continue, the union must look at the whole financial picture of the public agency, and not just accept the management's excuses that there is no money.

* * * * * * * * * * * * * * * * * * * *

As union members evaluate their loyalty to the Democratic Party, it is worth knowing the history. The unions have been closely allied with the Democratic Party since 1936, when union officers made a strong commitment to the re-election of President Franklin D. Roosevelt. Initially, however, "CIO head John L. Lewis and Amalgamated Clothing Workers of America

---

[165] Leanne Garfield. "These Cities and States Are Throwing Hundreds of Millions at Amazon." *Business Insider*. November 27, 2017.

General President Sidney Hillman formed Labor's Non-Partisan League (LNPL) to mobilize working-class support for Roosevelt. Forming an independent organization allowed Lewis and Hillman to co-ordinate support for the Democrats without being forced to subordinate labor goals by bringing their organization under the aegis of the Democratic Party."[166]

After the huge Democratic Party win in 1936, the Roosevelt administration supported The National Labor Relations Act (NLRA), which for the first time on a national level—with significant exceptions for domestic, agricultural and public sector workers—proclaimed that "It is declared to be the policy of the United States . . . protecting the exercise by workers of full freedom of association, self- organization, and designation of representatives of their own choosing, for the purpose of negotiating the terms and conditions of their employment or other mutual aid or protection."

While many historians focus on the Act itself, and on the Roosevelt administration, it is important to recognize that unionism in the mid-1930's was an energetic and potentially revolutionary social movement that used sit-down strikes—where workers seized their factories --as leverage. The 1936-37 UAW sit-down strike in Flint, MI is the most famous one but in 1936, there were 48 sit-down strikes and in 1937, there were 477 sit-down strikes, involving 400,000 workers. Fearing a similar movement in the steel industry, US Steel voluntarily signed an agreement with the Steelworkers Organizing Committee (SWOC) in March, the Supreme Court ratified the NLRA in April, 1937 and the union movement began to find a "normal" place in the US economy and social structure. This shift was one point in a long decline during a period when unionism shifted from a social movement to a "special interest" lobbying group.

A closer look at this language, and in the administration of the NLRA, shows that the whole purpose of the Act was to channel the tumultuous union movement into a state-regulated structure, one of the first steps to establishing the Servicing Model. The administration of the law, and amendments like the Taft-Hartley Act and Landrum-Griffin, which restricted unionism, have dramatically weakened unionism.[167]

As one example, and to prove the point that when workers find a powerful way to organize, the employers make it illegal, on February 27, 1939, the Supreme Court decided in the case of *NLRB v. Fansteel Metallurgical Corp.* that sit-down-strikes were illegal, creating a national precedent for the no-strike clauses in virtually every union contract.

The unbreakable bond between the officers of major unions and the Democratic Party was sealed, even though John L. Lewis left the coalition before the 1940 election to support Republican candidate Wendall Wilkie. The support of the government, and of the Democratic Party, began to drop away, starting with the passage of the Taft-Hartley Act in 1947. One critical election came in 1948, at a time when the CIO was collapsing after Red Scare attacks. Unhappy

---

[166] Robert E. Cook. "TWO-HANDED FIGHTING: RHETORICAL APPROACHES TO THE PRESIDENTIAL ELECTION OF 1936 IN THE ADVANCE AND AMERICAN FEDERATIONIST." December, 2005.
[167] Joseph McCartin. "As Long as There Survives: Contemplating the Wagner Act after Eighty Years." *Labor-Studies in Working-Class History*. May, 2017.

with President Harry Truman, a number of union officers supported the Progressive Party campaign of former Vice-President Henry Wallace but the fear of a Republican victory, intensified by the lesser-of-two evils campaign strategy, meant Wallace received only 2.4 percent of the popular vote.

Because of the loss of political power, there have been very few laws passed in the past 70 years that explicitly supported the growth in numbers of unionism. One attempt at labor law improvement came in 1977, when the unions endorsed Jimmy Carter, even though Carter had supported Georgia's open shop law, originally passed in 1947. Michael Harrington even claimed that "if Carter wins, he will owe his victory in considerable measure to the working class politically organized as a class. . . . Resistance to unionization skyrocketed. A decade earlier, many companies had acquiesced in the face of unionization elections, declining to challenge the results 42 percent of the time. By 1978, firms were contesting 92 percent of such elections. Companies also resorted to playing dirty more often, firing pro-union employees at rates that far exceeded those of previous decades."[168]

The AFL-CIO proposed minimal improvements in the NLRA that would have increased penalties for unfair labor practices during organizing campaigns, but the opponents filibustered for five weeks and the Democrats—with no push from Carter—refused to invoke cloture and the legislation died. "The proposed labor law revision was directed largely at what supporters called a clear-cut pattern of denial by a few companies of their employees' right to organize. Pointing to the well-known example of the textile manufacturer J. P. Stevens, advocates of the bill argued that some employers had found it cheaper to defy the law than to allow even the chance of union organization. The death of the bill was the most stinging humiliation for the unions in a Congress that was marked by a string of defeats for labor. "[169]

A final attempt to expand union power was The Employee Free Choice Act, first introduced into Congress in February, 2007, which would have allowed card check, would have required that an employer begins negotiating with a union with a view to reaching a contract within 90 days, and if not, the two sides would be referred to compulsory mediation and to binding arbitration. Importantly, the law would have increased penalties on employers who punished workers for being involved in a union campaign by assessing an employer triple damages. After repeated failures to get the legislation passed, union officers hoped that the election of Barack Obama in 2008 would be a turning point.

Strong union support for Obama should have brought an improvement but, as Thomas Frank stated, "Labor, they worked real hard to get him elected, as they always do for Democrats, but a little bit harder in 2008. It was a great year. They come to him, 'This is our one request. This is our one piece of legislation that we really want to get passed.' No, not interested. Not interested. Let it die. . . . Obama had supported it as a senator, had voted for it as a senator. But

---

[168] Paul Heideman. "It's Their Party." *Jacobin*. February 4, 2016.
[169] "Filibuster Kills Labor Law 'Reform' Bill." *CQ Almanac*. 1978

as president, no, he didn't lift a finger for it. . . . stronger unions was not something Wall Street wanted."[170]

"There was this 'Hey we just got you elected and now you owe us' way of thinking about the world," said Ken Jacobs, chair of the Labor Center at the University of California, Berkeley. "Obama at some point said, 'You'll have to make me do it,' and that was not taken seriously to the degree it needed to be. To do something that will significantly shift power relations in the U.S. cannot be done quietly as a negotiated deal, it cannot happen without a loud clamor for it. It needs to be big enough and presented in ways people can understand."[171]

And the unions happily supported Obama for re-election in 2012.

There have been several new laws passed to expand union membership. In a case of history from the 1930's repeating itself, more than 210,000 postal workers struck for eight days in 1970 after a Congressional decision to raise the wages of postal workers by only 4%, at the same time as Congress raised its own pay by 41%. After calling out the National Guard, President Richard Nixon proposed the reorganization of the US Postal System and provided collective bargaining rights for four major unions, expanding union membership by hundreds of thousands.

In February, 2011, the Federal Labor Relations Authority ruled that the 41,000 workers at the Transportation Security Administration (TSA), founded after 9/11 attacks, could have collective bargaining rights, fulfilling a promise made by Obama during the 2008 campaign. The representation election was won by the American Federation of Government Employees (AFGE) which now claims 19,000 members at TSA. The administration of George W. Bush had originally declared federal airport security screeners would not be allowed to unionize so as not to "complicate" the war on terrorism.

One Op Ed in December, 2017, asserted that there is a renewed effort by Democrats to strengthen legislation to expand unionism. "Senate Democrats have indicated a willingness to propose bold solutions for restoring a balance of power between workers and corporations as a part of their 'Better Deal.' Their labor bill would ban 'right to work' provisions, which permit workers who are represented by a union to pay nothing for that representation; restore workers' right to engage in solidarity activism; and expand the National Labor Relations Act to cover public-sector as well as private-sector workers and create financial penalties to bosses who willfully break the law."[172]

It is not clear which Democrats have proposed this legislation, or which ones would support it, but clearly it had zero chance of passing Congress and appeared to be simply another

---

[170] "Obama Chose Wall St. Over Main St. The Real Network (interview with Paul Jay) December 27, 2017.
[171] Rachel M. Cohen. "How the Labor Movement is Thinking Ahead to a Post-Trump World." *The Intercept*. January 21, 2018.
[172] Moshe Z. Marvit and Shaun Richman. "American Workers Need Better Job Protections." *New York Times*. December 28, 2017.

bait-and-switch. Legislators can count, and know the legislation will never pass, but want to tap into union political action funds for the 2018 elections.

* * * * * * * * * * * * * * * * * * *

These are the only major laws to expand collective bargaining rights and increase union membership since 1937. Other laws, like OSHA and ERISA or federal minimum wage, protect all workers but do not explicitly increase union membership. It can be argued—consistent with the Servicing Model of Life-- that there has been a gradual shift among workers to dependence upon the federal government, away from movement for self-help and organizing that got these laws passed in the first place. When non-union workers encounter a problem at work, their reaction is to try to sue or to find a government agency to step in and make the situation right, rather than planning to organize into a union. For private sector union members, calling upon the Labor Board for help is almost a reflex action, especially if officers are getting guidance from union lawyers.

A major strategic decision to consider is how much power unions should exert for laws that could benefit all workers instead of laws that will help the union movement grow. Historically, many unions, especially the craft unions that have private pension and health and welfare funds, have used participation in those funds to build loyalty among the members. In the early 1800's, when union membership was still considered to be a criminal act, the unions established sickness and accident funds and death benefits. When the Social Security Act was being considered in 1935, some unions opposed it because it would spread a union benefit to all workers, reducing the importance of the union.

Supporting a minimum wage increase has the same challenge—if someone wants a wage increase, let them join a union, right? The direction of the Fight For $15 reflects this contradiction since it encourages many union members and supporters to demonstrate outside fast food restaurants, and tries to get local legislation passed, but does not try to get the workers to join the union.

The industry is a complicated one, with franchises and irregular hours and a stereotypical workforce of teenagers and students, living with their parents, who prefer part-time work and don't need benefits like health insurance. The shift in the economy has transformed this workforce into working adults, who need fulltime work with a living wage and benefits. The Fight For $15--even if the raises are spread out over the next 5 years—did provoke some cities to raise the minimum wage but the campaign was not an organizing campaign, since getting union representation was not part of the strategy. The fast food workers became, in effect, spectators, passively watching a media show outside their workplaces that they hope will benefit them. The direction of the Fight For $15 is especially a questionable strategy since the SEIU, according to LM-2 reports, spent more than $15 million in 2016 to support the movement, after it had laid off a substantial part of the international organizing staff.

Another episode in this discussion is political support for legislation that would establish "just cause" legal protections for all workers, advocating the law because it would prevent some of the sexual harassment or the irregularities of the gig economy. "A just-cause rule would give workers greater freedom to say no to requests that have nothing to do with their jobs, like 'Can you pick up my dry cleaning?' or 'Come up to my hotel room.' It would provide workers more power to resist unfair schedule changes, like an attempt to cancel a preapproved vacation. . . . Just cause — a legal right to your job — should be an essential part of any package of reforms to restore workplace dignity and fairness."[173]

Obviously, a "just cause" clause is a fundamental part of every union contract and a major issue in every new organizing campaign, a clear difference between working union and working non-union. If legislation were to pass (in your dreams, right?) it would eliminate one of our best organizing issues. In the real world, this not even a topic for debate. If unions still represented almost 40 percent of the workforce, with political muscle to match, the movement might have some possibilities. Not in 2018, however.

"Recent decades have witnessed a collapse in confidence in government and recurrent populist uprisings in America. . . . On Election Day, 2016, fully 69% of voters were either dissatisfied with or angry at government. . . . a systematic and recurring reaction by an upset and frustrated electorate. It was the manifestation of years, in fact of decades, of rising levels of discontent by a growing number of disaffected voters. And into the midst of that discontent entered two immensely unpopular candidates for president."[174]

This anger does not inevitably lead to action by angry workers. In fact, many of our co-workers don't pay much attention to political issues since our union contracts protect us from a lot of the dangerous changes. When a co-worker has a workers' compensation case and can't collect, or your owner declares bankruptcy and tosses away your pensions, or when a plant closes and suddenly we have no health insurance—then our friends are suddenly aware of how tilted the political system is but, at this crisis point, it is usually too late. As a reflection of this passivity, only about 55% of voting age citizens cast ballots in 2016, the lowest turnout in a presidential election since 1996, when 53.5% of voting-age citizens turned out.

In the controversial Alabama senatorial election in December, 2017, when Democratic Doug Jones defeated Republican Roy Moore, voter turnout was only 25 percent of registered voters. And Jones stated right after the election that "of course," he will consider voting with Republicans on certain issues once he is sworn into the upper chamber.

* * * * * * * * * * * * * * * * * * * *

As the relentless anti-union political movement grinds on, candidates at both state and national levels openly run as union busters and get elected, especially as the economy so drastically changes. They use their power to directly attack unions, passing open shop laws and legislation restricting public employee bargaining. Neither of the two major parties makes any effort to support the expansion of unionism or the protection of non-union workers. The challenge is not just the election of Donald Trump but the long decline of the union movement's political power.

---

[173] Moshe Z. Marvit and Shaun Richman. "American Workers Need Better Job Protections." *New York Times*. December 28, 2017.
[174] Todd Eberly. "We Know 'What Happened.'" *The Baltimore Sun*. October 5, 2017.

So what can we do? There are two critical challenges: first, the procedures involved in the Servicing Model of Politics [Appendix 3], which lets the officers make political endorsements, or deals, for "the Union" and spend the member's PAC funds with virtually no participation from those members. The members are expected to dutifully show up to vote—spending about 20 minutes every couple of years on "political action"—or maybe even to volunteer to be boots on the ground for a candidate. Very few officers poll their members so that "the union" can speak for a large number of members and the debates that should have been sponsored in every local, considering the election returns in 2016, never happened.

The union movement must become a movement again, politically independent and strong, and not just another "special interest" lobbying group, so that our issues and numbers become important in this complicated world.

Secondly, the current political approach is the tortured relationship with the Democratic Party, which—union officers tell their members—is "the party of labor." We have allowed the officers and candidates of the Democratic Party to turn against us, while they still sop up millions of dollars in campaign contributions, even as a significant percentage of union members vote against Democrats.

How, or whether, the officers, who control the PAC funds, will respond to this discontent is not clear yet. As one organizer remarked to me: "Yeah, after their Pres Lily [Eskelsen García of the NEA] early endorsed Hillary, following AFT's undemocratic lead. How do you think we should be pursuing the issue of changing how unions make their political decisions internally? We need to inject a dose of democracy into it? I think nearly all the unions would have endorsed Bernie with a full discussion and a fair referendum, like CWA did. OK, maybe not the building trades, but maybe some of them too."

One CWA member wrote to me: "On another note, I'm sure you saw CWA endorsed Bernie. Lots of people are angry. In the past, we have always waited until the primaries were completed then put our support behind the democrat who received the nomination. Lots of

people are saying Hillary is going to get the nomination and then screw us because we didn't support her initially. I don't know what the answer is Bill, but I do know what we've been doing is not working. I was very excited to see CWA send each of us a survey on specific issues along with the candidates positions on those issues (dem and rep). It was nice to hear staunch republicans in the workplace say how disgusted they were with their candidates position on things aside from guns and god. We need to spoon feed this stuff to the membership nonstop and I think the survey was a great idea. It's generated smart discussions. Workers are going to get screwed regardless of when they decide to endorse a candidate."

One historian remarked that Hillary Clinton's support for unionism was "transparently shallow and instrumental. This became clear when Clinton campaign chief John Podesta's emails leaked. The transcripts included exchanges such as when, in response to a request that Clinton take a stand against right-to-work laws, her political director Amanda Renteria demurred, saying 'I like staying more at platitudes about what unions have done for workers.'"[175]

Ironically, in the opening months of the Democratic and Republican primaries for the 2016 presidential election, Hillary Clinton's campaign strategy promoted Trump as the Republican contender in the general election, thinking—and hoping--that Trump's racism and sexism would make him easier to beat than a more mainstream candidate, like Marco Rubio.

While the Democratic Party expects loyalty and financial support from the unions, the reality is different, as Jennifer Klein described it.

"So Donald Trump, the multi-millionaire celebrity businessman, won the 2016 Presidential election. Liberals have sought to blame a resentful class politics. Yet what about their own relationship to class and labor politics and its complicity? No official of organized labor had a prime-time billing at the Democratic National Convention—despite the fact that at least a fifth of the delegates were labor people. . .. AFL-CIO President Richard Trumka and Mary Kay Henry, President of the Service Employees Union (SEIU), each gave short afternoon speeches. . . Compared with evening speeches that ran from fifteen to forty minutes a piece, the two major labor leaders were each granted two minutes. And neither exactly used their time to vigorously defend unionism."[176]

One commentator called the union support for Hillary Clinton a reflection of "the Stockholm Syndrome, "feelings of trust or affection felt in certain cases of kidnapping or hostage-taking by a victim towards a captor."

"In the 2016 Democratic primary, US labor unions overwhelmingly endorsed Hilary Clinton and invested millions of dollars in ensuring her nomination. Few eyebrows were raised, despite Clinton's questionable record and platform towards workers. Why not? Organized labor's support for political enemies of unions and workers is so common it has become expected. The labor movement suffers from a political Stockholm syndrome, embracing the very politicians who attack them. The embrace of Hillary Clinton, openly hostile to the current campaigns of some of the very unions who endorsed her, exposes the self-destructive absurdity of the situation. An intervention is needed or unions will be hard-pressed to reverse their current decline if they do not shake the Stockholm syndrome and adopt different political strategies.

---

[175] Barry Eidlin. "Election 2016: Labor, Politics and the Imperative of Organization." *Labor Studies Journal*. September, 2017.
[176] Jennifer Klein. "Talking About Inequality" without Talking about Power: Organized Labor and the 2016 U.S. Presidential election." *Labor Studies Journal*. September, 2017.

Endorsing less-than-friendly politicians is nothing new for US unions but the widespread endorsement of Hilary Clinton is a *reductio ad absurdum* of the practice. Clinton, in addition to maintaining a general anti-labor slant, has opposed the principal campaigns of some of the very unions endorsing her. . . how did the United Food and Commercial Workers (UFCW), who dedicated years and millions of dollars to organizing Walmart workers, respond to Clinton's seven-year tenure on the Walmart Board of Directors, during which she uttered nary a word on the corporation's infamous anti-unionism? Also with an enthusiastic endorsement."[177]

As part of support for The Employee Rights Act, modeled on state laws that enforced an open shop and required regular recertification votes, anti-union consultant Richard Berman gloated after the election: "For Big Labor, it was a harsh reminder that union membership's political preferences are far less monolithic than union leadership's. Employees rejected their union representatives' staunch support for Hillary Clinton, demonstrating that they can act in their own self-interest — even when it diverges from the union elite's. . . . But any challenge to union leadership's tight grip on power is always shouted down from the top."[178]

* * * * * * * * * * * * * * * * * * *

> @ctown2thdoc @TetrologyGaming @Apple @Twitter 7:31 PM - 9 Feb 2017
> this country doesn't need normal. Normal wasn't working

The argument from many union officials that "things will never be the same" is unintentionally positive: the so-called *status quo* has been moving in the wrong direction for more than 70 years, so any upheaval provides the opportunity to revive and to reshape the political movement. The Koch Brothers, are relentless and smart—when one campaign fails, as measured by election results, they re-evaluate their strategy and reorganize, in ways that union officers have not done. Yes, they have millions to pour into these campaigns, but unions spend tens of millions of dollars in every electoral cycle and what do we have to show for it?

The political shift that the Trump campaign exposed is also an opportunity to break away from old habits that have been harmful to us. One fundamental question for union members today is: support the white *macho* campaigns of the Republicans, stay with the Democratic Party and hope that it will be miraculously transformed into a "labor party" or work to bring a third party into power.

There are opinions from both supporters and opponents about sticking with the Democratic Party. One side insists that the Democratic Party is the only game in town. The newspaper *In These Times*, supported financially by officers of several major unions, is probably

---

[177] Andrew Tillet-Saks. "Labor's Stockholm Syndrome: Why Unions Must Stop Backing Anti-Labor Candidates in the Primaries." Truth Out. August 3, 2016.
[178] Richard Berman. February Union support for Donald Trump gives Big Labor chance to catch up." *Washington Times*. February 6, 2017.

the loudest voice for not getting too radical. Daniel Moraff argued that a third-party simply cannot generate the votes that a Democrat can and therefore

"Primary campaigns provide real opportunities for leftists to compete and win. Campaigns off the party line, in all but the rarest cases, do not. . . . The Democratic Party establishment is vulnerable—to primary challenges. The recent record of third party competition in partisan races in the United States is one of unmitigated failure at nearly every level. Thanks to the Sanders campaign, the case for left challenges within the Democratic Party has never been stronger. . . . Thousands of local left-to-progressive formations are springing up or growing, from DSA to Indivisible to the Working Families Party. Many of them will, in 2018, have the ability to draft and run candidates for office. They will have two choices: one, run a candidate in the Democratic primary, with a far lower win number than the general, no spoiler issue, no third-party stigma, and a chance to win—joining the long list of leftists elected as Democrats. Two, go the independent route and hope that where hundreds upon hundreds of left third-party challengers have failed, they will succeed. . . . The 2018 election cycle is an enormous opportunity. Choosing this moment to adopt electoral strategies that have virtually no prospect of winning elections in 2018 would squander the opportunity at hand. "[179]

As an echo, not a choice, Jacob Swenson-Lengel minimizes the success of the Tea Party since 2009, asserting that it "only ever represented a tiny faction of Americans," and that the demonstrations in early 2017 indicate "already there are signs that we're organizing at a scale that dwarfs the Tea Party." While he boldly proclaims the creation of "a new American majority," his strategy is conservative: "First, we should aim to take over the Democratic Party wholesale and make it into a vehicle for the working class. In addition to electing real progressives to office, this means building a greatly expanded coalition of active voters and a genuinely progressive policy platform. . . . Where possible and without compromising progressive principles, we should aim to peel off sections of the Republican coalition to join our side."[180]

"The anger and fear provoked by the advent of President Trump have led to explosive growth for progressive advocacy groups determined to oppose the president's agenda and, crucially, to elect Democrats to local office — groups like Indivisible, Run for Something, Emerge America and Color of Change (through its PAC). At the end of 2017, the 'resistance' within the Democratic Party has become more ambitious, and foreshadows a once-in-a-generation reorganization of the American left that could dictate the tactics and ideology of the Democratic Party for years to come. If the newcomers prevail, they could pull the party further to the left, leading it to embrace policy positions like those advocated by Mr. Sanders, including single-payer health care and free tuition at public colleges. . . .there are three dozen

---

[179] Daniel Moraff. "Want to Elect Socialists? Run Them in Democratic Primaries." *In These Times*. March 7, 2017.
[180] Jacob Swenson-Lengel. "Forget Building Our Own Tea Party. The Left Can Win So Much More. *In These Times*. March 10, 2017.

outfits that have started or reconfigured themselves since the election to try to harness the surge in anti-Trump activism."[181]

"The 2016 Democratic primaries also heightened the contradictions between those who have accepted the neoliberal world order as inevitable versus those who want to build a new social democratic alternative to neoliberalism, and the Trump administration will certainly intensify these differences. So far, the AFL-CIO has not proven to be a good forum in which to hold these debates. It has taken a hands-off approach and tried to sweep the contradictions under the table. But these contradictions persist nonetheless. They show up in debates over who to support for DNC chair and in the growth of informal caucuses of the left, right, and center. The decline of the collective bargaining regime and the growth of these tendencies based on very different visions of the role of labor in the age of Trump can only accelerate the demise of a Federation model that was crafted in different times for different purposes."[182]

Advocates for working-from-within include Naomi Klein and, of course, Bernie Sanders and the misnamed group, Our Revolution. The group *RootsAction* posted a plea on November 13: "'The Democratic Party can either continue to serve its corporate donors, or it can build and sustain coalitions that can actually win,' says Naomi Klein, the author of *No Is Not Enough* and *This Changes Everything*. She adds: 'The stakes have never been scarier -- but we also haven't seen this much potential for a truly transformative progressive politics in decades. If Democrats want to be a part of it, they should give this report a full and honest airing and act on its findings.'"

Sanders posted a statement on November 11, 2017 on *Politico* headlined "How to Fix the Democratic Party": "At a time when we have a Republican president and Republican Party whose leadership and agenda are strongly opposed by the American people, now is the time for real change. It is critical that we come together and reform the Democratic Party. When we do that, we will win local, state and national elections and transform our country."

This conservatism is unfortunate because Sanders stimulated a significant movement in early 2016, even provoking the rare disagreement among international union officers. Presidents of at least five unions openly supported the Sanders campaign and made some noises about challenging the power of the Democratic committee at the convention. Unfortunately, as

---

[181] Kenneth P. Vogel. "*The 'Resistance,' Raising Big Money, Upends Liberal Politics.*" New York Times. October 5, 2017.
[182] Mark Dudzic. "The AFL-CIO "On The Beach." *New Labor Forum*. June 1, 2017.

Sanders personally collapsed and endorsed Clinton, so did this movement but even this endorsement found opposition from union members.

As a strong support for the Democratic Party, The United Association of Journeymen and Apprentices of the Plumbing and Pipefitting Industry (UA) endorsed former Labor Secretary Tom Perez in the in the race for chairman of the Democratic National Committee. "Tom Perez believes in American workers and that in the future of the Democratic Party will once again be the champion of the middle class," Mark McManus, the union's president, announced. "Tom understands the problems that working men and women face each and every day, which is why he has worked so hard to level the playing field, provide greater access to education and skills training and crack down on employers who cheat workers out of their wages. These are the top priorities for the UA and for the entire country. I'm confident that Tom will provide the leadership to reach and empower working class Americans as chair of the DNC."

> **Donald J. Trump** ✔ @realDonaldTrump Sad to watch Bernie Sanders abandon his revolution. We welcome all voters who want to fix our rigged system and bring back our jobs. 11:04 PM - Jul 25, 2016

The other side says break: Nick Branna, who was National Political Outreach Coordinator on Bernie Sanders' presidential campaign, and a founding member of Our Revolution, left this organization shortly after it was founded.

"Because Bernie, I think, like the rest of us, understands that reforming the Democratic Party is something that is becoming increasingly bleak. . .And I think it's become very clear that Progressives don't have the leverage with the party in order to be able to enact any of the things or to make them take us seriously, as well--. . . it's something that we all espoused and agreed upon on Bernie's campaign, and that's the idea that the politicians themselves, not necessarily the DNC being hooked onto corporate money, that's certainly true, but the politicians, Democratic politicians themselves being hooked on the corporate lobbyist and Wall Street billionaire money. And that was never even contested in the party, you know? And that to me... for it not to be even on the table, you know, tells me that the party is really not going to be the institution through which we can effect Progressive change."[183]

At the top of the union movement, one positive sign was the Resolution 2, called "An Independent Political Voice," passed at the national AFL-CIO convention in October, 2017, which stated:

"For decades, the political system has failed working people. Acting on behalf of corporations and the rich and powerful, the political system has been taking away, one after another, the pillars that support working people's right to good jobs and secure

---
[183] Interview with Paul Jay on The Real News Network. March 10, 2017.

benefits. Our opponents know that unions are the last bulwark for working people, and so set as their top priority taking away the freedom of working people to negotiate for a better life. Moreover, politicians restrict voting rights, legalize unlimited contributions and gerrymander in order to entrench themselves and preserve the corporate status quo.

Against this, we have one choice. We must give working people greater political power by speaking with an unquestionably independent political voice, backed by a unified labor movement. The time has passed when we can passively settle for the lesser of two evils. We must aggressively foster a new generation of elected representatives who share our aspirations for growing the labor movement and meeting the challenges of globalization and the emerging 21st century workplace."

Only time will tell if this resolution was simply posturing or if union officers are serious about affiliating with a new political party or—more radically—reviving unionism as a political movement, reaching out to non-union voters on workplace issues.

As a sign of the continued revolving door between the AFL-CIO and the Democratic Party, however, when the officers started a new Mobilization Hub in February, 2018, to focus on the 2018 elections and beyond, they hired Julie Greene directly from the Democratic National Committee. Greene, who formerly worked at the AFL-CIO as a Deputy Political Director, proclaimed that "the Hub will use its resources to back union-supportive candidates for the congressional midterms. Beyond 2018, it will recruit and educate union members interested in running for office at all levels of government." As a reflection of a change in structure, "The AFL-CIO started forming the Hub in 2017 during the beginning of its still on-going reorganization, which has included layoffs and department consolidation. Roughly 75 staffers will report to Greene but that number can grow as the federation expands, an AFL-CIO representative told Bloomberg Law. The Hub is the largest department at the AFL-CIO."[184]

The appointment was met with skepticism from at least one union member, who posted: "Ahhhhhh!!! Okay, the big federation is so tied to the Dem Party but now, given the shady doings during the 2016 primaries and the insidious control of the Clintonistas--the AFL-CIO has chosen to ignore the millions of workers who decidedly wanted a socialist (even a luke-warm variety) alternative (no pun intended Socialist Alternative folks). Rank and file union members must demand a change at the top. Gompers was a socialist before he was co-opted. With this hiring, the AFL-CIO demonstrates that it is planning for another defeat in 2018. And then blame it on 'white workers'. Hey, it's not the shade of skin or religion or heritage--its the political ideology."

* * * * * * * * * * * * * * * * * * *

Another positive sign is that the officers of the AFL-CIO are looking at one alternative: running union members for office. Wrapped in loyalty to the structure of the Democratic Party, political "action" invariably meant using the union's resources—financial and boot-on-the-ground—for whatever candidate survived the Democratic Party primary election. At the AFL-CIO National Convention meeting in St. Louis in October, 2017, a resolution "Encouraging

---

[184] Jaclyn Diaz. AFL-CIO Gears Up for Midterms With New Political Office." Bloomberg Law. January 24, 2018.

Union Members to Run for Local Public Office," submitted by the Committee on State and Local Labor Councils and Community Partnerships and the AFL-CIO Executive Council. . . .Charles Wowkanech, president of the New Jersey State AFL-CIO, spoke glowingly of a program in his state aimed specifically at helping union and pro-labor candidates run for elected office, strengthening the political mechanism by which progressive legislation can pass. . The New Jersey Labor Candidates Program has been effective: Over the past 20 years, 919 union members have been elected to public office in the state, ..." [185]

At the same time, campaign schools have been exclusively supporting the Democratic Party.

Maryland State and DC AFL-CIO "Taste of Emerge" (4/5/2017)
Exclusively for registered Democratic women in Maryland:
This one-day training includes workshops designed to show you how to get a head start on your political aspirations and help you determine the
next steps you need to take in becoming an effective leader in your community, whether or not you run for office.
Pre-registration is required

On-line, union members posted interesting comments about the political conflict.

"Breaking the power of right-wing populism is a long-range task. In the short term, a critical marker of progressive strength will be the capacity to limit Trump to one term. Defeating Trump in 2020 is the single most important step to set back Trumpism. We need to be clear-eyed and laser focused on this objective. This is our 2020Vision. As long as Trumpism controls all three branches of government, we are on the defensive and no progress can be made on winning progressive reforms. Defensive fights -hanging on to what we have already won – are likely to be bitter and protracted."

The consideration of recruiting our members to run for office is a positive and proactive step because it replaces several generations of failed policies. The ultimate in Servicing Model political action is "call your Congressperson" or other elected representatives or sign an on-line petition (and donate to the organization). Or demonstrate outside their office, exhibiting the preference for endless protesting rather than taking power. It is ridiculous to carry on this "political action" because elected representatives are, like most of us, unswayable—that is, we hold certain truths to be so self-evident that we will not change, no matter how many calls or letters we get. Union members will better to emulate the Tea Party and run our own candidates.

Union members in office is obviously not always the Perfect Solution. In New Jersey, a bizarre confrontation took place in the fall of 2017 between the New Jersey Education Association (NJEA) and a union member elected to public office. NJEA's super PAC, Garden

---

[185] Eric A. Gordon. "More union members needed in public office, says AFL-CIO." *People's World*. October 23, 2017.

State Forward, has raised $1.1 million and spent about $521,000, according to IRS documents obtained by the AP, with a significant amount used to support a Republican candidate, Fran Grenier, who was running against state Senate President Steve Sweeney—the former union president of an Ironworkers local. With a membership of more than 200,000, the NJEA attacked on Sweeney "as a Christie crony and faux Democrat," for his program to force state workers to increase pension and health insurance payments, growing from a major problem of the underfunded state pension plan. Obviously the unions as a whole have allowed the situation to slide for many years and now find a solution in endorsing a candidate who supported Donald Trump! The one positive remark was that "everybody knew if you crossed the NJEA, they were going to come after you."[186]

Another repeated failure is simply making a strong moral statement in favor of a position with no political muscle to back it up, either with supporters already in office or ready to run. Single Payer is a perfect example—John Conyers kept introducing it, unions and central labor councils keep passing resolutions in favor of it, laying out all of the advantages. Are we any closer to having it a reality than in November, 1945 when President Harry Truman first proposed it? Worse, after President Obama officially announced that "single payer is off the table" in the discussions about national health care, which eventually became The (Un)affordable Health Care Act, union members obediently fell into line to support his re-election. And then began passing resolutions proclaiming the value, and importance, of Single Payer! Sad!

Finally, it is clear that, for a large number of people, the political issues will be solved by Someone Else and they can just sit home and watch it on the evening news. There is talk of Impeachment—that is, depending upon Congress to eliminate President Trump— or some judicial action, like prosecution for obstruction of justice. In every one of these, a passive attitude leaps out. We should know that expecting Congress to clean itself up, or that judges who are appointed by the same party structure, will correct it, is a fantasy. The swamp will not drain itself.

One component of changing our political approach is expanding beyond supporting candidates to creating ballot issues, as referendums, so that we get out on our terms, and then demanding that any candidate who wants union financial support campaign on our issues.

In Massachusetts, for example, the Massachusetts Nurses Association is out collecting signatures for a referendum in November, 2018, demanding a nurse-to-patient ratio that will apply to every health care institution. Of course, the union can bargain for this ratio in the hospitals it represents but this is a way of bringing an issue which is a union issue, a family issue

---

[186] Brent Johnson. "Why does N.J.'s top teachers union hate Senate President Steve Sweeney so much?" New Jersey Advance Media. September 16, 2017.

and a public health issue and making it central to the election period. Just the process of collecting signatures—and being pushed out of public parking lots—brings great union visibility and makes our union issue a public issue.

In South Dakota, for the November, 2016, the Laborers Union got a ballot referendum: "''Notwithstanding any other provisions of law, an organization, corporate or nonprofit, has the right to charge a fee for any service provided by the organization." As one news source reported "The product of the nearly 15,000 signatures, the ballot initiative reflects the concerns of South Dakotans who want to see Right to Work repealed and labor rights restored. The results have left many labor proponents applauding the efforts of labor groups in the state."[187] Obviously, passage would have repealed the state open shop law and, of course, the ruling class went berserk. The referendum failed but it was proactive union campaign that should be carried on in every open shop state.

* * * * * * * * * * * * * * * * * *

Unlike union political strategists, the Koch Brothers know how to adjust a losing strategy. They started a political action movement, Americans for Prosperity (AFP) in 2003, after an internal dispute among the multi-millionaires began to shift political discussions. AFP was closely allied with the Tea Party, funded by the tobacco industry, and was the latest of a succession of right-wing groups that began in 1994 with Newt Gingrinch's Contract With America.

"When the Koch Brothers gathered their supporters in 2010 to look at what they considered to be a failed strategy, they looked at state and local elections, which would be coming up immediately. Their success is shown in the numbers, which show the Republican Party to be stronger than it has been in 80 years! The numbers tell the tale: in Congress, the Democrats lost 69 seats (and their majority), in the US Senate, they lost nine seats (and their majority). Democrats had 10 fewer governorships in 2016 than they did in 2008, reducing their total number of state executives from 28 to 18. Republicans now control 31 governor's mansions, their highest total since 1999 and three shy of their high-water mark since the turn of the 20th Century," reported Politico last year."[188]

They were originally focused on electing a Republican as president and tried to raise $ 88 million with the goal of defeating President Obama for a second term. The donations by the Koch Brothers "surged from $7 million in 2007 to $40 million in 2010 to $122 million in 2012. In the 2012 election cycle, AFP was a key component of the Kochs' estimated $400 million political network, receiving large portions of its money from the Kochs' Freedom Partners and the Koch-linked American Encore (previously known as the Center to Protect Patient Rights) and Donors Trust. But after the Kochs failed to unseat President Obama in 2012, they decided to augment their ad wars with a much more significant multi-state ground game that includes a large and sophisticated voter dataset, micro-targeting, and a cadre of boots on the ground. 'One

---

[187] PR News Channel. Pierre, SD. August 31, 2016.
[188] Tim Alberta and Eliana Johnson. "Exclusive: In Koch World 'Realignment,' Less National Politics." National Review. May 16, 2016.

of the biggest things we learned and shared with our investors is that we can't parachute in the last couple months of an election cycle with a bunch of activists into a new state and expect to have the same impact that President Obama had by staying in those states for four years and being invested in the community,' Marc Short, the former president of the Kochs' Freedom Partners operation, told the *Washington Post* last year."[189]

The strategy of the right-wing has been to challenge in primary elections any reluctant supporter, creating a climate of fear among incumbents who might be tempted to oppose the extremist policies. "[No] Congressional Republicans have consistently resisted Mr. Trump or his agenda even though his approval ratings are already historically low for a new president. . . .More important, people who identify with the party overwhelmingly view him favorably. In districts represented by Republicans, fully 87 percent of registered Republicans view Mr. Trump favorably." [190]

"Democratic lawmakers in at least 30 U.S. states are either unveiling or highlighting legislation this week aimed at President Trump's working-class voters, in a nationwide coordinated rebuttal to the agenda the president will outline in his first joint address to Congress on Feb. 28. . . .It's an attempt to form the legislative spine of a state-level resistance to Trump's policies, Nick Rathod, executive director of State Innovation Exchange Action (SiX), which is overseeing the initiative, told USA TODAY. The timing creates a juxtaposition between Democratic economic security prescriptions for workers, such as raising the minimum wage and paid family leave, and Trump tax reform and federal budget policies that, Democrats say, are at odds with his populist campaign oath to prioritize 'forgotten' Americans from the factory floors of the Rust Belt to the sawmills of the Mountain West. 'If you work hard and play by the rules in this country, you should be paid enough to live on, to care for your family, and to retire securely,' Rathod said in an interview previewing the legislative 'Week of Action' that will spotlight more than 130 bills in states from Oklahoma to Alaska.

"Yet Democrats are also years behind their Republican counterparts who've successfully coordinated a state-level strategy to enact laws including voter ID requirements, income-tax reductions and anti-union 'right-to-work" laws.

"For instance, since Florida approved 'Stand Your Ground' gun legislation in 2005, more than 24 more states have adopted similar laws with the help of the National Rifle Association and ALEC, which provided legislative templates and media strategy. 'The left has really never had anything like that until now,' said Rathod. ALEC took in about $9 million in 2015, while SiX's budget is about a quarter of that. 'We're starting to chip away and we need to supercharge that with resources,' he said." [191]

---

[189] Matea Gold. Billionaire Koch brothers' network takes cue from Obama's playbook." *Washington Post.* July 29, 2015.
[190] Kyle Dropp and Brendan Nyhan. "Republicans Have One Big Incentive to Stick With Trump." *New York Times.* January 31, 2017.
[191] Heidi M Przybyla. "Democratic legislators in 30 states to rebut Trump." *USA Today.* February 27, 2017.

Another political model we could follow is the controversial Steve Bannon, who was leading the effort to shake up the Republican leadership. Originally with financial backing from the New York hedge fund billionaire Robert Mercer and his daughter Rebekah, Bannon, featured on a *Time Magazine* cover as "The Great Manipulator," clearly is determined to transform the political system, knocking off incumbent Republicans who are too cautious or too closely aligned with national Republican leadership. One report claims Bannon originally tried to create "a parallel structure" in the Trump Administration and then began to build one nationally, recruiting candidates like Erik Prince, the founder of the security contractor Blackwater, and Ann LePage, the wife of Maine governor, Paul LePage.[192]

Even though Bannon was disavowed by the Mercers, his strategies are still being followed by other right-wing groups that will target any elected official and will challenge them in a primary election from an extreme point of view. There is already a growing number of Republican incumbents at the state and national level who have announced that they will not run for re-election rather than face intense primary challenges.

Another successful political operation is the National Rifle Association (NRA) which threatens elected officials with challenges if they do not strongly oppose all gun control legislation. After the massacre in Las Vegas, the whimpers about expanded gun control were immediately met with threats from the NRA, which has developed the kind of political power that unions should have, given our numbers. In the past, there have been threats "to NRA" reluctant legislators—that is, to recruit and support opponents to incumbents, a threat that most Congresspeople take seriously, if gun control legislation is not stifled.

And when was the last time we heard of the threat "to AFL-CIO" an official who posed anti-union legislation? Or that union officers are recruiting primary challengers for incumbent Democrats?

The anti-union/anti-worker political organization have been enormously successful, unfortunately, over the past 50 years and certainly since the announcement of *Citizens United* in 2010. Yes, these campaigns are funded by the very wealthy but that will always be a fact of life. Unions will never have the disposable money to venture into such expensive campaigns, but we have to stop making excuses and create alternate campaigns.

As Bernie Sanders demonstrated in the Democratic primary, money can be raised, volunteers can be motivated, and new technology—like social media and on-line donations—can support a nationwide campaign. His campaign raised more than **$218 million online from 2.8 million donors so imagine what 15 million union members could do.**

---

[192] Jeremy Peters, Maggie Haberman and Glenn Thrush. "Erik Prince, Blackwater Founder, Weighs Primary Challenge to Wyoming Republican." *New York Times*. October 8, 2017.

One question which is still in progress is the strategic decision of many of the Sanders supporters who are members of Democratic Socialists of America (DSA). The organization, mostly young and radical, had a huge jump in membership during the Sanders campaign and is now trying to calculate a strategy that must answer the same basic question: continue to support the Democratic Party and hope for some relief or support a third party. There is no question that the Sanders campaign changed the dynamic and even made the word "socialist" reputable again so there is tremendous internal discussion within the DSA over remaining or seceding from the Democrats.

In the municipal elections in Sommerville, MA, in November, 2017, as two DSA candidates, Jesse Clingan and Matt McLaughlin, were elected to Somerville's Board of Alderman, hopefully reviving the "sewer socialism" tradition. One report exulted in the fact that voter turnout was "2.5 times greater than the previous municipal vote in 2015"—but turnout in the two alderman races was only 38 percent and 33 percent.[193] The general rule is that about half of the eligible voters are registered so the electoral "movement" still did not rouse significant numbers.

"But last night we saw a very different kind of wave, one that moves us towards a politics that rejects the horrors of Trumpism—and instead embraces a bold progressive vision for the future. Across the country, candidates running from the Left won—and many of them won big. . . These victories are not anomalies or flukes. Rather, they prove that embracing an explicitly socialist politics does not prevent candidates from winning in 2017. If anything, the socialist tag can show voters where candidates stand and what their values are. As Lee Carter explained to *The New Republic*, 'If you're to the left of Barry Goldwater, Republicans are going to call you a socialist anyway, so you may as well just own the label'"[194]

Even better, there is now even a meetup site, Date A Socialist "to get in touch with other Socialist people for love, romance or a hook up or you are a Capitalist and looking to meet friendly Socialist singles for fun and good times."

* * * * * * * * * * * * * * * * * * *

As union members leave the Democratic Party, it is instructional to look at the history of the attempts to found an independent Labor Party because, without a political alternative, workers will do what they did for Hillary Clinton on election day—stay home. This perverse and passive response simply magnifies the strength of the anti-union movement.

And who predicted it? Liddle Donald, who proclaimed in the spring, 2016, "Five, 10 years from now . . .you're going to have a workers party . . .a party of people that haven't had a real wage increase in 18 years. That are angry."[195]

---

[193] Benjamin H. Bradlow. "Somervile's Turn to 'Sewer Socialism.'" Common Wealth. November 18, 2017.

[194] Miles Kampf-Lassen. "Socialists Just Showed the Democratic Party How to Win Across the U.S." *In These Times*. November 8, 2017.

[195] Theo Andersen. "Move Over, Corporate Democrats. A New Wave of Left Populists is on the Rise." *In These Times*. January 4, 2017.

In 1996, after several years of organizing, more than 1,400 delegates met at a convention hall in Cleveland, OH, to establish a Labor Party, a reflection of the changes that had taken place at the top of the AFL-CIO after the election of John Sweeney in 1994. Supported by officers of the Oil, Chemical and Atomic Workers (OCAW), whose survey of International staff, local union officers, and rank-and-file members found that 65% of members agreed that, "Both the Democratic and Republican Parties care more about the interests of big business than they do about working people." The delegates reflected "A growing fury among union members against the Democratic Party's support - via Bill Clinton's version of neoliberalism - for NAFTA, the first of many trade agreements that implemented a globalization program that enriched a global elite at the expense of workers everywhere."

Even Sweeney stated ""I would be the last person, however, to discourage the dedicated brothers and sisters who are organizing the Labor Party movement from taking their best shot and I hope the progress they are making sends a clear signal to a Democratic Party that has moved away from working families just as surely as it has moved away from the old, the young, the disabled, and the poor."

"These unions, by and large, were also organized in a top-down fashion. This meant that participation was mainly limited to officials and staffers, and very few of these unions embraced the more expansive educational and mobilization projects that we were involved with in our core unions."

Over the next 10 years, members of the Labor Party talked about fusion, about education and about mobilization but was never able to stand on its own. "Unfortunately, the labor movement was in such an advanced state of decline at this point that little new support or resources materialized. The lack of resources and the rise of Obamamania, particularly among the state's African Americans, made it impossible for the party to launch a serious candidacy in the 2008 elections, and the party died on the vine."[196]

One problem was the Labor Party's financial dependence upon the top officers of the international unions, who were still loyal to the Democratic Party and strongly opposed running independent candidates. It is once again worth noting that the Bernie Sanders campaign in 2017 raised $ 218 million from 2.8 million donors so new organizations can be financially independent. There is energy, and money, out there.

The discussion on fusion led to the formation of the Working Families Party, financially supported by officers of major unions, especially the SEIU, as another way to prop up workers support for the Democratic Party. While the working Families Party has occasionally run candidates under its own name, it generally offers a third ballot line, occupied by a Democratic candidate like Obama or Andrew Cuomo, so supporters cannot "support" the Democratic Party while voting for its candidates.

---

[196] Derek Seidman.. "What Happened to the Labor Party, An Interview with Mark Dudzic." Jacobin. October, 2015.

As one apologist stated: "It is not realistic to demand that today's labor movement completely disengage itself from its current ties with the Democratic Party. However, the ongoing economic crisis, and the failures of the Obama administration seem to provide an opening to begin to challenge labor to move some of its resources towards long-term projects that would advance a broad working-class program that goes beyond the next election and is geared toward building independent political power for working people. We could launch such a project if labor contributed just 10 percent of the resources and finances that it spent in the 2012 election cycle."[197]

* * * * * * * * * * * * * * * * * *

A major political controversy, not just for the present but for the long-term change in the union movement, is whether the officers of the Democratic Party can manage to control all of the anger and energy that the Trump election has provoked. Many of the union officers and activists who Felt the Bern are frantically trying to block any discussion about independent action. It is disturbing to find some of them who held their noses and voted for Hillary now proclaiming themselves to be Our Revolution.

As demonstrations on so-called "social issues" expand—those that seem to be disconnected from our workplaces and therefore not "union" issues—the leadership of the Democratic Party, and groups affiliated like 350.org, are trying to steer the energies into the 2018 campaign to support Democratic candidates. At the demonstration in Washington, DC, to mark the 100 days of the Trump administration, the featured speakers were Working-Class Heroes like Al Gore and Richard Branson. In Baltimore, the first Women's March in 2017 was wonderful because there were not scheduled speakers—just angry people in a crowd of about 5,000, attacking the political structure. Fast forward one year and it was totally controlled: an elaborate podium in front of City Hall, a parade of Democratic politicians, including the Mayor who vetoed the minimum wage bill and a conservative City Council member who proclaimed himself "a fighting feminist."

These rapid changes once again present union members with both a danger and an opportunity but the future is uncertain because the union movement has been so tied to the two major political parties. Either the two parties will pull back together and the duopoly—"the center"-- will continue or they will splinter, both within themselves and in the general population.

As one union member said to me: "By now, I think most people are realizing that the Republican Party is actually two, and probably three or more, separate parties that are at serious odds with each other. I don't think I am alone in not expecting they will accomplish anything significant with their nominal control of all of the levers of the federal government. That said, I can also identify at least the same number of factions within the Democratic Party that are also at loggerheads with each other. Maybe it's time for some honest splits in the parties, formation of some new parties, followed by some attempts at coalition building. You know, like they do in lots of other democracies around the world."

---

[197] Mark Dudzic & Katherine Isaac. "Labor Party Time? Not Yet." Labor Party. December, 2012.

With the series of elections in 2017—the governor's race in Virginia and New Jersey, and the senate race in Alabama—and with the overwhelming presence of Trump and his administration, the obvious next campaign by the Democrats to create the Blue Tide is ABT—Anyone But Trump--as a way to pressure dissident elements into returning as loyal supporters. Joe Biden? Oprah? C'mon.

This move would reboot the cycle of "the lesser of two evils" that has been going on since 1960, as a Republican presidency brings a more conservative Democrat, driving out new energies, new policies and new political parties. Too bad.

As the SEIU announced its political plans for 2017,

"Two people briefed on the initiative said the overall budget would approach $100 million, though that figure includes a substantial portion of money that the union was already likely to spend in these states [in the Midwest]. Even so, the initiative ensures that the political spending will primarily support outreach to voters on key issues, which would not necessarily have been the case. By comparison, the union spent about $70 million on all federal political activity in 2012 and again in 2016, though the sums rose considerably once spending on local candidates and other nonfederal costs was included. Beyond the Midwest, the initiative will be aimed at a small number of competitive states elsewhere in the country, like Colorado, Florida and Nevada. But the effort comes after the union indicated last year that it was reducing its budget by 30 percent, and some labor officials may question whether a focus on politics, whatever its short-term benefits, will divert the union from solving its more profound challenges."[198]

You cannot solve a problem by not talking about it, right? One bad strategy is not engaging members in political discussions because of the extreme feelings. In 2016, "some longtime leaders in Iowa admitted reluctance to engage members on the subject of the presidential race at all, having calculated such communication as too risky based on isolated instances of vitriolic outbursts, or threats to withdraw membership in response to the union's endorsement of Clinton."[199] There are all kinds of internal divisions in our unions but squashing any open discussions does not make the problem go away, it just starts circulating as destructive rumor and gossip. It would be better to have open debates at union meetings, with members who support the different candidates and other members and their families in the audience asking questions.

As one union officer posted: *"Watch how some of your coworkers get quiet when the conversation about this idiot that we have in Washington. They have strong opinions about everything else but is quiet when this subject comes up. Lol i be*

---

[198] Noam Schreiber. "Service Union Plans Big Push to Turn Midwest Political Tide." *New York Times,* August 24, 2017.

[199] Jennifer Shearer. "Midwest Labor and the Working-Class Vote: The Case of Iowa." *Labor Studies Journal*. September, 2017.

observing can't fool me i know your undercover."

The apparent surprise at the significant percent of union members who voted for Trump shows that we must completely reorganize our political approach. Our unions must be a place for political discussions—hopefully rational and cordial--because our futures, and those of our non-union neighbors, depend on regaining our strength. With our lousy track record over the past 70 years, every option should be up for discussion. In the words of the immortal Steve Bannon, "We need to stop playing footsie with the establishment. They're going to string you along, pat you on your head, and send you on your way."

"The US labor movement, thankfully, is not yet dead and soon unions -- from Locals to Internationals to the AFL-CIO -- will face the recurring question of political strategy. Labor leaders could again choose to support the corporate Democrat out of despair or by convincing themselves that they are just being practical, strategic or politically sophisticated. There will be temptation to choose the path of little struggle and seemingly little risk: the customary endorsement of the most likely Democratic victor. But as any labor organizer worth their weight in salt knows, the easiest path is seldom the right path. Labor must gather our courage and senses and choose a different path. Given the obvious dead end of our current course, we have nothing to lose and everything to gain."[200]

NOW GO DO IT

1. Evaluate your union's political support over the past two election cycles, at both national and local levels? What have you gained?
2. How do your co-workers feel about the political situation today? What do they plan to do about it?
3. What debates has your local sponsored for the members on political issues on specific campaigns?
4. What political discussions have you had at work?
5. Have you ever considered running for office yourself? If not, why not?
6. Take a poll of the members in your department? What are the most important issues for them?
7. Look at your local PAC fund? How is the money distributed?
8. Have you looked at the history of third parties in the US?

---

[200] Andrew Tillet-Saks. "Labor's Stockholm Syndrome: Why Unions Must Stop Backing Anti-Labor Candidates in the Primaries." *Truth Out*. August 3, 2016.

CHAPTER 8-- DEALING WITH DISPLACED MEMBERS

> "How is it that a country as rich as ours is yet pinched for the common necessaries of life? A vigorous and healthy and intellectual population, yet bowed down with gloom and despair . . . with ruin and starvation before their eyes."
> Horace Greeley, *Recollections of a Busy Life*, 1868

One ugly aspect of the new economy, discussed in Appendix 5, is the "displaced" worker, whose industry may be gone, whose lost job may be permanent, whose secure public-sector job may have been subcontracted--all reflections of the dramatically changing economy and political system. The economy is entering such a fast moving and fluid period that the union will be faced with crisis after crisis, providing opportunities as well as dangers.

For decades, layoffs were accepted, even welcomed, as part of our normal work world. Some of the best union contracts had SUB pay, to add to unemployment compensation, so workers' incomes could be almost as high as their regular pay while they were laid off. Benefits like health insurance continued and there were recall rights, enforced by union stewards. We knew that any industrial downturn was only temporary since the economy was cyclical—if it went down, of course it would come back up.

No more.

Jobs lost now can be gone forever and with such a small number of union contracts, displaced workers have no benefits and no guarantees of recall or transfer. The economic and social consequences of these enormous changes are reflected in the large majorities that Trump got from workers in the "rust belt," from industrial workers who live where industry has disappeared. The candidate who promised to Make America Great Again by bringing back these jobs was impossible to resist, almost like tabloid gossip.

The social consequences of these displacements—like opioid addiction, domestic violence and despair leading to suicide—are marked. There is even a class-based addiction to cigarettes, with inevitable mortality problems. "In a 2008 Gallup poll of over 75,000 Americans, the rate of smoking among people making less than $24,000 a year was more than double that of those making $90,000 or more. . . . once the health risks of smoking became widely-known, the better-off began kicking the habit: high-income families decreased their smoking by 62 percent from 1965 to 1999, versus only 9 percent for low-income families."[201] About 158,080 Americans were expected to die from lung cancer in 2016 so the consequences are devastating.

For the many displaced workers who were not union members, the resources—both financial and social—have been small and are being cut. For union members, as the economy changes, the phrase "a member always a member," is more important than ever. Unions need to adjust their strategies and operations to deal with these structural and permanent—as opposed to

---

[201] Keith Humphreys. "Why the wealthy stopped smoking, but the poor didn't." *Washington Post.* January 14, 2015

temporary—layoffs. The economy is entering such a fast moving and fluid period that the union will be faced with crisis after crisis, providing opportunities as well as dangers.

Union officers and members have, of course, major work to do inside the workplace with ongoing negotiations and enforcement of the contract, so a member who is out of sight is often out of mind, especially when the laid off member is no longer paying dues. It is important to hold the union together by representing workers who are out on the street because the laid off members are still union brothers and sisters who should not be deserted. Unionism should not be a movement restricted to the active members and to the workplace but should include all workers, their families and their communities.

Bad times, in fact, can be good times to build unionism so a union needs to get out of its defensive posture—hoping to prevent the worst from happening—and look at this catastrophic economic situation as an organizing or mobilizing opportunity. An energetic effort to bring together active members, laid off members, retirees and all of their families can be a big part of rebuilding unionism.

Workers usually don't turn to their unions as a source of strength in the midst of the collapse because they do not feel that their unions belong to them, or that they are part of a movement. In the past when people were laid off, especially if the layoff was permanent—because of a plant closing, for example--workers and their union drifted apart. The union was a job trust, only helpful if the worker was employed and covered by the union contract. In several industries, like auto and steel, where the contract mandated supplemental pay or a continuation of health insurance if a worker were laid off, there was some contact, if only to make sure that the benefit was protected. In many building trades locals, unemployed members would gather at the hall, looking for a referral but also enjoying the social relations of the trade. The union is part of their lives.

Unions can grow at the very time when it looks like they should be shrinking. Other institutions, like churches, are actually trying to expand by offering services to unemployed workers. One minister—practicing the Organizing Model of Religion--said that offering job counseling to people in the community was an important social service, but that "we just hope they'll decide to stay and worship with us."

The union steward, for example, whose responsibilities used to involve simply processing grievances also must grow—ready or not—into organizing on a much broader scale. As notices begin to circulate about workers being laid off, there may be a transition period. The union needs to use this time to set up information networks, realizing the enormous stress that these workers and their families are suffering.

It is also important that workers understand that they, and their unions, are not the cause of this depression. In the 1930's, historians found that many workers displaced during that Depression internalized their situations, as if each worker, as an individual, had failed, rather than recognizing the failure of a system in which they were unfortunately caught up. An individual worker has not lost a job because of some personal failings or because of some scapegoats, like immigrant workers but is obviously vulnerable to the blame game, as the 2016 election showed.

Members also need to appreciate that it not the union who is laying them off even though the bosses try to shift the blame to us for every plant closure. Over decades, unions have lost any power to control management decisions so the closing of a location, the installation of job-replacing automation, or other harmful decisions cannot be confronted in "normal" ways—through a grievance or a legal challenge filed by union officers and union lawyers. These opposition gestures are usually futile because a structure is in place to protect the power of the boss.

Too often, as the election of Trump reflected, workers who are displaced never consider taking positive and collective actions to protect themselves—fighting a plant closing or stopping the assignment of work to a non-union facility. Workers need to collectively struggle to protect their jobs, using imaginative strategies and leverage diagrams, participating in every action and not simply sitting back and complaining that "The Union" didn't do anything.

One extraordinary example of workers action was the takeover of the Republic Windows and Doors factory in Chicago in 2008 when the owners abruptly closed the factory and tried to lay off the whole work force without even the required 60-day notice. The workers, represented by UE, occupied the factory, initially to get their back pay but the factory was sold, and they returned to work for a new owner, Serious Metals. Three years later, Serious Metals also announced the closing and once again the workers responded dramatically, with support from the Occupy Movement, and created the New Era Windows and Doors Cooperative. In 2016, after a law suit filed by the union, the workers got $295,000 in a bankruptcy settlement.[202]

Your activities may not be so dramatic but here are some basic areas for the union's attention.

- Union reps should be vigilant so that all money owed to your members, even when on layoff, is paid in full. Some contracts require the boss to supplement unemployment payments, to continue health insurance coverage or to subsidize educational programs for defined lengths of time. Make sure that these accounts are regularly checked so that a laid off member is not cheated of a contractual right or stranded without support. Make sure all accrued benefits, like vacation or sick time, are accounted for. Often members who worked regularly paid no attention to these contract clauses, so union officers need to help out.
- Be aware that these benefits are often the first ones attacked if the boss wants to reopen the contract, hoping to split the active members from the ones on layoff. The UAW/GM negotiations over the past 10 years provided an illustration of this trend as supplemental unemployment benefits (SUB) and the JOBS Bank, where laid off workers would be placed at full pay, were immediately—and publicly—under attack. It's a test of union

---

[202] Kari Lydersen. *Revolt on Goose Island: The Chicago Window Factory Takeover and What it Says About the Economic Crisis.*(2009)

solidarity for the active members to keep their laid-off brothers and sisters in mind. If active workers show any inclination to agree to benefit cuts for laid off workers, they should be reminded—principles of solidarity be damned! —that the benefits they protect for other workers today could be their own benefits tomorrow.

- Is a worker facing a layoff eligible for retirement? If so, what financial losses might be involved? What's the pension look like? How about Social Security or Medicare? The local should have both information and contact numbers available to answer these questions.
- A number of employers participate in Employee Assistance Programs (EAP), either in-house or through an outside service provider. The union should try to guarantee that members on layoff can use this EAP because their personal and emotional concerns often take a sharp turn downward if the layoff lengthens. If your contract doesn't guarantee the access of members on layoff to the EAP, demand to negotiate some new language to broaden the coverage. If the boss refuses to pay up for the service, the union should look around for providers and for funds—either from the health insurance carrier, from the union or from public assistance—to get the EAP program started. If all funding sources fall through, the union could negotiate with a private EAP provider for discounted rates, using the potential volume of clients as a lure. In some industries, union members are trained as EAP counselors so the local could provide space at the union hall for these counselors to meet troubled members, even if they cannot pay.
- A big responsibility for the union is trying to keep up the morale of members on layoff, who could otherwise become discouraged. Make sure that you develop a contact network with any members who are laid off so that you can continue to represent them. Members may need help with issues that fall under the union contract, like health insurance coverage, or with public issues, like home foreclosure or utility shutoffs and will appreciate personal contact and won't think "the union" has forgotten them.
- Give each laid off worker a check list of benefits and resources so each one can keep track of all entitlements.
- Setting up a contact network, with members spread out, may compel the union to develop new ways of maintaining contract with its members. Does your local have a web site where the latest information can be posted? Do you have cell phone, text message or e-mail contacts for all of your members? No matter where they are, you need to reach out to them—and they to you? How about a discussion board so that everyone can share information about possible recalls, procedures for collecting unemployment or even new job opportunities in other industries?
- One local set up a separate web site with potential job openings in the area so members could trade information. The members were also encouraged to look out for their fellow workers—if members got jobs, they could refer other members to the same business. After all, networking—an acquired skill in the building trades—is taught at business

schools. The practices can apply to workers in other industries as well, especially if they never thought they would be facing layoffs of such proportions.

- If your workplace closes, the union should demand that all records from the employer be preserved or turned over to the union. Certifications or other job skills records can help workers find another job, but only if they can prove their skills.

- The local that wants to sponsor educational activities can often find support—and sometimes funding—from public agencies to teach classes in resume writing, computer skills or even college credit courses. For some industrial unions, the economic collapse has hastened the inevitable loss of jobs that would eventually fall victim to new technology or plant relocation so members need to realize that some of these jobs are not coming back. Offering classes in new skills—and teaching the classes at the union hall—helps your members and builds that sense of solidarity.

- Laid off members may need financial aid or guidance, so the union should develop a list of community agencies and legal resources to pass along. Each member could face some kind of financial hardship so why make each one reinvent the wheel? The best plan is to have a central contact number—like a hot line--at your union hall so that members can have a one-stop shop for a variety of these personal and financial issues.

- With the wide range of individual savings plans, like 401(k)'s, you should post information about how—or if—members can withdraw money in case of financial emergency. Each plan is different so you need to make sure the information you send along is precise.

- Laid off members will also pick up every rumor of a recall, no matter how farfetched, so be ready to give accurate information. Honesty is a quality that should be part of the gene pool for a local officer but sometimes it's hard to keep repeating bad news—like, "no recall in sight." Raising false hopes for your members doesn't help anyone, and eventually discredits an officer and the union as a whole. Officers should therefore demand regular and accurate information from the employer and should speak as one when passing on information to the members, both active and laid off.

- Be alert to political changes that can affect your laid-off members. In some financial stimulus package/bailouts in the past, there were provisions to subsidize COBRA payments or to eliminate taxes on unemployment compensation payments. Make sure you follow these changes and that the information is immediately passed along to your members. Tell them how to pressure their elected representatives to pay attention to workers, and not just to bankers.

- You could also create special fundraising events for special causes—helping with retirees' health insurance, for example, or special activities for the children of laid off members. You could also ask your local Food Bank—especially if you have been a sponsor and donor in good times—to come to the union hall.

- Also in the category of bad times leading to good things, the union should be alert for new organizing opportunities at your workplace or in your industry. Are there unrepresented office workers or non-supervisory workers who are suffering double? They face a layoff but without the seniority protections of a union contract, a boss who can pick and choose with no recourse for the affected workers. Talk with these unorganized workers about joining the union so their difficulties will be at least modified, even if "Minimize your misery" may not sound like a great organizing leaflet. Unionized workers often forget the additional pressures that non-union workers suffer when the boss, uncontrolled by a union contract, is all-powerful.

- And let's not forget the organizing possibilities if your members suffer a permanent displacement. They will go to work somewhere else and—by the numbers—it will probably be a non-union workplace. If they complained about the union before, now they get to experience first-hand what the world is like without union protection and they may want to get it back. Keeping in touch with all of your displaced members and emphasizing organizing strategies can build the union at the very time it seemed to be in danger. And the more programs your union had in place to help displaced members will spread the value of a union throughout the non-union workplace.

One of the most disturbing aspects of any layoff is the sense of isolation—the exact opposite of solidarity--that displaced union members feel. Cut off from normal social relationships, at work and in the union, and facing extraordinary challenges, these members become depressed and resigned to their apparent fates. They then do stupid things, like voting for Donald Trump. A strong program by the union can change this atmosphere and rebuild the sense of community that provided the basis for unionism in the first place.

An important campaign for the union to carry on is the revival of the union hall as a center for social and political activities. Back in the day, when unionized workers all lived in a community near the workplace and had to scrape by even with a contract, the union hall was a focus of activity that created a sense of solidarity. There were social activities, like holiday parties for children or sports leagues. Thanks to the union and to the interstate highway system, workers are now dispersed far from their workplaces but think about reviving the tradition of coming to the union hall as a habit for all of your members. If your local does not have a decent-sized hall, borrow one from another local or look around for a public building that you can use. The union can be the center of no-cost activities, inviting active, laid off and retired members to activities at the hall. Have guest speakers on current topics—financial planning, changes in unemployment laws, COBRA proposals—and you will be delighted at the turnouts.

- You can sponsor inexpensive social activities—weekly cookouts for laid off members and their families, for example, keep the union community together and at a very low cost. Un a labor movie with free popcorn. Even if laid-off members just show up to play cards or to argue sports or politics, the union is still a part of their lives. Be proactive, as always.
- Even if the finances of your local are tight, figure out a way to get your laid off members together and to keep their spirits up. If you need to raise some money, run a 50/50 raffle among the active members to create a "food fund" for these activities.

- Bring back the tradition of holiday parties to celebrate any occasion—Christmas or Hanukah or the end of Ramadan, 4th of July and, of course, Labor Day. Encourage members to bring their families.
- Negotiate reduced rates for outside activities, like bowling leagues to give your members and their families fun and relief from the worries about the economy.
- Work with local merchants to set up discounts for necessary goods and services. The business community will appreciate any support and your members can certainly use the break.
- How about social activities or trips? Retirees groups are a guide to some of the best programs available.

Many of these activities are reactive—simply trying to hold on and make the best of the bad situation. An organizing union, however, needs to be proactive and aggressive, so layoffs can provide the push for some important political changes. The social "safety net," especially health insurance, which active workers usually take for granted has been severely damaged by politicians who are more interested in bailing out bankers than in really helping workers. Your laid off members now have the time and the sense of urgency to demand political changes—for extended unemployment benefits or health care coverage, for assistance in job retraining classes and for other public assistance.

It is astonishing that some governors were eager to refuse federal assistance for extended unemployment benefits during the 2008 recession or for health insurance under the ACA and figured they could ride out the political storm. Your members can be a foundation for the movement that changes their mind—or changes their chances for re-election. Make 'em pay! Such a campaign—extending unemployment benefits to part-time workers, for example—would re-establish "justice" unionism that represents and defends all workers, tilting the political structure in our favor and creating potential contacts for organizing campaigns in the future.

Get your members together to pressure their elected representatives to pay attention to workers, and not just to corporate executives. The bad news about being laid off is often too much free time. This free time can now profitably be used for visits or vigils to pressure politicians at all levels to respect the needs of workers. political campaigns could include pushing for extended unemployment benefits or higher weekly allotments.

Even the bad times can lead to good things. A major problem for workers on layoff is loss of health insurance. Now can be the time when they get interested in political campaigns for national health insurance. If your union has locals in Canada, use the Canadian single-payer system as an example of what the U.S. needs because Canadian workers, even on layoff, have health coverage.

In many locals, which have never experienced significant layoffs, the status of the laid off members has never been carefully spelled out. Should these laid off members even be considered "members?" If so, should they pay dues? If so, how much? What about voting in local elections or contract ratifications? What about eligibility to run for office?

Unions have survived tough times before so it's up to each of us to make sure that, in the future, workers will look back at this period and see that, yes, unions not only survived then but grew stronger.

NOW GO DO IT

1. **Has your union experienced a significant layoff? What activities do you plan to meet this abrupt challenge?**
2. **What language do you have in your contract to protect members who are laid off?**
3. **What campaigns did your union run to try to block layoffs?**
4. **What programs has your local started to keep in contact with displaced members?**
5. **What other kinds of assistance can your union officers to displaced members?**
6. **Has your union created political campaigns to increase benefits, like unemployment compensation or health care, for displaced workers?**

CHAPTER 9 -- UNION EDUCATION

> "Rarely do we find men who willingly engage in hard, solid thinking.
> There is an almost universal quest for easy answers and half-baked solutions.
> Nothing pains some people more than having to think."
> Martin Luther King

As I do union training and ask participants to introduce themselves, I put out two questions:

"How many of you have read material, or watched a video, or had instruction, in how to improve your job skills?"

Every hand in the room goes up.

"What was the last book you read/video you saw/instruction you got that helps you improve your union skills?"

Silence.

As we look at changing ourselves, and our unions, labor education and training is an important part of the process. To improve your union skills, as well as your enthusiasm, you have to learn about all of the union functions covered in this book. A great buzz word is "autodidact"—it means people who can teach themselves and learn on their own. Since you are reading this book, you are one. It is the first place to start since there is no work rule forbidding you from reading a book, watching a video or sharing your experiences with other members—or with members of another union—as part of the important self-education process described in Chapter 2.

In some areas, there are formal college labor studies classes but the availability is dwindling, a victim of both right-wing political attacks and the failure of union supporters to sign up for classes. Look around your area for a class and, if you can't find one, start down the list in Appendix 6.

You could start your own class by getting a dozen of your co-workers together to talk about union issues and to figure out what changes you can make in your union to respond to the crisis. At the beginning of the 20th century, workers in cigar factories in the Tampa area pooled their money to hire a *lector,* a reader, who would sit on a bench in the factory and read to the workers. Often the workers heard the local newspapers but they also heard classics of literature and even radical political books. As a union collects dues for its efforts, workers paid the *lector*. In one case, a factory owner tried to fire a *lector* and the worker struck until he was reinstated. As historians George Pozzetta and Gary Mormino describe it, "manufacturers replaced [the lectors] with radios, the final symbolic victory of the new industrial order over the cherished artisan privileges that had for so long sustained Tampa's cigar workers."[203] The important point is

---

[203] Rodney Kite-Powell. "Readers Played an Important Role in Cigar Factories." *Tampa Bay Times*. January 30, 2017.

that these workers—most of them immigrants, many of them not speaking English—wanted to have some control over their working conditions and, as importantly, wanted to learn. This is a habit YOU need to acquire if we are going to turn around the decline of the union movement.

Many unions unfortunately do not have Education Directors, responsible for creating classes and for encouraging members to attend. In unions which do offer education programs, they are usually structured so that only a miniscule number of members can attend—short classes at district conferences or summer schools or international conventions to provide some union skills. Some unions do sponsor occasional trainings for a day or two at local union halls, with more membership participation.

Some large unions, using new technology, have expanded their on-line educational programs so that every member, if motivated, can get some basic union education. Unfortunately, in The Servicing Model, members do not demand to know more, and to learn more, so there is not the bottom-up demand for union education.

As a rule, union training classes follow a common formula: how to process a grievance and take it to arbitration, how to cost out a contract (which assumes that the boss is willing to offer any money), how to be a "leader." In some areas of training, this conventional classroom approach is practical since the instructor is often providing knowledge or skills that the members do not already have—filling out LM-2 reports, parliamentary procedure or preparing an arbitration. For most of the classes, like grievance handling/steward training, contract negotiations or political action, however, the participants already have experience--they have seen grievances filed and dealt with union stewards, they have been through contract negotiations as members, and they have certainly had political discussions at work.

The limited number of education programs reflects The Servicing Model of Unionism, in which a limited number of officers "know everything" so they make all the decisions and control the union's resources. The union education classes reflect this structure: one person stands in the front of the room and spreads knowledge, rather than encouraging a discussion. Members in the classes are called "students," rather than "participants," whose union experience is an important part of the class. There is usually no follow-up to see if the union members changed their strategies and practices after having the class. The classes are not education for organization.

There is seldom a discussion about the Big Picture--the real situation of unions today and about what strategies the union officers and members should use to reverse this downward direction. The urgency of increasing membership participation—even with the *Janus* decision looming—is not considered a union priority. In fact, some union officers often fear education programs because members might begin to think—ah, the horror—that they could be better union officers than the incumbents. Union education is simply one more method to reinforce the *status quo* and to maintain this control.

Change is constant, and moving faster, so we have to adjust our educational programs to keep pace. There should be an education program in every union at every level—local, district and national. Each union should commit to every member's participating in a variety of trainings—not only to spread strategies and skills but for members from different areas of the workplace to get to know each other. Familiarity creates solidarity, right? The classes should be on a regular basis—every month for stewards and officers, and regularly for the members. While some members will complain about such a heavy schedule, we are digging ourselves out of a deep hole and need new knowledge and skills—and a better attitude-- to make it happen.

The structure of "education" also needs to be changed so that union education happens every day on the job and involves every member, trading opinions and strategies on how to move the union forward. Talk about how the union won certain benefits or describe how the union lost  some of these benefits through concessionary bargaining. Instead of arguing about the football point spreads, argue about how to build leverage for your next negotiations or how to blunt management's anti-unionism. Every member should be talking to every other member—and also trying to include non-members, as part of the internal organizing program.

With new technologies, sharing classes on-line, or by text or apps, is easy and cheap and appeals to the millennials, whose loyalty to their unions is a major challenge. On-line classes or webinars can also bring together union members who are geographically separated—members of state-wide local or district council, for example. These officers and members deal with the same contract, with the same management but only see each other a couple of times a year and have no method to keep up on best practices. Stewards are often surprised to see that management attacks in their department which appear to be the nasty personality of their local supervisor are actually part of a coordinated state-wide or nationwide attack on the union. The supervisors have been carefully trained because management figures a financial investment in breaking the union will pay off later. As importantly, creating a webinar for a whole state will begin to break down geographical antagonisms between often white rural areas and more diverse urban districts to demonstrate that we have common problems and should find common solutions.

As described in Chapter 3, both the AFL-CIO Economic Power & Growth Hub (https://sites.google.com/a/aflcio.org/training-videos/) and the Labor Research & Action Network (https://lranetwork.org/) have run a series of union instruction classes and both sites emphasize learning Best Practices from a variety of unions. LRAN provides an excellent discussion of strategies for turning new hires into strong union members, illustrated by a combination of research—how do new hires respond to various union recruiting attractions—and personal organizing experiences.

One important element of these training programs should be labor history. Too often, new hires come into the workplace and think that the higher rates and benefits are simply a gift from a benevolent boss or are offered as a reward for the training that the individual worker has gone through to develop some skills. While a history of the union movement would be great, a history of the local is immediately more relevant, charting how each benefit was negotiated—sometimes with a strike or organizing campaign—so that members understand that the Cash Value of My Union Contract [See Appendix 8] did not come without a fight.

Attractive parts of this labor history are videos from local union members, describing their experiences in the union. In every meeting I have attended over the years, there has always been one remarkable personal history from a longtime member, told in such a compelling way. These little narratives—rich in emotion and detail-- were so extraordinary that I urged the local staff to make videos and post them for wide and easy distribution.

Ask the participants what they will do differently because of this program and follow up—30 days, 60 days, 6 months after the class-- to see if there was any impact. Such a follow-up—from the officers, from the staff or from fellow students—requires a proactive attitude and recognizes the importance of changing union strategies before we are obliterated.

One failure of the education programs is not reaching the newer members of your union. If an education program is offered at a state or district meeting, or even at an international convention, the members attending have many years of union experience and, for different reasons, recognize the importance of their union. With new hires, and especially younger workers, this value is not clear, especially because most of them come with no union background. Any education program should include new member training, starting the first minute a new hire hits the time clock. Union history should be included as part of every apprenticeship program. As an apprentice in night school, I heard the instructor—a longtime union member--state" I am going to show you the skills but it's the union that makes sure you get paid for them!"

Explaining the language of the union to these new hires, who have no union vocabulary, and usually don't know the difference between third step and third base, is a challenge that many union education programs will not face. Start an education program for these new hires and be patient—it is sometimes necessary to stop after every sentence, almost as if you were speaking in a foreign language, to ask if the participants understand. It is an investment of resources—union time and dues money—that will pay off in a stronger membership. A couple of good IBEW videos directed at new members are in a new Baltimore local https://www.youtube.com/watch?v=3OTHL7pb99I and in Johnstown, PA http://ibew459.org/union-media.

* * * * * * * * * * * * * * * * * *

> "I am the Shop Steward Coordinator for Local ATU 843 out of Bellingham, WA. I have been a shop steward for about 10 years, and one of the things I have learned is that you are never too old to learn!" Mel Lolkema

It is also important to encourage members to attend outside training programs, if there is one in your area. The number of "pure" labor studies programs—those which operate separately, with a distinct staff of union educators at a college--is drastically dropping. Many of the programs have been combined with industrial relations programs, or even with business administration departments over the years but there are still brave and dedicated teachers around the country (including Hawai'i) who still offer union skills training to workers and union officers. Some of these programs have been attacked as part of the relentless anti-unionism movement, so there are now only an estimated 30 centers in the country.

In September 2016, for example, the longstanding labor studies program at the University of Massachusetts-Amherst lost funding and its director "abruptly departed, "either forced out or resigned. This program was "founded in 1964 after the AFL-CIO's president, George Meany, visited the campus and encouraged it to create a labor studies program, similar to those at many other land grant universities. The UMass center has since become nationally renowned for training labor leaders and activists. . .. Nevertheless, the center is not profitable and until now has relied on a patchwork of university funds to open its program to needy students. Following previous tumult in 2010, it was folded into the sociology department. 'We can't continue to do the work that we have done if we can only accept [students] who can afford a $60,000 master's degree," [former director Eve] Weinbaum said Tuesday in a phone interview.'"

Some of the labor studies programs have just withered and died. One of the contentions at the UMass program was that "Enrollment in the program has declined for years, said John Hird, interim dean of the College of Social and Behavioral Sciences, which houses the sociology department. It has two new students this year and 16 total, down from 30 total a decade ago, according to data from Hird."[204]

Union officers in some states, like Massachusetts--where the president of the state AFL-CIO president stated that he "was deeply troubled to learn about the recent attacks on this program"-- support the labor studies programs. Many of these programs, however, are considered a threat to the officers of unions, who refuse to support them or to encourage their members to participate in union education classes. When I had a job interview in 1996 for the position of Director of Labor Studies at Dundalk Community College, a steel town outside Baltimore, the president of the Baltimore AFL-CIO Central Labor Council was on the search committee, and said he had only one question to ask: "Why should I send any member to your class if they will then run against me for office?" Some union officers tried to blacklist the program, preventing classes from being held at union halls or training centers, even though other officers enthusiastically participated.

One important training center was The George Meany Center For Labor Studies, which opened in 1969 on a 47-acre campus in Silver Spring, MD. Financially supported by the AFL-CIO as a residential school that trained thousands of union officers, the school was transformed in 1997, by the John Sweeney administration, into The National Labor College. As part of internal disputes within the AFL-CIO Executive Council, and with declining membership and revenues, the financial support—estimated at 40% of the college's budget-- dropped by 2010. By 2012, there was a debt of $30 million on a conference center and an estimated $ 6 million annual

---

[204] Laura Krantz. "UMass labor center loses director, some funding." *Boston Globe*. September 7, 2016.

operating deficit, which the AFL-CIO had subsidized. A closure plan was accepted in December, 2013.

One challenge was that college courses were offered for credit, at $ $297 per credit hour for members of AFL-CIO unions and their relatives. With a 3-credit course, or several of them for a week, plus lodging at the college, travel expenses and lost time, a week at the NLC could cost several thousand dollars, a figure that excluded most union members unless their unions were covering the costs.

The property was put up for sale, combined with an effort to offer only on-line courses, but there were still only 599 on-line students at the end. The college was closed officially on April 26, 2014 and the facility sat desolate and dilapidated until the ATU brought it in 2015 for its national headquarters.[205] Students were encouraged to transfer to Empire State College (part of the State University of New York), Penn State University, Thomas Edison State College or Rowan University. A small successor, The Bonnie Laden Union Skills program moved to the AFL-CIO but that has also been dissolved.

One comment on an article in the *New York Times* about the closing stated: "Shame on the supposed labor leaders who are on that Board. Shame Shame, Shame. They have defected on the future of the labor movement. They should all be required to notify their membership of the status of the institution."[206]

To its credit, the ATU has used its new national office to host comprehensive training programs for its members, offering week-long courses where members stay in the residential halls. The union also offers short classes for members in the DC area and is trying to create a kind of union "think tank" by letting other groups, like United Students Against Sweatshops or the Industrial Areas Foundation, use the building.[207]

* * * * * * * * * * * * * * * * * * *

A union is an organization and every organization that experiences challenges, or even failures, will either change its approach or it will continue to fail. While it is essential to share Best Union Practices, it is also helpful to pay attention to the other organizations in our lives—social groups, like clubs or associations, or churches, political parties or even neighborhood associations and PTA's—that depend on attracting voluntary members, who will both financially support the organization and donate their energies to make the organization stronger. Most of us participate in groups like these and have the same strategy discussions so we can learn from them.

We can also look at The Other Side—at companies which face severe challenges and how they adjust, or not. We can learn from the thought processes of our bosses, who keep making us learn new skills in response to constantly shifting workplaces and patterns of ownership and control.

---

[205] Ry Rivard. "A Small College's Demise." *Inside Higher Ed.* November 14, 2013.
[206] Eugene L. Meyer. "Square Feet: A Campus Built by Labor is Going on the Block." *New York Times.* August 1, 2012.
[207] Full Disclosure. I have taught in the ATU educational program.

As one example, the 2017 Mid-Atlantic Lean Conference, held in Baltimore in November, 2017, promised "Four keynote presentations by leaders of change and cultural transformation and thirty-two presentation sessions to choose from, spanning process improvement, operational excellence, leadership, people-centric culture, change management, and more."[208] We have suffered the consequences of groups like this in our workplaces—job combinations, union avoidance, speed-up-- but they focus on *change* and *innovation* and we should duplicate the process even as we challenge their decisions.

Another local conference, "Managing Unionized Workforces in a Recessionary Economy" offered topics like "Negotiating Collective Bargaining Agreements that Save Money and Increase Efficiencies" and "Interpreting and Implementing the Agreement to Take Advantage of a Down Economy." Many company representatives and lawyers could get instruction on how to screw unions as well as exchanging strategies.

And if these brutal approaches did not work, there was also a program "Removal of the Union as a Bargaining Representative," with specific guidance on "Employer Initiated Elimination of Union."

The success of the anti-union movement is not an accident and shows once again that the anti-union groups are much better at developing strategy and training its participants that the union movement is. The schedule for the National Conservative Political Action Conference in late February, 2017, is an excellent example of the relentless movement. While the news media—soon to be banned from all official meetings--focused on conflicts at the time between the alt-right and Donald Trump, or on whether Steve Bannon and Reince Preibus could ever be friends, the consideration of political strategies was more important to the participants. The program was scheduled less than one month after Trump's inauguration and already looked to the 2017 and 2018 elections.

Among the programs at the Activist Boot Camp on February 22—advertised as "Learn the Necessary Skills to Advance the Conservative Message in your community. This track will give you the skills to become a better grassroots activist and organizer"—were topics like

- Liking Your Way to Victory: Facebook Recruitment
- What Just Happened? 2016's Lessons for Future Activism
- Hold Their Feet to the Fire: Holding Elected Officials Accountable
- Campaign Technology Matters More Now Than Ever
- Case Study: How the Cruz Campaign Motivated Activists to Get Involved
- Sharing Freedom by Telling Your Story

The dazzling workshops we all should have attended were "The Revolt of the Deplorables," and "If Heaven Has a Gate, A Wall, and Extreme Vetting, Why Can't America?" although The Next Generation Happy Hour on February 24 also sounded exciting.[209]

---

[208] http://www.leanmaryland.com/2017Conference
[209] https://docs.google.com/viewerng/viewer?url=http://cpac.conservative.org/wp-content/uploads/sites/2/2017/02/CPAC-2017-Agenda-2.24.17.pdf

These workshops are extensions of a much more sophisticated political strategy, developed—and funded, of course—by the Koch brothers and called the Grassroots Leadership Academy. Even though they are among the wealthiest individuals on our planet, their emphasis is—as ours should be—on bottom-up organizing. I keep urging you **Learn From Our Opponents** and this academy is a excellent illustration—and it's all FREE, "due to contributions from our growing number of free market and limited government supporters." (The Koch Brothers have a net worth of $21.5 billion so they are not exactly dependent on the good will of their supporters.) While not defending the right-wing social order, the organizing techniques that the Academy offers are certainly useful, including workshops like "Social Media Best Practices," "Working With Legislators and "Mobilizing Fellow Supporters."[210]

If you have ever been to a union function—a district meeting or international convention—raise your hands if you ever attended such a strategic workshop.

Seeing no hands raised, we will move on.

NOW GO DO IT

1. **Figure out how many of your co-workers have attended a union education program—ever!**
2. **Look for a schedule of any union education programs and then ask your co-workers to join you in attending.**
3. **Ask each of your co-workers to bring in a clipping or news story of an organization that changed its strategies because it was not doing well.**
4. **Ask a local community college to offer a labor studies class.**
5. **Create a history of your local—contract negotiations, major grievances, strikes.**
6. **Post on your local union web page personal stories about the value of union education.**

---

[210] https://gla.americansforprosperityfoundation.org/

CHAPTER 10—FINANCES OF YOUR UNION

> "When an institution is in trouble, you cannot cut your way to health."
> Deborah Borda

Trump's victory in 2016, with his support from many union households, may have been a dramatic moment but the financial situation for unions has been in decline for many years. This squeeze is the result of many different factors. Changes in technology, like robotics, and workplace relocations to non-union sites have permanently impacted union incomes. In other cases, where dues are based on a percentage of income, rather than on a flat dollar amount, lower wages or shorter weeks created a shortage every month. The Recession of 2008-2010 brought layoffs, plant closures and company consolidations, a collapse far deeper than almost anyone predicted. This recession wreaked havoc on union administrations, catching some of them totally off guard while exposing, in other cases, the refusal of union officers to make tough choices.

Although the age of Trump may look like a new attack, declining union membership—and declining union revenues-- over the past 60 years is a problem that many officers have not wanted to confront.

The open shop campaigns in states like Wisconsin, Michigan and Illinois have cut into union membership, and the impending Supreme Court decision *Janus v AFSCME* will make a bad situation even worse in 2018 unless all union begin aggressive internal organizing campaigns.

With the total failure to organize new members in any significant numbers, unions at every level are faced with unpleasant decisions: cut activities to work with less income from dues and less return on any savings or investments or try to maintain all programs by raising dues, not the happiest set of choices. After all, money talks—and not having money talks even louder.

Financial questions are always tied to strategic decisions because unions must decide what programs should be supported financially, the proverbial bang-for-the-buck: how will every dollar spent build the union, both by expanding participation by our current members and by organizing new ones?

Unions face the basic question: who does what and who pays for it? In most unions, there are three tiers in the union structure: the local, the district and the International Union, each of which has a separate budget, a different set of officers and sometimes different priorities. Each union is different in how decisions are made and priorities established, how staff is assigned and which level of the union will receive the greatest proportion of dues income.

In the general political area, there is a comparable structure that may be more familiar to us as we see the spectacle of government at every level suddenly running enormous deficits, and demanding that the next higher level of government pay to make up the differences. In the city of Baltimore in 2017, for example, city schools faced a possible deficit of $129 million, and demanded that the state and federal governments make up this amount. At the same time, the state of Maryland projected a $400 million budget hole caused largely by inaccurate revenue estimates. Both the city and the state pressured Congressional representatives to supply federal money, from a government whose deficits have soared into the trillions. Politically, of course, this is not a workable model but it duplicates the challenges we face as union members.

Unlike the federal government, unions cannot simply print up more money. Local officers may want to shift expenses to the district or the international, but the decisions can become a big scramble with the potential to wreck the movement, just at a time when we need to co-ordinate all of our resources.

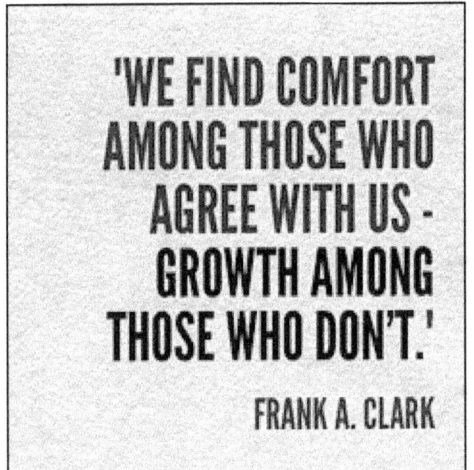

With the relentless attacks on the union's income, it is time for unions at every level to have strategic discussions, with realistic financial statements and projections, about how basic functions of a union could be jeopardized if funds are cut. How can we adjust to blunt the attacks? Once again, this is a discussion for the whole membership, not just a few of the officers, and every expenditure needs to be checked out. The discussions may be contentious, but disagreement can be healthy and besides, the challenges we face will not simply go away if we don't talk about them. We need to evaluate what campaigns need to expand, how to pay for them and, most importantly, can any of them be carried on with volunteers, especially retirees or laid off members, as described in Chapter 8. In fact, this *crisis* can generate an *opportunity* to bring more members into active participation in their union. Most importantly, every campaign should focus on increasing our membership so we can stop being the minority of the working-class (and generate more dues income).

The SEIU generally is one example of drastic measures that have been taken in this time of crisis. Several years ago, the SEIU officers decided that major expenses—like new organizing—should be carried by the locals and drastically laid off international staff. "'Because the far right will control all three branches of government, we will see serious threats to the ability of working people to join together in unions,' SEIU president Mary Kay Henry wrote in an internal memo, dated Dec. 14 [2016]. 'These threats require us to make tough decisions that allow us to resist these attacks and to fight forward despite dramatically reduced resources.'

After citing the need to 'dramatically re-think' how to implement the union's strategy, Henry's all-staff letter announces that the SEIU 'must plan for a 30% reduction' in the international union's budget by Jan. 1, 2018, including a 10% cut effective at the start of 2017."[211]

To carry out this plan, at the end of 2017, the SEIU—as management—was involved in intense negotiations with the staff union, OPEIU Local 2, over buyouts and layoffs, with criticism from the workers that both skills and institutional knowledge were being pushed out. Doing the numbers, the SEIU spent about $19 million in 2016 in the Fight for $15 campaign—which was not directly designed to bring in any new union members—and donated, from a different pocket, more than $60 million to Hilary Clinton's campaign.

Many of the lessons that the media passes out to help individual workers economize can apply to the union as well—with the same hazards: the way to cutting expenses is obvious but developing the will can be a real problem. The advice columns first encourage all family members to sit down and look together at their budget—income, necessary expenses, and discretionary spending, so everyone has all the crucial information, as if strict budgeting were easy. In a union, with different competing interests, the problem is ever more complicated but, like a family, everyone needs to participate.

Most union officers usually do not inform their members of the financial condition of their union, even though they are legally required to file LM-2 reports with the Department of Labor, which then posts the reports on-line. While the economy was strong, there was plenty of dues money and no one paid much attention to how it was spent. In some locals, conducting union business was regarded as a second job with lost time vouchers for every activity. Generally, the participation in these paid activities reflected The Servicing Model, with a few members or officers taking on most of the activities and generating most of the expenses.

If you question this statement, simply create a list of your members who, in the past year, have been paid out of local funds, and find this number as a percentage of the total membership. If the number exceeds 5 percent, your local is well ahead of the majority—and that is a dangerously low figure.

You can also list the number of members who volunteered for union activities to get a good breakdown of overall membership participation. As unions first developed in the US, they had no resources and relied on the commitment of time and energies from all of the members at a time when wages were low and hours of work were long. Members felt unionism was a cause, a crusade, *la Causa*, that they were carrying forward against enormous odds, so they gave their time—and sometimes their lives—to build the movement. Over time, unions evolved into financially stable organizations-- and employers--so officers acted as if they deserved to be paid for every activity, with the hope that nothing would ever change.

---

[211] Josh Eidelson. "Fear of Trump Triggers Deep Spending Cuts by Nation's Second-Largest Union." *Bloomberg Business Week*. December 27, 2016.

Once you start your financial discussions, here's a short list of some strategic functions that need evaluation. Remember that every financial adjustment also affects union strategies and should be focused on increased membership numbers and participation.

- What about arbitrations? One statewide union spent more than $1 million in 2016 for legal expenses, mostly arbitrations, which are both expensive and risky. A local union that routinely sent cases to arbitration, running up a cost of $ 10,00.00 for each grievance, now found that they were financially prevented from the usual routine. Does this mean the local simply gave up on important grievances? Not at all—members were mobilized to support important issues and force the boss to settle up and avoid an arbitration. The union can use the pressures of the economy to their advantage if the members stay strong. And think how many organizers the union could hire for $ 1 million a year!
- It may be time to look for volunteers and to try to eliminate as much union-paid lost time as possible. Officers who routinely are off fulltime should plan to go back into work for a day or so every week to save union funds and may even improve themselves by working around their members on a daily basis.
- Here's one of the most controversial policies: how about cutting—if temporarily—the salaries of the officers and staff? If the members are cut, or face furlough days, should the pain be shared equally?
- One easy mark is the union newsletter or magazine which many unions print and mail out on a regular basis to their members, who usually don't read them. Why not use the new technology and post the same material on a union web site, or send out a mass e-mail or text message, or create an app—or do all of the above? Not only will the costs drop dramatically but the response time for electronic communications can be almost instantaneous, as opposed to the long delays involved in printed material, and you will appeal to the millennials among your members.
- Some local officers proposed major changes in union functions while admitting that any proposals face strong—and selfish—opposition. Many unions have expensive district or international conventions—lost time at an expensive hotel or convention center, with travel and other expenses for just a few members. Delegates consider these "educational" meetings—often at gambling centers, by the way—to be justly-deserved junkets, a reward for loyal service in the union. These educational gatherings can continue but why not have them over a weekend to cut lost time? Why not look at using a local college, with dormitories and dining halls, to save money? Does your employer cover some educational expenses? Move your union activities to a location where the boss will have pay for sharpening union skills—a delightful proposal.
- Now is *not* the time to cut your new organizing program—in fact, now is the time to expand it by using your laid off members or retirees as volunteers. As non-union workers are squeezed and harassed, there can be increased interest in union

protections. Your union should make up a list of cuts that the contract blocked and a list of organizing targets—other branches of your employer, competitors, places that are close geographically—and go after them.

- What about your union hall? Is it a burden? If you owe on your union hall, the union can try—just as homeowners do--to renegotiate the mortgage. If your union is renting and it looks like the work will stay, think about buying a building at a low price. Renting out your union hall for functions can be part of a general fundraising program, for the local. Many groups need a good place to celebrate, especially if your hall has a bar, and the income would be helpful. You could even offer a discount to members as a way of increasing the sense of union support and solidarity.
- On the other hand, if your union is not organizing, it may be time to try to sell the union hall and move into a more affordable location.
- Finally, do not borrow just to maintain the "regular" operation of the union. Just as your household should avoid more debt, the union should work with the resources it has.

In general, the financial crisis will force the re-evaluation—*kaizen*--of every aspect of union activity and this is a good thing. Unions have neglected this skill in good times but now will be forced to take a hard look at how they function and how they spend the members' money.

* * * * * * * * * * * * * * * * * * * *

For craft unions, like the building trades or entertainment unions, there is an additional problem: what to do with the health and welfare and pension funds? These funds are, by law, jointly-administered, with an equal number of union and management trustees. The union officers, however, are the people who have to answer to the members, facing the anger if benefits are cut or postponed.

These funds are essential to the welfare and to the stability of the union, reflecting a tradition of self-help going back hundreds of years that builds loyalty among the members. Generally, the funds are set up on a per-hour contribution, diverted from the pay packet, supplemented—hopefully—by investment income to provide current health insurance and future retirement benefits. In most cases, the members pay no attention to the funds, simply assuming that "The Union" will take care of them.

As layoffs roll through the industries, however, the hourly contributions will drop significantly. In every case, moreover, the funds have taken major hits in investment incomes so there is less of a cushion. In multi-employer funds, the income has been affected by an aging workforce, and large employers pulling out of the plans.

Many are still dealing with significant losses incurred during the recession of 2008. As one example, the Teamsters Central States Southeast and Southwest Area Pension Fund is projected to become insolvent in the next 10 to 15 years. The fund lost 42% of its assets—about $11.1 billion in capital—in just 15 months during 2008 and early 2009. "If cuts are allowed, retired truck driver Glenn Nicodemus, 63, could see his monthly benefits fall from around

$3,300 a month to as little as $1,180. He retired in March [2013] after nearly 40 years on the road, and his only other source of income is $1,700 a month in Social Security benefits."[212]

This situation, of course, does not help the union organize non-union drivers.

According to the Pension Benefit Guaranty Corporation, which insures pension plans, up to 10 percent of the roughly 1,500 multiemployer plans will run out of money in coming decades. The conditions of public pensions funds, always underfunded, are in bad shape with states like Rhode Island and New Jersey or cities like Philadelphia losing hundreds of millions of dollars in 2016.

Once again, the issue is both the raising and the spending of revenue. The payment of benefits directly to the members should be the first priority. The trustees should look at every additional expense—consultants' fees, investment charges, trustees stipends—to see what money can be saved for the fund. Are there questionable investments? Some funds, unfortunately, have been used like private piggy banks for the trustees and have lost considerable amounts of money. When the stock market was rising and the fund's investments—on paper, at least—were rising with it, the problem did not appear so serious but now that funds are dropping, it's time for a very hard look.

Maintaining health insurance coverage for the members is critical, as is keeping up payments to members who have already retired, or those who had planned to retire in the near future.

Another hard choice may be asking for higher contributions from the participants in the fund. A fast run of the numbers may show that a small increase—cents per hour—could restore the fund to stability, protecting current and future coverage. This diversion, like contract articles, could be temporary and could be reversed if the economy comes back to life. A small amount—5 or 10 cents per hour—will hardly be missed by individual members but will generate a sizeable amount of income for the funds.

Some locals already have such contingency plans. One local of Steamfitters/UA long ago established "the penny fund," diverting one cent/hour from the active workers into the H & W Fund to provide money to cover workers who might be out of work for an extended period. Now the officers are considering increasing this amount, and also are discussing a similar fund for the pension plan, which was also devastated by the loss of investment income.

In sum, the way that a union handles its money reflects its strategic planning and its most basic operation, so the crisis can also be an opportunity—probably long overdue-- to re-evaluate every aspect of the local's operations.

* * * * * * * * * * * * * * * * * * *

One important first step to protecting the union's finances is to calculate how to break our co-dependence on our employers for the union's revenue stream. Two parts of this dependency are important clauses of many union contracts: union security and the dues checkoff. In the shrinking number of states where a union shop is still legal—a clause requiring every worker

---

[212] Melanie Hicken. "Retired union workers facing 'unprecedented' pension cuts." CNN Money. November 15, 2013.

covered by the contract to be a union member—many unions have grown careless about building union loyalty so that everyone will voluntarily join.

As was discussed in Chapter 2, as far back as the early 1800's, unions were voluntary and workers informally enforced the union shop by refusing to work with a non-members or by shunning them until they joined. During World War II, as the employers worked to control the militant unions that developed in the 1930's, they offered a deal: be good little boys and girls and we will agree to a "maintenance of membership," a clause that required any worker who joined the union to remain a member. After the war, this agreement expanded into the union shop clauses that are familiar to us today and unions grew enormously, both in membership numbers and in financial assets. This income allowed the development of fulltime staff and officers and was a major support for the expansion of The Servicing Model of Unionism.

At the same time, anti-union forces organized politically to attack this privilege, starting the movement cleverly called "Right To Work." The Taft-Hartley Act, passed in 1947, allowed states to enact a law prohibiting union security clauses. Today, 27 states are open shop, and other states may try to increase this number. There has also been national legislation introduced for an open shop law, with a consistent push to elect candidates who support RTW, taking advantage of the political weaknesses of unions, discussed in Chapter 7.

For decades, union shop clauses made The Servicing Model work because people could not drop out, no matter how dissatisfied they were with the officers. Now, in open shop states, it is embarrassing that many unions only have 50% membership, and some even lower. National unions that started in northern states with union security contracts have found it very difficult to adjust to the open shop when companies opened in the south or when traditional union states like Wisconsin and Michigan went open shop. The financial crises of the unions, compounded by the lousy economy, became much more severe as members dropped out.

Public sector unions which could not negotiate a standard union security clause in many states unions were able to negotiate or legislate "agency fees," requiring payments from non-members covered by a union contract. There is, of course, a logical argument as for the union shop or agency fee: the workers covered by the contract get all the benefits the union has negotiated, and the union must represent them, so it is only fair that they be required to financially support the union. Just as taxpayers whose children are grown pay to keep public schools open, the agency fees are fair financial support for a union.

Fairness be damned—anything that can cut off the union's income is a juicy target. The election of anti-union candidates like Scott Walker in Wisconsin, and Bruce Rauner in Illinois-- who would certainly never push to have taxes paid voluntarily--is part of the campaign but the court challenges, like *Friedrichs v California* and now *Janus v AFSCME*, could block the whole structure of guaranteed dues payments.

When the *Friedrichs* case was moving up in 2015, some unions started energetic internal organizing programs to build loyalty among all the workers covered by the contract but many officers were like deer in the headlights. When Justice Antonin Scalia died in February, 2016, and the case was blocked, many unions went back to the old ways.[213] With the *Janus* case set for the spring, 2018, if there were ever an urgency to The Organizing Model of Unionism, it is now.

The debate over union membership, and the devilish traps that management like Maine Governor Paul LePage set for us, are the best reasons to plan an internal organizing program, starting from the moment a new hire enters your workplace. Building up your membership helps in so many ways, and not just financially. Beyond the financial challenge, unions with such a low memberships are ripe for decertification campaigns.

The other dependency is on the dues checkoff, which became a fundamental part of union-management relations during World War II. Once upon a time, union stewards hand-collected dues from the members but the checkoff became more common in the 1940's. Even Henry Ford—exclaiming "Now I get to be the union's banker"—agreed to it in the UAW first contract. Usually in negotiations, the checkoff is offered as a package with the no-strike clause and an expanded Management Rights section but they became an accepted fact of union life and a critical addiction for unions. Many officers even allow personnel managers to pass out the dues authorization cards to new hires, guaranteeing that the new hires will be dues-payers, and that the union will have the steady revenue stream but not strong union members.

Some unions are now developing strategies to avoid the checkoff, using new technology like telephone apps to continue dues payments. The Massachusetts Nurses Association (MNA), for example, has a system for paying dues directly to the MNA called "MNA Direct," covering 75-80 percent of the membership. As one staff rep remarked about the direct deposit to the union "It totally cuts out the boss so that they have no knowledge of the number of non-Union folks in each unit." A big SEIU local in Minnesota created a checkoff using the telephone, a direct deduction of dues that skips the employer.

These bank deductions are developing in other unions, especially among high-paid workers, who are likely to have money in the bank. For lower paid workers, the payroll deduction worked best for the union because the money came before the member was forced to spend it on frivolities, like food or rent or childcare.

The new appointments to The National Labor Relations Board by the Trump administration makes the alternatives to the dues checkoff even more important for private sector unions. For many years, a favorite trick of the boss was to cut off dues checkoff if a union contract expired and a union, reluctant to strike, wanted to play "the inside game." Based on a campaign developed by UAW President Jerry Tucker during bitter negotiations at Moog Automotive in 1981-82, the "inside game" encouraged workers to keep working while finding leverage beside a strike to pressure management into a settlement. The campaign was described in the AFL-CIO/IUD pamphlet published in 1986, *The Inside Game: winning with workplace strategies.*

The bosses countered this strategy by stopping dues deductions, hoping to throw the unions into financial turmoil. When the unions challenged this policy as an Unfair Labor Practice (ULP), the NLRB ruled in 1962, in a case involving Bethlehem Steel, that the boss had to right

---

[213] See *Closing Up the Open Shop: A Guide to Internal Organizing* for the history.

to stop the checkoff because it was "created by the contracts and became a contractual right which continued to exist so long as the contracts remained in force."

Reversing this 50-year precedent in December, 2012, the NLRB ruled in a case involving WKYC-TV that "like most other terms and conditions of employment, an employer's obligation to check off union dues continues after expiration of a collective bargaining agreement that contains such a provision." [214]

As described in Chapter 7, however, the Labor Board is preparing for a major—and very negative—change to reverse a series of pro-union decisions. There is no question that the suspension of the checkoff when a contract expires, will be one of them so unions need to plan now for alternative methods of membership funding. For every bad thing the bosses try to do to us, there are positive alternatives we can develop—with the right attitude and strategy.

In all, how we deal with these financial challenges will show much close we are to revitalizing our movement.

NOW GO DO IT

1. Get a copy of your union's LM-2 report so you can see how money was spent. If you are in a public-sector union which does not file the report, ask the officers for the annual financial statement.
2. Calculate how many of your members were paid for activities in the union
3. Think about where you would spend money differently if you were an officer.
4. Are there obvious ways to cut back on some expenses?
5. Are there more effective ways for the union to collect dues?
6. If you are in an open shop state, or work for the federal government, do you have an ambitious internal organizing program so your membership grows?

---

[214] www.ilr.cornell.edu/sites/ilr.cornell.edu/files/WKYC-TV-and-NABET.pdf

APPENDIX 1

TWO MODELS OF UNIONISM

When unions were first organized, the workers' success depended on total membership involvement since the early organizations had no resources except the passions of the members and their communities. As unions became more established, this **Organizing Model of Unionism** gradually was replaced by **The Servicing Model of Unionism**, which became the dominant structure for unions. In the mid-1990's, as some union officers recognized the desperate situation for unionism, **The Organizing Model** was revived, at least as a discussion topic.

This chart shows the differences between the two models.

ORGANIZING MODEL	SERVICING MODEL
Proactive	Reactive
Independent of management	Dependent upon management
Actively involves members in all decisions	Union officers "solve problems" for members in response to complaints or requests
Creates many activities in workplace	Total reliance on grievance and arbitration
Constantly negotiating for improvements	Waits for regularly scheduled contract dates
Develops the skills and abilities of the members	Total reliance on union staff, "experts" and lawyers
Open communications channels	Union info is considered privileged and kept secret to a small group
Active membership	Passive membership
Decentralized union structure	Centralized union structure
Bottom-up decisions	Top-down decisions
Regularly supports other unions	Basically isolated from other activity

APPENDIX 2

WORKER/UNION LEADERSHIP

"Leadership means moving people, moving our coworkers. An elected or appointed union representative is not necessarily a leader."

--A Great Authority

Good Leadership	Bad Leadership
Kaizen	Is easily satisfied
Initiative	Passive
Proactive	Reactive
Works hard	Does the minimum required
Self-reliant	Dependent
Self-starter	Waits to be told what to do
Persistent	Quickly discouraged
Positive	Negative
Does not quit	Gives up easily
Sets goals	Bumps along
Does more than needed	Does the minimum to get by
Seeks new information	Closed mind
Absorbs and uses new information	See above
Ready to change	Resists change
Accepts pressure to improve	Resists pressure to improve
Finishes tasks in full, on time	Owns a bagful of excuses

WHICH ONE ARE YOU?

APPENDIX 3

TWO MODELS OF POLITICAL ACTION

Just as the operation of your local union reflects either The Organizing Model of Unionism or The Servicing Model, the crucial area of political action also follows each of these models.

ORGANIZING MODEL	SERVICING MODEL
Political activities used to increase membership involvement	Political activities restricted to a few officers who attend various expensive functions
Political decisions made by an open vote of members	Political decisions made by a small group
"Political action" means all sorts of activities—petitions, referenda, etc.	Political action limited to regular campaigns and endorsements
PROACTIVE—starts early political action, so union can set issues	REACTIVE—political action comes late in a campaign, after issues are set
Really works to build activities	Accepts low voter registration and turnouts
Holds elected official accountable for campaign promises	Timid of offending incumbents and easily "forgives" disappointing officials
"Political work" used to build the union	"Political work" considered 'separate"
Looks for members to run for office	Won't consider running labor candidates
Focuses members on common class issues	Allows "social" issues to divide membership
Emphasizes Labor-to-Neighbor campaigns	Makes no effort to communicate with people outside the union
Workers set the issues for politicians	Politicians set the issues and expect union to obediently support them
Looks at all political parties	Totally tied to Democratic Party
Understands the powers of the labor movement and makes union issues urgent	Afraid of being "Big Labor" and does not establish union issues in campaigns
Members involved in all strategies	Members only expected to follow orders

APPENDIX 4

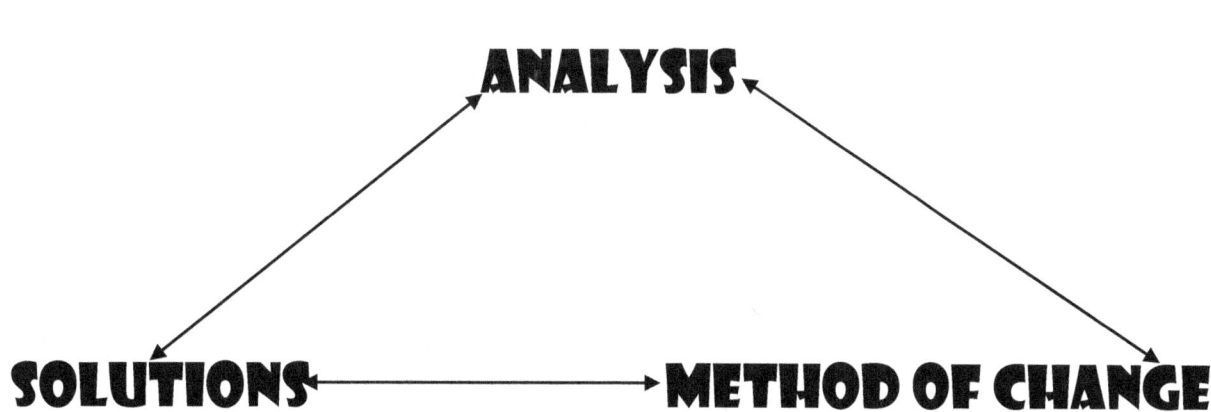

Any real political discussion must have all three components and, without all three, the discussion is both incomplete and usually a waste of time.

- Problems—while this is clearly the starting point, too many people see it as the end as well, as if listing problems, like "unionism is declining" is enough. It's also the easy way out because most people will agree on a problem, but really disagree on solutions or methods of change. Often the calculated description of the problem, like "the Bush recession" leads to a predetermined solution--vote for Democrats in the next election.
- Solutions—OK, we know what you think the problem is, what's your answer? Simply pointing out problems does not really move the discussion. People see the problem—they want to know what to do about it.
- Methods of Change—or "How do we get from here-to-there" is usually omitted and is the most important aspect of the discussion. Simply proclaiming moral imperatives, as in "Conditions for workers must be improved . . . " or appealing to sway the unswayables, as in "Congress must pass legislation protecting workers . . ." is conservative and avoids a real conversation about winning. Check Einstein's definition of insanity.

Provoking a discussion over solutions and methods is ESSENTIAL—simply putting out vague points that everyone agrees with does not create change—it simply locks you in your gated community.

It is also no value to be simply an "aginner"—that is, to be against war, or poverty, or various social policies. You have to propose positive social solutions and methods for change and be ready to organize around the principles.

APPENDIX 5

Baltimore Sun Op Ed   February 7, 2013

A farewell to jobs
If the employment decline is not temporary, bold action will be needed

By Bill Barry

In all of the clamor about deficit reduction and fiscal cliffs, the assumption is that the U.S. economy is basically fine. The "jobs slump" is just that — a slump — so with proper government intervention (or lack thereof), the happy days of full employment will return. After all, the "recession" is just temporary, isn't it?

There is a more devastating prospect: that the lost jobs are gone forever, leaving tens of millions of Americans, concentrated at opposite ends of the age scale, who may never work "permanently" again. If you think this is hysteria, ask your middle-age friends who have lost their jobs about their prospects. Consider that young adults under 25 have a much higher unemployment rate — and 85 percent of recent college graduates say they may have to move back in with their parents. In Maryland, the unemployment rate for ages 16-24 is the highest since World War II.

So where did all of these "permanent" jobs go?

•Technology: From factories where robots make all of the products to each of us who uses an ATM, BGE smart meter or E-ZPass, millions of jobs have been replaced by technology. The relentless push for even greater technology investment also means reduced employment.

•Corporate mergers: As businesses conglomerate, "operating efficiencies" eliminate many jobs that will never return.

•Increased productivity: As the recession of the mid-2000s deepened, employers were both laying off people and assigning additional work to the remaining staff. Gradually, the laid-off workers were permanently replaced.

•"Offshoring": The exporting for the past few decades of U.S. jobs overseas has eliminated millions of jobs at both ends of the skill scale. Not only are repetitive tasks like clothing manufacture and call centers shipped out, but X-rays, for example, now can be read anywhere in the world. As a measure of this loss, the U.S. trade deficit in November was $48.7 billion.

•Decrease in government jobs: Government was long considered the employer-of-last resort. No longer; in December alone, government jobs decreased by 12,000 as a result of decreased tax revenues. Increasing unemployment, of course, will further decrease tax revenues. "Sequestration" cuts would eliminate another 1 million jobs. So where will these displaced workers find another spot?

•The underground economy: With the surge of millions of undocumented workers into an already precarious economy, many "jobs" don't officially appear as such; they are day labor, cash only or private contractor.

•Part-time work: Especially in the hospitality sector, like fast food, there is no "normal," so nearly every employee is considered part-time. Workers face erratic and unpredictable hours. The announcement by some chain owners that they would further cut hours to avoid providing health insurance is simply an extension of industry practices. As work is de-skilled, it becomes not only possible but desirable for employers to bring in part-time or underground workers instead of full-time hires.

•The recession: the scapegoat that conceals the permanent loss of jobs. Yes, the recession has hurt, but it was in part the product of the change in the economy as demand from workers who are losing their jobs dried up.

So, the question is: Now what? We have to drastically change the U.S. economy to put people back to work. Here are some things we should do:

•Shorten the workweek. The eight-hour day was a union demand in the 1870s and the 40-hour week became standard in 1935, and even as productivity soared the hours have not dropped. All of the gains have gone to the top 5 percent as profit and dividends. John Maynard Keynes in 1930 predicted that technology and productivity would be so powerful that the 15-hour week would be "normal."

•Lower the retirement age to at least 60. In the 1930s, when Francis Townsend developed a plan for Social Security, one of his goals was to make it so attractive for people to retire that jobs would be opened up for younger workers. The numbers of workers filing for Social Security at younger ages today is a prime reflection the desperate economy.

•National health care. A grievous problem with the loss of a full-time job is the loss of health insurance. President Barack Obama's health care program is inadequate to the problem; only a national single-payer, "Medicare for all" plan would stop the anxiety that comes with unemployment when your children need to see a doctor.

•Increase the minimum wage. If the federal minimum wage had increased with inflation since 1968, it would be almost $11 an hour — not enough to live on, but enough to give a huge boost to economic demand. Raising the minimum wage to keep up with worker productivity would mean a rate of $22.00

•Expand unionism. All the numbers demonstrate that unionized workers get higher pay and better benefits, and that these standards are passed along to nonunion workers. This is the basic reason why the top 5 percent want to eradicate unionism from the U.S.

Would these proposals drastically change the US economy? Absolutely.

Would they — gasp! — redistribute the wealth? Positively.

Would they require a whole new political movement, away from the two parties controlled by the wealthiest 5 percent? For certain.

And yet without such a bold plan, the overall U.S. economy will continue to sink, propped up by unsustainable deficit spending that puts us eternally at the edge of the financial cliff, wasting trillions of dollars in interest payments that could otherwise be spent productively. More importantly, without such a change our children will never know the security and employment that we have known — a human element that should be the most urgent motive.

*Bill Barry is the retired director of labor studies at the **Community College of Baltimore County-Dundalk**. His email is **billbarry21214@gmail.com**.*

Read more: (177 comments)
 http://www.baltimoresun.com/news/opinion/oped/bs-ed-economy-jobs-20130207,0,7419413.story#ixzz2v6S26hPM

APPENDIX 6
PLACES TO LEARN

Once you decide you want to learn more about building you union, here are some good sources for strategies.

BOOKS

Boyer and Morais. *Labor's Untold Story*
Philip Dray. *There is Power in A Union*
Melvin Dubofsky. *Hard Work: The Making of Labor History*
David Prosten. *The Union Steward's Complete Guide*
Henry Kraus. *The Many and the Few: A Chronicle of the Dynamic Auto Workers*
Jack Metzgar. *Striking Steel*
Bornfenbrenner and Juravich. *Ravenswood: The Steelworkers' Victory and the Revival of American Labor*
Feldecker and Hayes. *Labor Guide to Labor Law.*
Howard Zinn. *A People's History of the United Sates*
Bingham & Gansler. *Class Action: The Landmark Case that Changed Sexual Harassment*
Karen Ertel. *A Grievance Guide (13th edition)*
Alice & Staughton Lynd. *Rank and File: Personal Histories by Working-Class Organizers*
William M. Adler. *Molly's Job: A Story of Life and Work on the Global Assembly Line*

MOVIES

Norma Rae
Bread and Roses
Salt of the Earth
The Killing Floor
Ten Thousand Black Men Named George
Silkwood
The Molly Maguires
Blue Collar

Matewan
The Organizer
North Country
Pride
El Norte
The Pajama Game
Erin Brockovich
I, Daniel Blake

DOCUMENTARIES

At The River I Stand
The River Ran Red
American Dream
The Great Sit-Down
The Inheritance Girl

1877: The Army of Starvation
Harlan County, USA
The Uprising of '34
Struggles in Steel
Heaven Will Protect the Working

You can get materials from Union Communication Services www.ucs.com or from The Labor Heritage Foundation www. http://www.laborheritage.org/

APPENDIX 7

Using the Recognition Agreement

Ever have a boss throw a grievance back in your face with the happy words: "Forget it, it's not covered in the contract. You haven't got a leg to stand on"?

Even worse than hearing those words is seeing a union steward accept this decision and fail to pursue justice on a reasonable issue-- giving up after carefully checking out every article and subparagraph, every comma and semicolon, of the union contract to see if there is some way to get the grievance onto the table.

The fact is that there may well be is a way to get your grievance up and running when it appears that the situation is not covered by any specific contract language. Consider using the recognition agreement (sometimes called recognition clause or article). Commonly the first article of every union contract, the recognition agreement is often unknown, or at least unappreciated, even by the most experienced union representatives who pride themselves on knowing every nook and cranny of the collective bargaining agreement.

The recognition agreement is incredibly important because it covers every situation in, around or related to the workplace. Usually the language is deceptively simple: a common recognition agreement simply reads that "the Union is recognized as the sole and exclusive collective bargaining representative (or agent) for the purposes of collective bargaining in regards to wages, hours and all other terms and conditions of employment."

What are "all other terms and conditions of employment"? Just like it says: everything at, around or relating to the workplace. "Terms and condition of employment" cover the hundreds of situations that arise every day in the unionized workplace. Some of the situations are *specifically* covered by the contract, some are *generally* covered by the contract and some are not even *mentioned* in the contract. That's the beauty of the Recognition Agreement -- it covers everything.

Understanding the recognition agreement is especially important because management always tries to extend its control of its workers and its workplace, almost trying to put people under a kind of 24-hour surveillance. There are an increasing number of grievances, for example, concerning "off-duty misconduct" -- that is, a worker does something away from the workplace, which may (or may not) be related to something or someone at work, and management tries to enforce discipline. Usually the boss uses the "management rights" clause as a right under the contract to take this action.

Well, the recognition agreement is the union's opportunity to do something similar -- to raise any issue as a grievance, whether it's specifically covered by the contract or not.

Once upon a time, a union had *only* a recognition agreement and had to organize to fight on various issues, leaving both opportunity and difficulties for the membership. For example, the original national agreement between the United Auto Workers and General Motors, signed on

February 11, 1937, after the big sit-down strikes, was little more than a recognition agreement and a commitment to start bargaining. This single sheet of paper covered 17 different GM facilities and more than 100,000 workers and was language good enough to launch the UAW in the automobile industry.

The recognition agreement is especially helpful when you are trying to resolve a grievance that falls under the category of "just plain unfair" or when you are working through an issue that has come into the workplace since the contract was negotiated -- introduction of a new piece of equipment or a new task, for example, or even new ownership.

The recognition agreement gives the union the legal right, both by contract and by law, to pursue *any* issue -- repeat, *any* issue -- affecting the bargaining unit workers. It is so broad that it lends itself to group grievances, which are helpful in pushing a "just plain unfair" grievance, by getting many members involved in the particular issue.

For supervisors, who are also used to a strict interpretation of the contract, the union's use of the recognition article will be an unwelcome surprise. Many employers hide behind the management rights clause as something that is supposed to cover, in the boss's favor, anything that is not specifically addressed in the union contract. In fact, the recognition agreement is the antidote to management rights. It could well be called union rights.

Employers and unions understand that a contract cannot specifically cover all possible incidents in a workplace, especially as contracts grow longer and longer in duration. Words like "reasonable" and "every best effort" are sprinkled through various articles, and both sides understanding that these are open to future interpretation.

Employers fight this use of the recognition agreement, but it's frequently used with great success. One good example involved a critical case for the Communications Workers of America (CWA), when arbitrator Glen M. Bendixsen ruled emphatically in the union's favor in a case involving the assignment of work at AT&T.

New technology led to "new work" at the company. AT&T assigned to management some work the union claimed had "contractually and historically" been assigned to its members. Citing their contract's recognition agreement, CWA claimed the work and the arbitrator agreed. The article specified that CWA is "the exclusive representative for those employees whose job titles were listed in the contract" and for those workers holding new job titles created under the contract.

The language not only helped the union beat the company on this issue but, went further. Using the same clause, Bendixsen directed the parties to negotiate over new work and told AT&T to provide necessary information to the union. These are two areas normally associated in the private sector with "refusal to bargain" charges through the National Labor Relations Board.

For stewards, however, this award offered a mixed lesson, which should be clearly explained to every member. While the arbitrator provided a "win" for the union, his remedy was only a "cease and desist," with no money awarded for back pay or lost work. More important, the original grievance was filed in 1994 and the arbitrator's award was issued in August 1998. So the violation continued for four years and the union members received not a cent in back pay. The point: win your fights by pressuring management whenever possible, not by filing grievances. Avoid arbitration if you can. But that's a lesson for another time.

Stewards should use the Recognition Agreement when filing an initial grievance. It is always recommended that a grievance refer to as many articles as possible in the contract, always using language like "including Articles such-and-such . . ." to make sure that every angle is covered and that nothing is omitted that might be helpful later on. The best course is to also refer to the recognition article as one of these clauses. "The Employer has violated the contract, including the recognition article . . ." The recognition agreement is the door that opens all of the other articles of the contact, and gives the union the right to raise as a grievance anything that happens around the workplace.

Although the most common part of the Recognition Agreement is for grievances, it can also be used for "Bargaining Between Contracts," or what is often called "Constant Bargaining." The interest of your members (and non-members if you have any) in their union usually peaks during contract negotiations because they all know that they will be affected—for better or worse. All of the workers show an interest in the union, come out to meetings and eagerly listen to any reports. The big problem is that once the contract is ratified, they all disappear again.

Bargaining Between Contracts gives the same jolt of energy and, most importantly, lets your boss know that there is a union. Using the Recognition Agreement, any time your employer makes a change, you should demand to bargain over it—even if you think the change is positive for the members. Your union has the legal right to negotiate over any change in, around, or related to the workplace and should step up and use these rights. If your boss wants to make a negative change—change insurance carriers, for example—in mid-contract, the union should send a written demand to bargain and start up the same kind of contract campaign used during regular negotiations. Even if it is a department issue, spread it through the whole workplace, build solidarity and see your union grow.

--Bill Barry. *The writer is Director of Labor Studies for the Community College of Baltimore (MD) County.*

This article is reprinted from *The Steward Update*
http://www.unionist.com/union-building-tools/steward-update-newsletter

APPENDIX 8
The Cash Value of My Union Contract

By law, an employer is only required to
1) pay federal minimum wage of $7.25/hour (some locals are higher)
2) pay OT at time ½ for all hours over 40 in a week
3) provide workers compensation

Everything else has been won by the union in negotiations. Let's add up our negotiated gains to see how much we got!

Hourly wages $_____(current wage)- $7.25/hour =_____ x 2080=$_____

Daily OT (over 8) or double time (x hours worked in year) $_____

Evening/night differentials (x hours worked in a year) $_____

Health insurance (employer's annual contribution) $_____

Other insurance -dental, life, etc. (employers' annual contribution) $_____

Pension (employer's annual contribution) $_____

Employer contribution to other fringes (401K, etc.) $_____

Paid holidays (Day rate x number of holidays) $_____

Paid vacations (day rate x number of days) $_____

Other paid days off (personal, sick days, jury duty, bereavement) $_____

Working conditions (work clothes, safety equipment, etc.) $_____

Other benefits (tuition, travel, etc.) $_____

                            TOTAL ANNUAL INCOME $_____
Now subtract your annual union dues (which are tax-deductible!) $_____

And the cash value of your union contract is $_____

www.ingramcontent.com/pod-product-compliance
Lightning Source LLC
Chambersburg PA
CBHW062215220526
45471CB00009B/3207